INSIDE ALLWAYS ™

Related titles of interest from Wiley:

INSIDE ALLWAYS ™·

The Spreadsheet Publisher

Corey Sandler
Tom Badgett

WILEY

John Wiley & Sons, Inc.

New York   Chichester   Brisbane   Toronto   Singapore

Publisher: Stephen Kippur

Editor: Therese A. Zak

Managing Editor: Ruth Greif

Editing, Design, and Production: Impressions, Inc.

This publication is designed to provide accurate and authoritative information in regard to the subject matter covered. It is sold with the understanding that the publisher is not engaged in rendering legal, accounting, or other professional service. If legal advice or other expert assistance is required, the services of a competent professional person should be sought.
FROM A DECLARATION OF PRINCIPLES JOINTLY ADOPTED BY A COMMITTEE OF THE AMERICAN BAR ASSOCIATION AND A COMMITTEE OF PUBLISHERS.

Portions of the sections on graph design appeared earlier in *Desktop Graphics for the IBM PC* by Corey Sandler, published by Creative Computing Press, and are used here with the permission of Ziff-Davis Publishing Co., New York.

LIBRARY OF CONGRESS CATALOGING-IN-PUBLICATION DATA

Sandler, Corey. 1950–
    Inside allways : the spreadsheet publisher / Corey Sandler and Tom
Badgett.
      p. cm.
    Bibliography: p.
    ISBN 0-471-50904-3
    1. Allways (Computer program) 2. Business—Data processing.
I. Badgett, Tom. II. Title.
HF554B.4.A44S26 1989
005.369—dc20   89-33080
                                  CIP

Printed in the United States of America
10 9 8 7 6 5 4 3

To Synergy,
in our personal and business lives.

Contents

Foreword

Allways is the first of an important new class of products for the business microcomputer. We call it "The Spreadsheet Publisher."

Desktop publishing has upped the ante on corporate communications. A well-designed document not only presents information more clearly than a drab one, but also gets taken more seriously. In an age when companies devote so much attention to their corporate image through the use of powerful desktop publishing hardware and software, it is amazing to see how ordinary and unimpressive a standard 1-2-3 spreadsheet printout can appear.

That is the problem we set out to fix with Allways. The Allways/1-2-3 combination is the most effective way to dramatically improve the way you look on paper, without changing your software, hardware, or the way you work.

And we're not just talking here about making the numbers on your spreadsheets more attractive, either. One of the strong points of Allways is its ability to work with text. You can use the product to make attractive financial reports, business forms, and other documents. And, you can improve the appearance of 1-2-3's limited graph repertoire and incorporate as many as 20 of those graphs into a spreadsheet printout.

Here are just some of the features of the product:

You can use as many as eight typefaces on any printout—using our built-in soft fonts, or the typefaces of your printer—and apply them cell by cell or throughout ranges. You can add emphasis with bold or underline attributes. You can highlight important information with light or dark shading. And, you can add drama with solid black.

You'll find out about all of the rest in this book.

Allways is the latest product from Funk Software, Inc., a company that has specialized in spreadsheet enhancements since its birth in 1982. At that time, VisiCalc was the king of the spreadsheet market. Lotus was about to come out with 1-2-3. I had just resigned my job at Data General. I was doing contract programming and consulting and trying to figure out what to do next.

One day, I was in a computer store watching a spreadsheet being printed in condensed mode on a wide-carriage dot matrix printer. The salesperson was saying that he kept that printer around just to print wide spreadsheets. As I watched, my good friend Ellen began amusing me with her parody of Frank Sinatra's song, "I Did It My Way." Ellen's version was "I Did It Sideways."

Her song was circulating in my brain as I watched the spreadsheet being printed. Then, the two ideas collided, and I asked, "Why not do it sideways with spreadsheets?"

Sideways prints in graphics. It creates a map of the data area in a matrix in memory, and instead of going from left to right, it goes from bottom to top, column by column, flipping the font.

At first, I began marketing Sideways as a VisiCalc add-on. Product sales grew slowly but steadily, and we got some very good reviews in the early computer magazines. Corey Sandler, one of the authors of this book, wrote the first review in PC Magazine in 1983. I still remember the lead: "Sideways is what Sideways does."

Around 1985 it was clear that 90 percent of Sideways sales were to 1-2-3 users, so we decided to do something special for 1-2-3 users, giving the product the look and feel of 1-2-3, while retaining the original Sideways function that just takes text files. That was a big success.

At that point we also customized it as a Symphony add-in. And then, about a year and a half ago, we made it a 1-2-3 add-in as well.

Today we have about a half million installations of Sideways. We expect Allways to be at least as successful.

Sideways was about presentation, in the sense that you don't want to present a spreadsheet held together with tape, staples, and glue. With Allways, we're saying, "Now that you've gotten rid of the staples and glue, what else can you do?"

We were very happy to assist Corey Sandler and Tom Badgett, two of the microcomputer industry's best-known authors, as they wrote this book about Allways. We hope it will help you use Allways in ways that go well beyond what you—and we—first expected.

Paul Funk
Cambridge, Mass.

Acknowledgments

The authors wish to note the contributions of a number of persons and companies who helped bring this book from concept to the bookstore.

Thanks to Tracy Smith of Waterside Productions for her capable agentry; to Teri Zak of John Wiley & Sons for publishing the book; and to Paul Funk, Jim Kinlan, and Steve Schwartz of Funk Software for their cooperation.

As always, we wish to thank our families for their understanding of the writer's life in the garret: Tom's is out by the cow pasture and Corey's is down in the catacombs.

We also wish to acknowledge the valuable assistance provided to the authors by a number of major hardware and software companies. We commend their products to your attention.

This book was researched and prepared using equipment and software that included the following:

≡ CompuAdd 80386/20 computer. A 20MHz 80386 microprocessor with 0 wait state, cache memory. CompuAdd Corporation, 12303 Technology Blvd., Austin, TX 78727. (800) 627-1967.

≡ COMPAQ Deskpro 386S computer. A 16MHz computer 80386SX microprocessor with 0 wait state memory. Compaq Computer Corporation, 20555 FM 149, Houston, TX 77070. (713) 370-0670.

≡ QMS-PS 810 PostScript laser printer with PostScript, H-P LaserJet + and Diablo emulations. QMS, P.O. Box 81250, Mobile, AL 36689. (205) 633-4300.

≡ Kyocera F1000A laser printer with H-P LaserJet II and Digital LN03 Plus emulations. Kyocera Unison, Inc., 3165 Adeline Street, PO Box 3056, Berkeley, CA 94703. (415) 748-6680.

≡ Allways. Versions 1.0 and 1.01. Funk Software, 222 Third St., Cambridge, MA 02142. (617) 497-6339.

≡ Hijaak and InSet software for image capture. Inset Systems, 71 Commerce Drive, Brookfield, CT 06804. (800) 828-8088. (203) 775-5866.

≡ WordPerfect Version 5.0 word processing software. WordPerfect Corp., 1555 N. Technology Way, Orem, UT 84057. (801) 227-4288.

≡ DESQview Version 2 multitasking, windowing software. Quarterdeck Office Systems, 150 Pico Boulevard, Santa Monica, CA 90405. (213) 392-9701.
≡ 1-2-3 Release 2.01. Lotus Development Corporation, 55 Cambridge Parkway, Cambridge, MA 02142. (617) 577-8500.
≡ Ventura Publisher, Desktop Publishing Software. Xerox Corporation, 360 N. Sepulveda Boulevard, El Segundo, CA 90245. (800) 445-5554.

Trademark Acknowledgments

≡ 1-2-3 and Symphony are registered trademarks of Lotus Development Corp.
≡ Compaq 386S and Compaq Expanded Memory Manager are trademarks of Compaq Computer Corporation.
≡ CompuAdd 386/20 is a registered trademark of CompuAdd Corporation.
≡ DeskJet and LaserJet are trademarks of Hewlett-Packard Co.
≡ DESQview is a registered trademark of Quarterdeck Office Systems.
≡ Graph Plus is a trademark of Micrografx®, Inc.
≡ Hijaak and InSet are registered trademarks of INSET Systems Inc.
≡ Intel® is a registered trademark of Intel Corporation.
≡ Kyosera F1000A is a registered trademark of Kyocera Unison, Inc.
≡ Microsoft Chart, Microsoft Excel, Microsoft Windows, and MS-DOS are registered trademarks of Microsoft Corporation.
≡ Selectric is a registered trademark of International Business Machines Corporation.
≡ SideKick is a registered trademark of Borland International.

1 Introduction

The electronic spreadsheet burst on the microcomputer world in the early 1980s. The first success was VisiCalc®, followed by—and soon many times surpassed by—Lotus 1-2-3®.

Some would say that it was the spreadsheet that gave the microcomputer a true reason for being in the business world, and with it was born the PC on the desktop.

The electronic spreadsheet is, basically, a gigantic yellow legal pad with each row and column linked together so that a change in one box can have an effect on all other boxes. It is a tool designed to allow the user to answer the question: *What if?*

What if . . .

≡ we reduced expenditures on research and development?
≡ we took out a new line of credit at a lower interest rate and increased the amount of money we borrow?
≡ we changed the percentage of gross revenues devoted to advertising?

Lotus 1-2-3 is one of those rare computer software offerings that captured the attention and loyalty of its users almost from the very beginning. Although VisiCalc and other spreadsheet products had warmed up the audience, it was 1-2-3 that took all the curtain calls. Lotus Development Corporation offered its customers just the right combination of features, easy-to-understand menus, and marketing to make 1-2-3 a hit.

But, time passes—especially in the rapidly evolving personal computer market—and yesterday's fabulous new evolutionary gain becomes today's dinosaur. The second generation of electronic spreadsheets—led by the Microsoft Excel® product—offered all of 1-2-3's data manipulation, adding a graphic screen-based ability to customize the appearance of the spreadsheet on the monitor and a set of sophisticated printer drivers to translate the screen image to polished hard copy on high-quality devices such as laser printers.

The new features possessed by the competition make electronic spreadsheets full members of the desktop publishing world. Users can employ proportionally spaced high-quality typefaces, draw rules and boxes, add shading and color, and otherwise manipulate their columns and rows of numbers and text with all of the capabilities of a professional typesetter.

Release 2.01 of 1-2-3, which was the current edition as spring 1989 began, remains a text-oriented product that was born in the days of monochrome monitors, before users came to expect creative graphics interfaces and color. The demand for 1-2-3 was still strong—Lotus was reported to be selling as many as 100,000 copies of the program each month—but the product's top-rank position was clearly under assault.

Into the breach between text-based 1-2-3 and the graphics-based new world leapt a small Cambridge, Massachusetts, company, Funk Software, with an "add-in" product that sits between the spreadsheet and the outside world (the monitor and the printer). Funk's product, Allways, brings releases 2.0 and 2.01 of 1-2-3 fully into the world of the "spreadsheet publisher."

Allways became an immediate top-seller early in 1989, as thousands of 1-2-3 users recognized the expansion it brought to their trusty old software.

Even as Lotus programmers feverishly applied finishing touches to release 3.0, a virtually new product that addresses many of the weaknesses of earlier releases and answers the requests of users for more power and a better user interface, the company made an important marketing decision: it launched a special campaign, giving new buyers of release 2.01 a copy of Allways.

Then on March 21, 1989, Lotus announced an agreement with Funk Software to include Allways as an integral part of 1-2-3 release 2.2. The functionality and features of Allways remained the same, but the Add-In Manager was included as part of the 1-2-3 menu structure. In addition, Funk Software promised to produce a release 3.0-compatible version of Allways.

About This Book

Whether you bought Allways to upgrade an existing copy of 1-2-3 or received a copy of the program from Lotus as part of a new purchase, this book is designed to help you become truly proficient at spreadsheet publishing. By learning how to use Allways to format spreadsheets for graphics-oriented printing, you will enhance the value of 1-2-3 and, as an enjoyable side benefit, make the venerable Lotus application more fun to use.

When you print a spreadsheet directly from 1-2-3, you can work hard and make it look like Figure 1.1.

When you format the spreadsheet with Allways before you print, you can easily make it look like Figure 1.2.

About Symphony

If you use Symphony® instead of or in addition to 1-2-3, then Allways still is for you. Funk Software has a Symphony version that is almost identical to the 1-2-3 version. The functionality is the same and the user interface is similar.

The only real difference you will notice in Allways for Symphony is how the function keys operate. Funk has mapped the keys to match the Symphony keys as closely as possible in the same way that Allways for 1-2-3 matches the 1-2-3 function keys. In 1-2-3, for example, F10 is the graph key, and in Allways for 1-2-3 the F10 function key turns the display of attached 1-2-3 graphs off and on. In Symphony, on the other hand, the F10 key is the name key and has that same function in Allways for Symphony.

In addition, the procedure for calling up Allways is slightly different. With 1-2-3 you use the Add-In Manager or a function key combination (hot key). In Symphony you can select Allways from a sheet menu. When you enter the / command with Allways installed, the Allways selection is the final item on the menu.

Finally, as with Allways in 1-2-3, you can use Symphony macros to conduct Allways commands and procedures.

Why Use a Spreadsheet as the Base for Charts and Graphs?

At first thought, it might seem unusual to use a spreadsheet as the platform on which to build graphs and text charts. Why not employ a specialized graphing program for the one and a capable word processor or presentation graphics program for the other?

The answer is this: Using an electronic spreadsheet to produce charts and graphs opens up the world of *What if?* to these efforts.

Change a number or a formula on a 1-2-3 spreadsheet, and the values in cells on that spreadsheet will also change. Change a number or a formula in the spreadsheet and update a .PIC file within 1-2-3, and the graph file—with enhancements—in your Allways file will also change.

What Is Allways and What Can It Do for You?

At its most basic level, Allways is a tool—a screwdriver, a drill, a wheelbarrow—needed to do your job.

If you use Allways as a tool, you probably are producing regular spreadsheet reports for inclusion in company annual reports, as part of client proposals, or to produce eye-catching overhead projection for marketing, financial, or

Figure 1.1
Sample
spreadsheet printed
directly from
1-2-3

	Three Months Ending		Six Months Ending	
	12/31/88	12/31/87	12/31/88	12/31/87
SALES				
Northeast	9,300,123	2,467,898	17,423,412	4,467,543
South/Central	7,454,890	1,987,234	14,234,678	3,567,123
West	1,864,234	492,567	3,456,321	975,123
Net Sales	18,619,247	4,947,699	35,114,411	9,009,789
OPERATING EXPENSES				
Cost of sales	4,123,498	432,567	7,789,234	789,234
Selling, general and ad	7,589,812	1,987,123	14,321,678	3,456,123
Research and developmen	978,123	324,765	2,000,123	525,234
Income from operations	5,927,814	2,203,244	11,003,376	4,239,198
Income from interest	156,123	107,654	234,123	125,678
Income (before Federal	6,083,937	2,310,898	11,237,499	4,364,876
Provision for Federal i	2,687,612	1,123,498	4,321,789	1,234,654
Net income	3,396,325	1,187,400	6,915,710	3,130,222

educational applications. Your solution before Allways may have involved sending 1-2-3 spreadsheets to a .PRN file, then loading that file into a word processor or desktop publishing package for enhancement before printing.

From our point of view, those for whom Allways is today a luxury will soon discover it to be a necessity. The world of business presentations has rapidly moved from typewritten documents to word-processed impact printer documents to medium-quality dot matrix output to today's high-quality (typically laser produced) desktop publishing hard copies.

With electronic spreadsheets now viewed as part of that desktop publishing world, you can see how a spreadsheet publishing product like Allways is well on its way to necessity status.

Doing It by Hand

Before we describe Allways, let's look at the "old-fashioned" manual way of cobbling a 1-2-3 worksheet to an outside enhancement product.

Figure 1.2
Sample spreadsheet printed after Allways formatting

Instant Millionaire Company, Inc.

Financial Report to Prospects

I
M

	Three Months Ending		Six Months Ending	
	Dec. 31, 1988	Dec. 31, 1987	Dec. 31, 1988	Dec. 31, 1987
SALES				
Northeast	9,300,123	2,467,898	17,423,412	4,467,543
South/Central	7,454,890	1,987,234	14,234,678	3,567,123
West	1,864,234	492,567	3,456,321	975,123
Net Sales	18,619,247	4,947,699	35,114,411	9,009,789
OPERATING EXPENSES				
Cost of sales	4,123,498	432,567	7,789,234	789,234
Selling, general and administrative	7,589,812	1,987,123	14,321,678	3,456,123
Research and development	978,123	324,765	2,000,123	525,234
Income from operations	5,927,814	2,203,244	11,003,376	4,239,198
Income from interest	156,123	107,654	234,123	125,678
Income (before Federal income taxes)	6,083,937	2,310,898	11,237,499	4,364,876
Provision for Federal income taxes	2,687,612	1,123,498	4,321,789	1,234,654
Net income	$3,396,325	$1,187,400	$6,915,710	$3,130,222
Net income per share of common stock	$0.32	$0.14	$0.30	$0.24

First quarter results for fiscal year 1988 show that the Instant Millionaire Company is well along the way to its corporate goal: to make its greedy founders rich at the expense of the consumer and shareholder.

Hurry. Time is running out. Send in your money to buy your own set of shares now, and take advantage of our free dish offer.

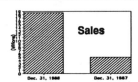

Application to Purchase Shares

Date	Name		
	Address		
Number of shares	City	State	ZIP

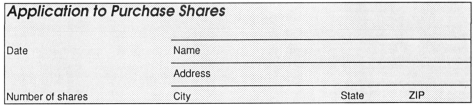

Making a change to an ASCII version of a worksheet you are formatting with another software package involves these steps:

1. Exit the word processor or desktop publishing software.
2. Load 1-2-3.
3. Call up the spreadsheet you want to change.
4. Make the modifications and save the file.
5. Export the changed file to .PRN format.
6. Exit 1-2-3 and reload the text formatter.
7. Load the modified .PRN file.
8. Redo all of the formatting already made before you decided to make a change.
9. Format the modified portions of the spreadsheet.

Of course, you can make simple changes to numbers or spacing inside the text formatter, but to make basic spreadsheet modifications, including formulas and dependent cell relationships, you have to return to 1-2-3. Besides, if you make even minor changes in the text version of your spreadsheet, then the original source file (the .WK1 worksheet) will not agree with the presentation version, so you probably will have to go through all of these steps in any case.

In addition, if you want to include graphics in your report, you must handle these as separate files. 1-2-3 does not save graphs as ASCII files, and it may be more difficult to load these .PIC files into your formatting program.

The Allways Alternative

Allways can include .PIC files as part of the main spreadsheet printout and, in addition, it simplifies the procedure for modifying an existing spreadsheet that you may already have formatted. To change an Allways spreadsheet after you have started formatting, you must return to 1-2-3, but because Allways is an add-in product, the process is much simpler.

1. Press ESC or the Allways "hot-key" combination to return to 1-2-3.
2. Make the changes.
3. Save the spreadsheet.
4. Press the hot key to reenter Allways.
5. Format the modified portions of the spreadsheet.

The formatting already accomplished up to the modification remains in place, and you can pick up where you left off.

Allways: A Descriptive Definition

What is this program that easily makes your spreadsheets easier to look at?

Allways is a postprocessor for formatting 1-2-3 spreadsheets. You can't use it to enter spreadsheet data, but with Allways you can

≡ select up to eight fonts and three typefaces for spreadsheet data.
≡ draw lines and boxes around cells.
≡ shade blocks and ranges.
≡ change column width and row height.
≡ print cells or ranges in up to eight colors.
≡ set display background, foreground, and highlight colors.
≡ select printers and do printer setup, including laser cartridge selection and orientation, from menus such as those in 1-2-3 and pull down windows.

When you press the Allways hot-key combination, the Allways screen appears. The screen contains the current 1-2-3 worksheet with the default screen and printing formats already set. The formats you select with Allways are linked to the spreadsheet currently displayed in 1-2-3, but Allways does not actually change the 1-2-3 worksheet. The appearance changes you make to the spreadsheet through Allways are stored in a separate file that loads with the spreadsheet. Because Allways is a graphics-oriented product, you can actually see the special fonts and other formatting specifications right on the screen. Allways is very close to a what-you-see-is-what-you-get, or WYSIWYG, product.

As already mentioned, Allways is a 1-2-3 add-in, which means it installs with 1-2-3 and is easily accessible through the **Add-In Manager** menu, or by pressing an ALT-function key combination. Which key combination serves as the Allways hot key is decided during Allways installation. You enter Allways by pressing the hot key and return to 1-2-3 through the Allways menu or by pressing the hot-key combination or ESC in the Allways ready mode.

The Need for Allways

It is into this environment that Allways has fallen. By providing WYSIWYG graphics, color, and pull-down menus for existing 1-2-3 spreadsheets, Allways makes up for many of 1-2-3's shortcomings. It is a natural addition for users who use 1-2-3 information for business presentations, who want to save time in spreadsheet design and preparation, and who want to make better use of today's laser and high-density dot matrix printers.

Allways helps you make better use of 1-2-3's graphics capabilities by moving a finished graph right into the spreadsheet for formatting and printing.

The limitations of Allways include the inability to enter spreadsheet data from inside the Allways graphics mode; you cannot generate graphs in Allways or do much to change the original graph produced by 1-2-3. In addition, much of the hard work you have put into existing spreadsheets to format the data is wasted. In fact, you may want to do some spreadsheets over from scratch, rather than spend the time required to replace 1-2-3 formatting in favor of the Allways features.

Nevertheless, Allways is a strong addition to basic 1-2-3 functionality and provides capabilities that you will learn and accept naturally. Once you have printed a few spreadsheets with Allways formatting, it will be difficult to go back to the way things were without it.

Using Allways to Enhance Graphs and Charts

A graph is a picture of numbers.

Like any other work of art, the representation of reality it can present can be realistic, it can be representational, it can be abstract, it can be good, and it can be bad. The principal difference between business graphics and art, though, is that graphics *must communicate* to be successful. In communication, there is no place for graphics for graphics' sake.

Although 1-2-3 is a most powerful manipulator of numbers, its abilities as a graph maker are considerably more limited. Here you have three choices.

1. Export 1-2-3 worksheet data to a specialized graph-making package, such as Harvard Graphics™ from Software Publishing Co. or Microsoft Chart® or Graph Plus from Micrografx®. These products serve users who need highly sophisticated and complex graph forms, including Pert, Gantt, bubble, and high-low charts. The 1-2-3 user must save the worksheet to a file, then enter the separate graph-making package and load the worksheet file. These graph-making packages will use the data to create new graphs, but they generally will not offer much in the way of enhancements to a 1-2-3 worksheet itself. Changes that must be made to the spreadsheet data require a trip back to the 1-2-3 program and the creation of a new file in both programs. Most will not allow the integration of a 1-2-3 worksheet and an associated graph into a single document.

2. Export a finished 1-2-3 graph, saved as a .PIC file, to a specialized presentation graphics program, where a limited amount of enhancement can be applied to the image. Products in this category include Freelance Plus®, from Lotus, and Graph Plus. Used in this way, these products do not add any new graph forms to the 1-2-3 arsenal. These products also do not offer much in the way of enhancements to a 1-2-3 worksheet itself, and they will not allow you to integrate a 1-2-3 worksheet and an associated graph into a single document. Once again, you have to reenter 1-2-3 to make any changes in data and then create a new .PIC file in 1-2-3 and a new graph file in the presentation graphics program.

3. Employ the Allways solution. Allways, as an add-in to 1-2-3, resides within the spreadsheet program itself. Allways will enhance both the 1-2-3 worksheet and the saved .PIC file. With Allways, you can integrate the finished

graph and worksheet into a single document, and changes to the data are easily accomplished. A shift into 1-2-3 is one keystroke combination away, and changes made to a 1-2-3 worksheet are immediately implemented in the Allways display. Changes made to a 1-2-3 graph and saved as a .PIC file will also instantly update the Allways version.

But Why Use Graphics at All?

If you have not already answered that question for yourself, take the time to do so now. No book, no high-priced consultant, no outsider at all can fully understand the nature of your business or the means by which you make your business decisions. One thing an outsider can surely say, though, is that clear and easy communication within your company and to your market and financial backers is critical.

What kind of reports do you need to prepare? Financial statements? Inventory reports? Analysis of personnel benefits and deployment? Payroll charts?

Are you using graphs now? Are they clearly designed and presented? Are they accurate? Do they include sophisticated statistical analysis of trends? Are you able to determine correlation between variables?

In this book, you will learn about the types of charts available to you, and what kinds of data are best suited to each design.

Remember, no matter how capable the computer and printer, it will still be up to *you* to decide which type of chart will best communicate your information: a line graph, a bar chart, a pie graph, an XY chart, a histogram, a scatter plot, or one of dozens of variations.

The program will also not be of much assistance to you in the gathering of information. What kind of data should you seek? How do you know if the data is valid? Is there some way to "massage" your data to enhance your message?

The 1-2-3/Allways combination will enable you to draw in almost any color, using a wide range of crosshatch, dot, line, and solid patterns. But you'll still have to make the design choices. Which colors, shapes, designs, and other devices communicate your messages most clearly? Are you setting up the viewer for a mistaken preconception before he or she studies the picture?

Allways: Evolution and Background

Funk Software, Lotus Development Corp., and their respective products have been linked together almost from the start. Paul Funk's foreword to this book gives a bit of the corporate history. Of course, all of Funk's products work with or within the 1-2-3 product. Some of the top executives and programmers at Funk came out of Lotus.

Allways has a short and interesting history. Paul Funk and the programmers at Funk Software first seriously considered a product with the functionality of Allways in March 1988. The idea was based on the success of a printer utility for 1-2-3 that made it easier to send control strings to a printer. Of all the Funk utilities, print enhancement routines seemed the most popular, even though the offerings at that time were severely limited compared to Allways.

Work started almost immediately and a reasonably finished product was ready to go out the door about seven months later. Allways became popular quickly, not only because it offered functionality that nearly all 1-2-3 users wanted but also because of the close ties between Funk Software and Lotus Development Corporation. These close relations led to the packaging of Allways with 1-2-3 during the first quarter of 1989 as well as to the promotion of Allways by Lotus as the presentation graphics add-in of choice for the package.

In addition, Lotus purchased the rights to Allways to include the program with release 2.2 of 1-2-3. Although release 3.0 contains enhanced formatting techniques, it does not show fonts and other presentation enhancements on-screen. A Lotus release 3.0 version of Allways will correct this shortcoming.

The newest release of 1-2-3 (release 3.0) will be available midway through 1989 and will include some—but not all—of the Allways functionality. We expect that Allways will continue to sell thousands of copies to the existing base of users of 1-2-3 releases 2 and 2.01 for some time afterwards. Corporate users who already have thousands of dollars and untold personnel time invested in earlier releases will adopt the new release cautiously, and individual users may neither see the need nor be able to justify the additional investment of upgrading to release 3.0. And, we expect Funk to continue to find ways to enhance Lotus products, including release 3.0 of 1-2-3.

Why a Book on Allways?

Among the things you will notice about Allways is that the company-provided documentation is quite good at showing you how to install Allways and how to use product features. But software user manuals do not normally provide much information on the philosophy of the software design. They do not offer instruction on when to use certain features, on why certain techniques are desirable and others are not, or on how to overcome shortcomings in the product. Much of this information comes from users themselves, people who have experience in the field and can supplement the original design intent with real-life experience.

With this in mind, this book was designed to be part tutorial and part user feedback. We will show you why Funk provided some of the features included in Allways and how to use these features for optimum spreadsheet enhancement.

How to Use This Book

This book is both tutorial and reference. You can start at the beginning and follow through to the end, learning about 1-2-3 and Allways as you go, each section building on the information of the previous one. On the other hand, we have organized the book so it can serve as a direct access reference for you as you use Allways.

Refer to the table of contents to find general topics, for example. You can use the index to help you find specific topics to answer questions about Allways as you use it. Turn directly to Figure 5.1 to help you determine quickly what features are available in Allways and how to access them; then, if you need additional information, look up the topic in the index or table of contents.

The last section of this chapter provides a brief summary of each following chapter.

System Configuration

Although you can use Allways with diskette-based systems, especially the newer, high-density drives, most 1-2-3 users who have add-in programs such as Allways use a hard disk. Although we show you how to configure Allways for a floppy system, the procedures we describe in this book will be based on a hard disk installation. Refer to Chapter 3, "Technical Details," for help with your floppy installation.

Conventions We Use

To reduce the number of repetitive entries and explanations and to limit the possibility of confusion, we use certain descriptive and display conventions throughout this book. Table 1.1 provides a list of some of these conventions.

Most menu selections and other program commands require that you press the ENTER or RETURN key. In describing these procedures we assume that you will press RETURN or ENTER as part of the command, and we won't tell you to do so.

1-2-3 macros must be preceded by an apostrophe (') label prefix. You don't see this prefix displayed in the spreadsheet cell, and we don't include the

Table 1.1
Externs Commands
Keyboard Notation

Element	Style	Examples
Single-key functions	All capital (uppercase) letters, bold when pressed now	RETURN and ENTER SHIFT CTRL ALT ESC F1, F5 TAB DEL INS
Multikey function	Connected with a single hyphen.	ALT-A CTRL-A SHIFT-A
Menu command sequences	In bold type with slash and full name of each menu item. Menu selections in upper- and lowercase; menu sequences in bold type	**/Range Name Create** **/Format Font Use** **/Layout Options** **LineWeight Normal**
Macro command, special key notations	All uppercase	{FOR} {QUIT} {UP} {BEEP}
Macro range names	Shown with backslash (\), name in lowercase	\c \a \z
Range names	Bold with initial caps	**Sales** **Total** **Input**

apostrophe in macro entries. You must use the prefix, however, or instead of writing a macro you will carry out the command sequence.

Allways and 1-2-3 menu command sequences begin with the forward slash (/). You then select a menu route by moving the cursor to highlight the desired option and pressing RETURN, or by entering the first character of the command sequence.

How This Book Is Organized

This book is divided into 14 chapters, plus a comprehensive index, which we believe may be the single most important design feature of the book. A detailed index that contains major headings and cross-referenced terms is an invaluable aid in using any text. It is an imperative portion of a book that you use regularly as reference or tutorial, as this book is intended to be used.

Chapter 1 is a general introduction to Allways, together with a discussion of how this book is organized and how it can best be used. Chapter 2 gets you started using Allways in a hurry. You will learn how to format data in an existing spreadsheet, how to set up your printer, and how to print a worksheet. More details on these functions follow in later chapters.

Chapter 3 gives you an inside peek at the way Allways works and various technical tips. It details the salient features of Allways, lists system requirements, shows you how to install the Add-In Manager and how to attach Allways, and offers some additional application hints.

Chapters 4, 5, and 6 provide specific information on how to use Allways to enhance your spreadsheet and graphics material from 1-2-3. We give instruction on a step-by-step path through the operation of the program, and we take a look at the underlying concepts of the menu tree.

Chapters 7, 8, and 9 explain the types of charts and graphs you can create with 1-2-3. You'll learn about what to include and exclude in your .PIC file. Chapter 10 shows you how to use Allways to enhance the images imported from 1-2-3.

Chapter 11 should whet your appetite for using Allways to create a range of business forms and documents, from simple memo pads to complex questionnaires.

In Chapter 12, you'll learn the details of printer settings and configurations. The entire purpose of Allways, after all, is to produce enhanced printouts.

Understanding 1-2-3 macros is an important part of getting the most out of Allways. Although Allways, itself, does not have a macro language, you can enter Allways commands in a 1-2-3 macro to automate many of the formatting or printing operations of Allways. Chapter 13 introduces you to 1-2-3 macros and Chapter 14 shows you some Allways-specific examples.

The comprehensive, cross-referenced index helps you find the precise topics you need as you learn Allways and as you work with your own spreadsheets.

2 Quick Start

If you are like most computer users, when you get a new piece of hardware or software you don't want to wade through the entire users' manual before you can do something useful with the new product. Fortunately, Allways is the kind of software package that comes up fast and shows immediate results.

This chapter shows you how to install Allways quickly, how to format your first spreadsheet, and how to print. Later chapters will provide more detail on installation and operation, but for now, let's get Allways up and running.

Installing Allways

You have to go through a simple installation process before Allways will run. If you are familiar with the Lotus INSTALL program, installing Allways should be very easy. If you already have installed your copy of Allways, skip this section and go directly to "Starting Allways."

The Allways Package

The Allways package consists of the user manual and five 5.25-inch diskettes that contain Allways programs, fonts, printer drivers, and sample files. You will learn more about what each of these diskettes contains in Chapter 3, "Technical Details," but for now the only one you need to be concerned with is **Disk 1—Installation**. It contains the INSTALL program **AWSETUP**, which provides a Lotus-like **Install** menu that automates the process for you.

Remember that Allways uses the Lotus ADD_MGR program and therefore is compatible only with Lotus 1-2-3 release 2.0 or later. If you are using an earlier version of 1-2-3, you will have to upgrade to a more recent release before Allways will run.

When using add-in programs with 1-2-3, you just about have to have a hard disk. It is possible to run add-in programs from a floppy system (we will give you some hints on doing that in Chapter 3, "Technical Details"), but the level of frustration can be rather high. For this quick-start section we assume you are using a hard drive.

Starting the INSTALL Program

We'll assume that you encounter no problems, that you have a fairly standard computer configuration, and that you receive no error messages. If you need more help, refer to Chapter 3, "Technical Details."

NOTE: Before you begin the install process, make sure you have at least 1.5 MBytes of free space on your hard disk. You can determine this by typing **DIR** at any prompt and noting the amount of free space at the end of the directory listing.

To start the install process, insert the Allways Disk 1—Installation diskette into drive A:. From the hard disk prompt, type

A:

Press **RETURN** and type

AWSETUP

Press **RETURN**.

The Allways **Install** menu will be displayed. (See Figure 2.1.)

Notice that the option **First Time Installation** is highlighted. Press **RETURN**. Allways asks for the path on your hard disk where 1-2-3 is installed. C:\123 is the default. Enter

C:\Lotus

or any other appropriate path to point to the installed version of Lotus 1-2-3 if it is other than the default.

Allways next wants to know the name of your 1-2-3 driver set. This file contains information about your configuration. Unless you have modified

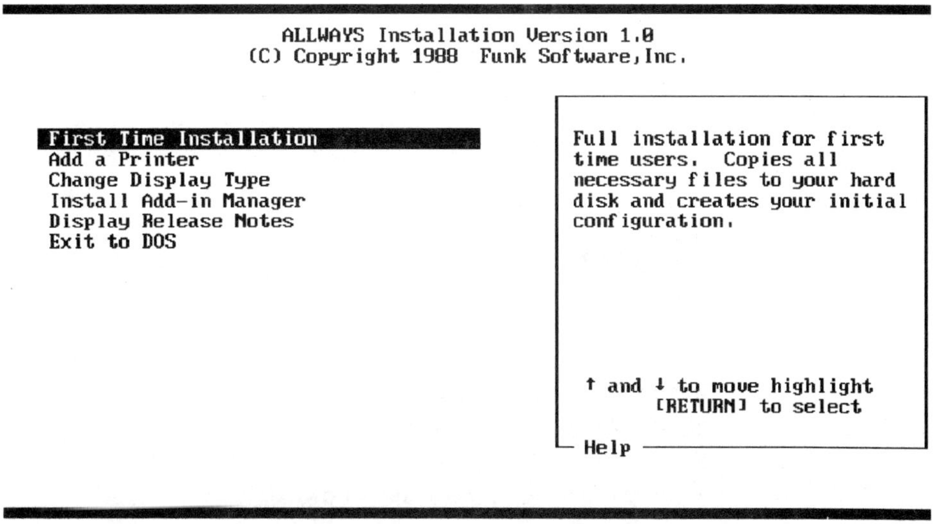

Figure 2.1
The Allways Install
menu

```
                        ALLWAYS Installation Version 1.0
                        (C) Copyright 1988  Funk Software,Inc.


        ┌─────────────────────────────┐    ┌──────────────────────────────┐
        │ First Time Installation      │    │ Full installation for first  │
        │ Add a Printer                │    │ time users.  Copies all      │
        │ Change Display Type          │    │ necessary files to your hard │
        │ Install Add-in Manager       │    │ disk and creates your initial│
        │ Display Release Notes        │    │ configuration.               │
        │ Exit to DOS                  │    │                              │
        └─────────────────────────────┘    │                              │
                                            │                              │
                                            │                              │
                                            │  ↑ and ↓ to move highlight   │
                                            │     [RETURN] to select       │
                                            │                              │
                                            └─ Help ───────────────────────┘
```

1-2-3, the name of the driver set is **123.SET**. Just press **RETURN** when Allways gives you that prompt.

The next prompt is for monitor type. Allways is smart enough (probably) to select the appropriate monitor type for your system. If the displayed prompt is correct, press **RETURN**. If the incorrect monitor type is displayed, select **No** and answer the questions.

Next, use the displayed menu window to choose the type of printer you are using. Use the up arrow and down arrow keys to highlight the proper printer choice, then press **RETURN**.

You will install only one printer at this time, so choose **No** at the next prompt.

The **Hot-Key** menu is next. If you have other ADD_MGR programs installed, the menu reflects these previous choices. Otherwise, Allways simply asks which of the three available hot keys you want to use to invoke Allways. Choose one from the list.

Allways will copy the required files to your hard disk, including the Lotus ADD_MGR (if you haven't already installed it). You will be asked to insert different diskettes as the program needs information from them. Allways tells you when the installation is complete, and you can then select **Return to DOS** from the **AWSETUP** menu.

You now are ready to run the program, but before you do, insert Allways **Disk 5** into the A: drive and change the active hard drive directory to the one where your worksheet files are stored. If you store your files in the same directory with 1-2-3 programs and that directory is named **Lotus**, type

CD\Lotus

Next, type

COPY A:AWSAMPLE.*

This command copies two files from the Allways disk to your Lotus subdirectory. You will use them in a few minutes to demonstrate what Allways can do with a plain 1-2-3 spreadsheet.

Starting Allways

When you first load 1-2-3 with Allways attached, a **WAIT** message is displayed in the Status box, then the screen clears and an Allways box with a copyright notice and the serial number of your Allways software is displayed. This is the ADD_MGR attaching Allways to 1-2-3 so it will be available when you press the hot key you selected during installation.

Allways works with 1-2-3 and uses the current spreadsheet, so to start Allways you must first load a spreadsheet into 1-2-3. For this example, load the sample spreadsheet you copied from the Allways Disk 5 by typing

/frawsample

NOTE: Later in this book we use the expanded command notation to ask you to enter such commands. For example, here we would tell you to enter the command **/File Retrieve AWSAMPLE**. For the present the exact keystrokes are given to step you through the process.

The slash bar (/) calls up the 1-2-3 menu. **F** selects the **File** option and **R** chooses **Retrieve**. The name of the file is **AWSAMPLE**. The Bestway Shipping Corporation balance sheet for October 1, 1988, appears on the screen. This is a typical 1-2-3 application and is a good one to help you learn about Allways.

To set up a standard of comparison, let's print the sample spreadsheet from 1-2-3. Enter the following commands:

/pprA1..K47<RETURN>G

In long command notation this sequence is

/Print Printer Range A1..K47 <RETURN> Go

If you have set your printer up for compressed print, you should get a spreadsheet printout that looks like Figure 2.2. If your printer is set for 10 characters per inch, you will get a two-page printout, page 1 of which looks like Figure 2.3.

This probably is the way you are accustomed to seeing Lotus 1-2-3 spreadsheets on your printer. The only difference is that if you plan to show the results to someone else or include them in a report, you probably included some additional formatting characters. For example, you might have used the '/= sequence to draw a double line under some headings, or you may have used vertical bars (|) to separate some columns.

When you design a spreadsheet for Allways, as this sample was designed, you don't put in these formatting characters in 1-2-3. They are installed with Allways.

Your First Pretty Spreadsheet

To see how Funk Software programmers formatted the basic spreadsheet with Allways, press the hot-key sequence you established during installation to switch to the Allways screen. If, for example, your hot key is ALT-F9, hold down the ALT key and press F9. After a short pause, the spreadsheet is displayed in the Allways format. (See Figure 2.4.)

Figure 2.2
Compressed print
version AWSAMPLE
in 1-2-3

Bestway Shipping Corporation
Balance Sheet
October 1, 1988

ASSETS

	This Year	Last Year	Change
Current Assets			
Cash	247,886	126,473	96%
Accounts receivable	863,652	524,570	65%
Inventory	79,071	53,790	47%
Prepaid expenses	9,257	11,718	-21%
Investments	108,577	31,934	240%
Total Current Assets	1,308,443	748,485	75%
Fixed Assets			
Machinery and equipment	209,906	158,730	32%
Vehicles	429,505	243,793	76%
Office furniture	50,240	36,406	38%
(Accumulated depreciation)	(101,098)	(64,394)	57%
Total fixed assets	588,553	374,535	57%
	$1,896,996	$1,123,020	69%

LIABILITIES AND SHAREHOLDERS' EQUITY

	This Year	Last Year	Change
Current Liabilities			
Accounts payable trade	426,041	332,845	28%
Notes payable	45,327	23,486	93%
Accrued liabilities	34,614	26,026	33%
Income taxes payable	88,645	51,840	71%
Total Current Liabilities	594,627	434,197	37%
Noncurrent Liabilities			
Long-term debt	488,822	349,253	40%
Deferred federal tax	147,844	92,101	61%
Total Noncurrent Liabilities	636,666	441,354	44%
Shareholders' equity			
Common stock	1,000	1,000	0%
Opening retained earnings	246,469	82,531	199%
Profit (loss) for the period	418,234	163,938	155%
Total Shareholders' Equity	665,703	247,469	169%
	$1,896,996	$1,123,020	69%

Figure 2.3
Standard (10 cpi)
version AWSAMPLE
in 1-2-3

```
Bestway Shipping Corporation
Balance Sheet
October 1, 1988
```

```
                                     ASSETS
                                            This Year     Last Year
Current Assets
Cash                                           247,886       126,473
Accounts receivable                            863,652       524,570
Inventory                                       79,071        53,790
Prepaid expenses                                 9,257        11,718
Investments                                    108,577        31,934
             Total Current Assets            1,308,443       748,485

Fixed Assets
Machinery and equipment                        209,906       158,730
Vehicles                                       429,505       243,793
Office furniture                                50,240        36,406
(Accumulated depreciation)                    (101,098)      (64,394)
             Total fixed assets                588,553       374,535
                                            $1,896,996    $1,123,020


                          LIABILITIES AND SHAREHOLDERS' EQUIT
                                            This Year     Last Year
Current Liabilities
Accounts payable trade                         426,041       332,845
Notes payable                                   45,327        23,486
Accrued liabilities                             34,614        26,026
Income taxes payable                            88,645        51,840
             Total Current Liabilities         594,627       434,197

Noncurrent Liabilities
Long-term debt                                 488,822       349,253
Deferred federal tax                           147,844        92,101
             Total Noncurrent Liabilities      636,666       441,354

Shareholders' equity
Common stock                                     1,000         1,000
Opening retained earnings                      246,469        82,531
Profit (loss) for the period                   418,234       163,938
             Total Shareholders' Equity        665,703       247,469
                                            $1,896,996    $1,123,020
```

Because Allways is (mostly) what-you-see-is-what-you-get, you should see fonts, shading, and other enhancements just as they will print on your printer. Try moving the cursor around the spreadsheet, just as you would in 1-2-3. Most of the commands you are familiar with also work in Allways, though you will notice some differences in the way Allways handles formatting and other features. As you will see later, however, these changes are mostly for the better.

Formatting with Allways

How did Funk do the things it did to this sample spreadsheet? As you move the cursor around the spreadsheet, notice the upper left-hand corner of

Figure 2.4
Sample
spreadsheet
AWSAMPLE in
Allways

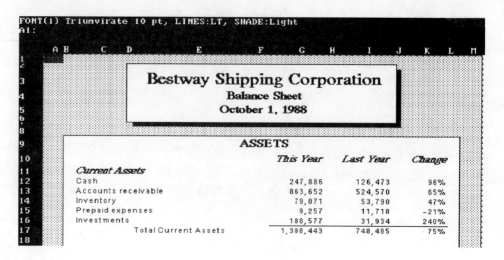

the Allways screen. In addition to the cell references and range format information you are used to in 1-2-3, you see data about font names, font sizes, shading, and perhaps other information.

Move the cursor to cell F3, for example. The information at the top of the screen shows that the format is:

Font(8): Times 20 pt Bold

NOTE: If you don't know what **Times 20 pt Bold** means, don't worry. A full discussion of fonts appears later in this book.

Allways uses a set of eight fonts for each spreadsheet. This font set is numbered 1 through 8, and you actually set the fonts for each cell or range by selecting the font number from a pull-down list in the Allways menu. This approach makes changes to broad areas of the spreadsheet easy, because you only have to change the definition of one of the numbered fonts to change the appearance of each range that uses this font number.

Cell F3 contains the company name, centered in the cell with the leading caret (^) in 1-2-3. Notice the width of this cell. You can check the width with the **/Worksheet Column Set-Width** command sequence. The width of F3 is two, but Allways interprets the center caret to mean "Center around this cell." That's why the company name, in the large, 20-point font, hangs to the left of its cell of origin.

Next, move the cursor to cell F7. The format of this cell is the default for this spreadsheet, Font (1) Triumvirate 10 point, but it includes a solid shade. Notice the height of this row. You can tell that there is something unusual about this row if you look at the row number at the left of the screen. The number 7, and the 6 for the row above, are distorted and incomplete. To check the row height, enter the **/Worksheet Row Set-Height** command sequence. As you can see, the row is set at 5 lines high, making it very thin compared to the rows around it.

This answers one of the most common questions about this sample spreadsheet, "How did Funk get the shadow box around the company name?" By establishing a very thin row below the company name box and a very thin column on the right side (column J with a width of 0.60), then shading these areas with the **/Format Shade Solid** command in Allways, you end up with a shadow box and a very impressive spreadsheet.

Let's try changing the font on the **Assets** label at the top of the first data block, just to give you an idea of how easy it is to make any spreadsheet pretty in Allways.

First move the cursor to cell F9 where the centered **Assets** label is entered. Next, enter the following command sequence:

/Format Font

This will display the font window (Figure 2.5), showing you which eight fonts have been selected for this spreadsheet.

You can see from the top of the display that the selected font for this cell is **Times Roman 14 pt**. This font selection appears in the font window as entry number 7. Use the cursor movement keys to select one of the other fonts available in the font window. Just to keep things simple, don't choose a font that is larger than the one already specified for this cell because a larger font will cause row 9 to become wider, possibly changing the way your spreadsheet prints.

Suppose you decide to change the **Assets** cell to the Times Italic 12 pt font. Move the highlight bar to line number 6 in the font window and press **RETURN**. Allways asks you what range of cells you want to specify for this font.

Figure 2.5
Allways font
window in
AWSAMPLE
spreadsheet

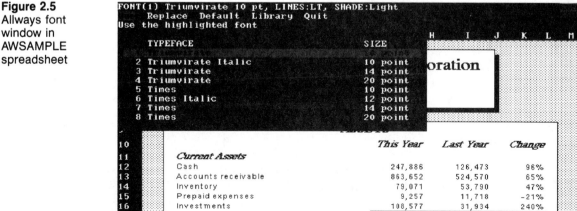

Simply press **RETURN** to accept only the single cell that contains the **Asset** label. You will see the display change immediately to the new font.

Overall, formatting your 1-2-3 spreadsheet with Allways is just that easy. You can use the Lotus-like menu structure to select fonts, cell widths, row heights, display and print colors; to draw boxes and lines; and to conduct a number of other relatively simple formatting functions that will make your spreadsheets stand out from the ordinary.

Printing with Allways

Obviously, the ultimate goal of all this formatting work is to get your spreadsheet on paper or acetate. If you have used 1-2-3 to print a spreadsheet, you can do it in Allways even easier.

Enter the **/Print Range Set** command sequence to specify the range you want to print. Either enter a discrete range (such as A1..K47) or use the cursor keys to highlight the range you want to print.

> **NOTE:** Although you may already have specified a print range for a spreadsheet in 1-2-3, you must establish a new print range in Allways. Print ranges set up in one program do not carry over to the other.

Notice on your screen that Allways marks the range with a dashed line. On larger spreadsheets you will see other dashed lines that mark the page boundaries so you can tell where the right and bottom margins are.

When you are satisfied with the selected range, press **G** for **Go**, and the spreadsheet will print.

The Allways print facility is much more complete than the print facility in 1-2-3, permitting selection of printer drivers, interfaces, resolutions, and other print characteristics right from the print menus without exiting Allways.

Exiting Allways

You can leave Allways the way you came in, with the hot-key combination you specified during installation, or by pressing the ESC key from the main menu or in the Allways mode (analogous to 1-2-3's Ready mode), and by selecting **123** from the main menu.

Remember that you do not conduct any file operations from within Allways. All file-loading and file-saving operations are done from within 1-2-3, so one of the first things you want to do when you get back into 1-2-3 from Allways is to save the current file. When you do, a companion file, *.ALL, which contains the formatting specifications you established in Allways, also is saved. The next time you load this file from within 1-2-3, then switch to Allways, the same formatting will be recalled from this format file.

As a user you don't really have to be aware of the format companion file; just be sure you save the current worksheet before you load another file or exit 1-2-3 so the Allways formatting will be retained.

A Tour of Allways Menus

Allways uses menu commands that are similar in structure to 1-2-3. As you have seen, when you press the slash bar (/) the main Allways menu is presented. You can select menu operations deeper and deeper within the menu structure by first using the cursor movement keys to highlight the desired selection, then pressing RETURN, or by pressing the first letter of the menu choice, in which case the selection will be made immediately.

This section describes each of the Allways menus in detail. You can return to this part of the book at any time when you need to study the Allways menu structure, or for a refresher on what any single menu selection actually does.

The Allways menu structure makes accessing the power of this spreadsheet postprocessor relatively easy; however, because of its complexity, the program sometimes can be difficult to follow and remember. Allways contains approximately 220 different menu and selection box choices. (The number varies slightly with the type of display you have and the printers you are using.)

If you imagine the Allways menu structure as a tree or an outline with major branches or headings, with smaller and smaller branches or subheadings attached, then you can get a mental picture of the menus.

The most basic structure (Figure 2.6) shows the major menus without all of the submenus or branches. Illustrations in later sections will show you the more complex submenus within each major heading.

The Main Menu

The **Main** menu is the one displayed when you press the slashbar. (See Figure 2.7.) It provides the gateway to all of the many menu selections within Allways. It contains eight basic selections, each one of which leads to additional choices. Four of these eight choices lead to other major menus in our subdivision scheme. The following four **Main** menu choices are self-contained.

Worksheet—Opens the **Column**, **Row**, and **Page** selection bar from which you can set column width, change the height of a row, and insert page breaks along a row or a column.

Graph—Operates to **Add**, or **Remove** graphs from the worksheet display; **Goto** a named graph range in the worksheet; change the **Settings** on any graphs associated with the worksheet, including colors, location, and fonts; view or change the **Font Directory**—the disk directory that contains fonts associated with the graphs.

Figure 2.6
Allways basic menu
structure

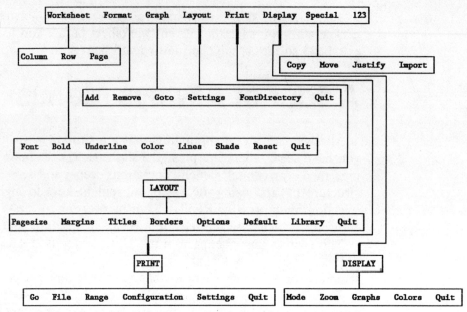

Figure 2.7
Allways Main menu

Special—Operates to **Copy** or **Move** formatting information from one cell or range to another cell or range; **Justify** text labels (operates differently from 1-2-3); **Import** formats from another worksheet.

123—Exits Allways and returns to the 1-2-3 Ready mode.

The Format Menu

The **Format** menu probably is the one you will use most often. (See Figure 2.8.) From this menu you select fonts for cells and ranges; set cell characteristics such as bold, color, and shading; and draw lines on the worksheet.

Font—Selects fonts for a worksheet range from the list of current fonts (up to eight at a time); installs a new font in the font list; restores or updates default settings; manipulates the font library; returns to ready mode.

Bold—Sets or clears boldface attributes for a cell or range.

Underline—Sets or clears underline for a cell or range.

Color—Selects one of seven colors, or red-on-negative, for printing a worksheet range.

Lines—Draws lines around cells.

Shade—Sets or clears the shading for a cell or worksheet range. Can select from light, dark, and solid shades.

Reset—Removes previous formatting for a cell or worksheet range.

Figure 2.8
Allways Format
menu

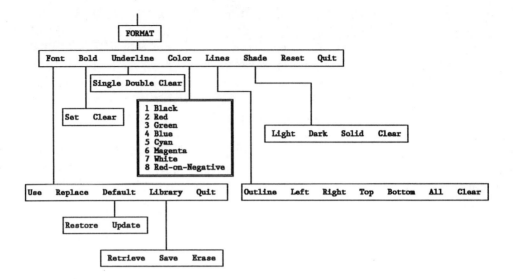

Figure 2.9
Allways Layout
menu

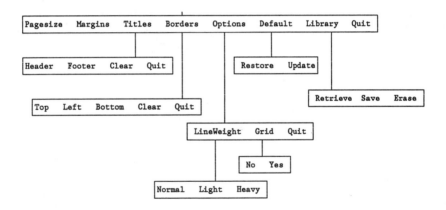

Quit—Returns to Allways Ready mode. Bypasses stepping backwards through the menu tree. You can use ESC to move through menus in reverse order; **Quit** returns immediately to Ready mode.

The Layout Menu

The **Layout** menu (Figure 2.9) establishes such spreadsheet characteristics as page size, margins, and line weight, and establishes many of the worksheet defaults as determined in Allways.

Pagesize—Tells Allways what size paper you will use to print the spreadsheet. Standard and wide widths are available from the menu, as well as standard, legal, A4, and A5 lengths. If you use an unusual paper size, you can program a custom form.

Margins—Sets top, bottom, left, and right margins.

Titles—Establishes header and footer text for spreadsheet printout.

Borders—Establishes rows or columns that will be printed as borders on mul-
tipage reports. **Borders** lets you print the title cells for a range, for example,
so that the contents of following rows and columns are labeled on the
printout.

Options—Sets line weight for boxes and lines; turns the Allways grid display
on and off.

Default—Restores or updates default page layout. Allways establishes default
format when a spreadsheet is first loaded. You can reformat the spreadsheet,
then establish the new format as the new default. Use **Default** to return a
modified spreadsheet to the original format.

Library—Stores and retrieves spreadsheet formats in a disk library. You can
recall the layout for a specific spreadsheet with the **Library** function.

Quit—Returns to Allways Ready mode.

The Print Menu

The **Print** menu (Figure 2.10) resembles the print menu in 1-2-3, but you
have more control over printing operations in Allways. In addition to setting
the print range for printing, you also can select and control printers and specify
how many copies to print.

Go—Begins the print operation.

File—Establishes file name when a spreadsheet is to be printed to a file.

Range—Sets print range. As with 1-2-3, with Allways you can specify a cell
range or you can highlight the area you want to print.

Configuration—Selects and controls printers.

Settings—Sets number of pages to print, specifies which pages to print, and
specifies whether Allways will delay printing between pages so you can
manually feed paper.

Quit—Returns to Allways Ready mode.

The Display Menu

With the **Display** menu (Figure 2.11) you can customize the Allways screen
for your own taste, establish the display mode (text or graphics), and turn the
display of graphs that are merged with the spreadsheet on and off.

Mode—Sets Text or Graphics mode. Graphics mode is the default and displays
onscreen the results of Allways format settings. The Text mode displays
the spreadsheet in 1-2-3 format.

Zoom—Sets the relative size of the display in Graphics mode. You can adjust
the display from about 60 percent of normal size to about 140 percent of
normal size.

Graphs—Turns graph display on and off.

Figure 2.10
Allways Print menu

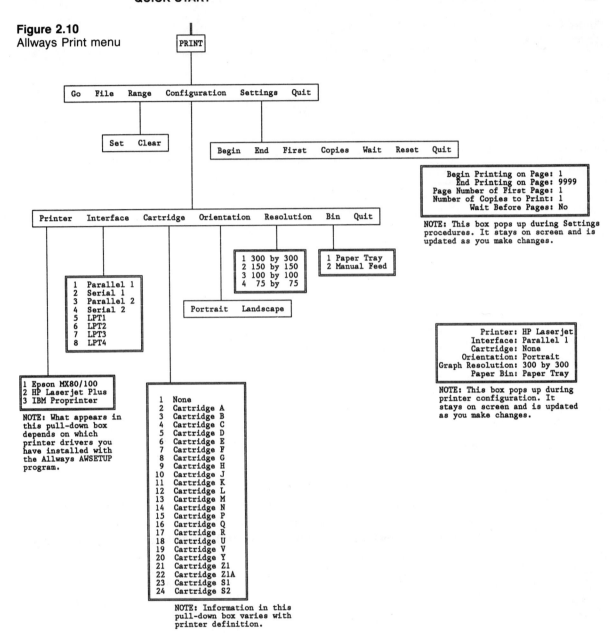

Colors—Establishes background, foreground, and highlight colors for the All-
    ways graphics display.
Quit—Returns to Allways Ready mode.

Figure 2.11
Allways Display
menu

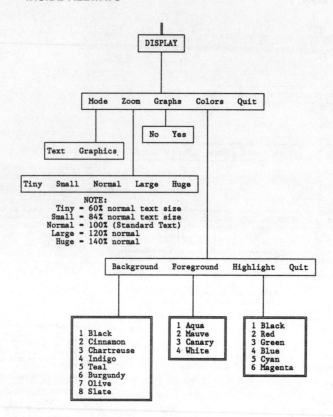

Summary

This chapter was designed to get you started. Some of this material is repeated in greater detail in later chapters, but you should be able to use the material here to install Allways and begin formatting and printing spreadsheets.

For more information on installation and configuration, refer to Chapter 3, "Technical Details."

③ Technical Details

The bulk of this book is about how to use Allways and 1-2-3. This chapter takes a step back and shows you how Allways does what it does and what it requires of your system.

It also answers some of your questions about how Allways uses your system resources—what memory Allways extracts, what storage it requires, where it is compatible, and where it is not.

Requirements

First, you should know that Allways is an add-in product that runs with 1-2-3 and, as such, is compatible only with 1-2-3 release 2.0 or later. An add-in program is accessed through the Add-In Manager utility, itself a memory-resident add-in program that gives third-party software access to 1-2-3 internals.

If you use an earlier version of 1-2-3, you should consider upgrading anyway, even if you don't want to run Allways. The upgrade cost is modest and your gains are well worth the price. For one thing, Lotus reports that a majority of commercial users have made the switch, which means that the core of users who promote third-party software support are using release 2.0 or later.

It means, too, that the majority of experienced users who are doing real work with this spreadsheet package are writing macros and using features that are compatible with the newer software. Therefore, if you wish to exchange spreadsheets with other users, chances are you will need that release 2.0 compatibility.

Our discussions in this book assume you are using 1-2-3 release 2.0 or later for the obvious reason that Allways won't work with anything else.

Versions of Allways

Version 1.0 is the original release of Allways. It is the one Funk supplied as part of its agreement with Lotus Development late in 1988 and early in 1989. During the first quarter of 1989, Funk released version 1.01, a maintenance release that fixed some minor bugs and offered some enhancements over the original release.

For example, version 1.0 showed up a bug in the Hewlett-Packard LaserJet™ emulations offered by some laser printer vendors. To make more efficient use of font download time, Allways normally downloads only blocks of an entire font as specific characters are needed. Some HP LaserJet clones, however, incorrectly interpret each download of a group of font characters as a complete font download and force a new page. That means that on some complicated spreadsheets a printer may eject 3, 5, 10, or more pages as the various characters are downloaded.

If you haven't encountered this problem, your printer may not have it, or you may simply be using relatively plain spreadsheet formats. You can find out whether your printer exhibits this characteristic by printing the AW-SAMPLE spreadsheet supplied with your Allways software.

Version 1.01 of Allways changes the way it downloads fonts for printers that are known to cause trouble. This technique may require more time for the initial printing to begin, but it eliminates the extra form-feed commands that cause your spreadsheet to be distributed across several pages.

In addition, with version 1.01 Funk supplies the Allways Expanded Memory Manager (AWEMM) program to control Allways' use of expanded memory. (See additional details on expanded memory and the AWEMM utility in the section of this chapter called "Extended/Expanded Memory.")

Version 1.01 also offers support for additional printers and enhanced graphics support for some existing printers. Version 1.01, for example, supports additional models of the Toshiba line, and the graphics handling on the HP DeskJet® was improved by a factor of at least four, speeding up graphics output on this printer significantly.

System

Allways should run with any hardware and software configuration that is compatible with 1-2-3 release 2.0 or later. Allways will require more RAM and disk storage than 1-2-3 alone, and as a graphics-based application, Allways may conflict with some terminate and stay resident (TSR) programs. Funk Software officials say they know of no conflicts with the very popular, well-known TSR programs, including other 1-2-3 add-ins and SideKick®, but you may encounter problems.

If you discover a TSR conflict, you should remove the TSR while using Allways and notify both the vendor of the TSR and Funk Software. Software vendors constantly are responding to user needs and requests, and your particular problem may already have been discovered and a fix provided from one or both vendors.

Even if Allways loads and runs properly with TSR programs in memory, you may not be able to use these programs successfully or in the normal way when Allways is using the screen. This is because Allways uses the graphics screen mode, and many popup TSR utilities assume a text mode when they execute.

In some cases you may have to exit Allways, then return to it to repaint the screen. If this does not work, you may have to return to DOS and remove the TSR from memory, either through commands or functions inside the TSR or by rebooting your system.

Figure 3.1 shows how the popular SideKick program, for example, modifies an Allways graphics screen. When you invoke SideKick with Allways running, the screen is cleared until you exit SideKick. Then, if you attempt to move around the Allways screen, bizarre things happen to your display until you exit Allways and restart. Actually, both programs behave rather well, because even when the Allways display is damaged, no data is lost, no error messages are sent, and you can continue to use both programs without rebooting.

If you use Allways in the Text mode, you should not encounter these difficulties. You also can return to 1-2-3 to pop up such software, reentering Allways when you are finished with that application.

You may encounter similar problems when you try to operate Allways from Microsoft Windows® or some other windowing environment. Some users have told us they had slight problems during installation; others that problems showed up during operation. Of course, Allways is not really a Windows product and there is no real advantage to using Allways from inside Windows, but some users establish Windows as their default operating environment and run all programs from that environment.

Figure 3.1
SideKick on an
Allways graphics
screen

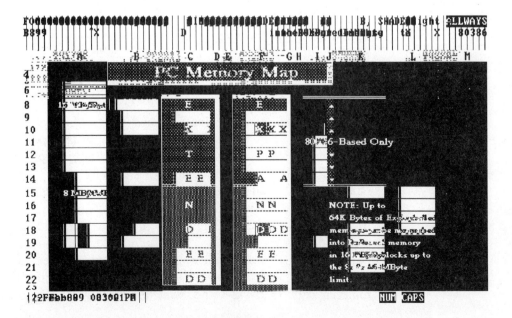

Funk Software advises that Allways be loaded outside a windowing environment, but you can experiment with that configuration and probably get good results most of the time. We encountered no problems in running Allways with the popular DESQview® program, for example.

Storage

Realistically, you need more than one megabyte on your hard disk to install and use Allways. The programs, fonts, help, and other files require about 1.03 megabytes, but you need room to store the Allways format files, in addition to your spreadsheets. Remember, Allways does not modify the original spreadsheet file. Rather, it attaches a separate format file to the spreadsheet.

Each of these format files requires a minimum of 721 bytes of storage, even if you don't change the Allways default formatting. Each cell you format uses another 12 bytes or so. Allways assumes some font and format defaults, which accounts for the minimum 721 bytes of storage required for the format file as soon as it is attached to the spreadsheet, even if you don't make any custom additions.

Allways is basically an efficient program and normally requires only a fraction of the total storage space of the original 1-2-3 file to retain its formatting information. Allways uses four bytes for each cell that has a change of format. In addition, four bytes are used for the row definition. A continuous group of cells with the same format requires only an on code and an off code.

For example, if you format a single cell in a single row, you will add 12 bytes to the basic 721 bytes required for the minimum format file: four bytes to define the row, four bytes to turn on the cell format, and four bytes to turn off the cell format.

The good news is that the same four bytes for each cell definition are used, regardless of the number of cell attributes you turn on. You can specify a single font, and the cell definition requires four bytes; or you can turn on a font, set it bold, outline the cell, and shade it, with the same four bytes. Moreover, you can format all of the cells in a row with the same group of formats with only 12 bytes.

The extra good news is that Allways is smart enough to know that contiguous cells in a row have been set previously to the specified format, even if you enter new formatting information later. For example, it is fairly common during format design to set a font or shade for a range of cells, then decide later to extend that same font or shade to more cells. As long as the same attribute is used with contiguous cells, Allways does not issue another attribute on code; the code set at the head of the range will hold, and you will require no more memory.

Nevertheless, you do not want to format spreadsheet cells needlessly. For a sample of how fast Allways can eat up disk space if you use format command unnecessarily, load 1-2-3 and enter this line in cell A1:

This is a font test

Now enter Allways and issue the **/Format Font Use** command. Select a font that is different from the default (Position Number 1) font. When Allways asks for the spreadsheet range, press the **END** key followed by the **Right Arrow** key, then the **END** key followed by the **Down Arrow** key, or enter the discrete range **A1..IV8192**.

This causes Allways to paint the whole spreadsheet range, every cell possible in 1-2-3, and format these cells for the font you selected. Now exit to 1-2-3 and save the file. Go into DOS and do a directory of the file name with a wildcard extension. Suppose you named the file **Testfont.WK1** when you saved it. Type

DIR Testfont.∗

You should see two files: One is the .WK1 file, the 1-2-3 spreadsheet, and the other is the .ALL file, the Allways format file. The .WK1 file occupies about 1463 bytes, while the .ALL file requires about 66,290 bytes. Even as efficient as it is, Allways requires storage space to format cells.

RAM

1-2-3 release 2.0 requires a minimum of 256 KBytes of RAM from the lower 640 KBytes (sometimes called *conventional memory*) just to load the program and leave room for a small spreadsheet. Later releases require more memory. Allways loads with 1-2-3 when it is attached, and requires another 40 KBytes or so of memory. After you have invoked Allways with the hot-key sequence to display an Allways-formatted screen, the Allways/1-2-3 combination takes even more memory, up to 65 KBytes. Depending on what other RAM-resident programs you have installed, you may not be able to return to the system from 1-2-3 after you have attached Allways and viewed at least one formatted screen.

You can either use the **Add-In Manager** menu to detach Allways, then exit to the system, or simply quit 1-2-3, conduct the necessary DOS operations, then restart 1-2-3 and Allways.

Extended/Expanded Memory

1-2-3 can grow spreadsheets into high-end memory; therefore, Allways users can benefit from 80286- and 80386-based machines that have memory above the conventional 640 KBytes. You won't need this memory as long as your spreadsheets are small enough to fit in the memory left after you load DOS, 1-2-3, Allways, and any other add-in or RAM resident (TSR) programs you may be using.

As soon as you begin to run out of user RAM, however, your spreadsheets will grow into high-end memory, if it is available. If you don't have any expanded (high-end) memory, when you try to load a spreadsheet that is too large, 1-2-3 will report an out-of-memory error and cancel the operation.

Expanded memory is special memory addressed above 1 MByte that can be mapped in chunks of 16 KBytes (up to 64 KBytes at a time) into a portion of reserved memory. Reserved memory is memory addressed between 640 KBytes and 1 MByte. DOS uses this reserved area for its own purposes, including video ROM and disk controllers. The Lotus/Intel®/Microsoft (LIM) Expanded Memory Specification (EMS) describes how this extra memory will be addressed and used.

1-2-3, and therefore Allways, can use expanded memory that adheres to the LIM standard. This can be as much as 8 MBytes of memory on a PC/AT®-compatible machine, and up to 16 MBytes on an 80386-based machine.

Don't confuse *expanded* memory with *extended* memory. (See Figure 3.2.) Extended memory also is addressed above 1 MByte, but the system can only use it for RAM disks, print spoolers, or disk cache memory, and, in each case, special software is required to make this memory available to the CPU.

If you use an 80286-based computer (PC/AT class), then you need a special memory board that uses the LIM standard to have expanded memory. This may be true even if you have 2, 3, or more megabytes of memory on the system or mother board. Most PC/AT-class computers can use this system memory only as extended memory, not as expanded memory. Some newer PC/AT-compatible machines, however, include an expanded memory manager program to map this high-end motherboard memory as expanded memory. Read the instruction manual for your computer or contact your dealer to find out if your machine has expanded memory or if you need a separate board that is LIM-compatible.

On an 80386-based computer, an expanded memory manager, such as the Compaq Expanded Memory Manager® (CEMM), can map the system board memory as expanded memory compatible with the LIM standard.

The Allways and 1-2-3 programs load and execute in conventional memory, but both programs can store data in expanded memory. Allways, at least, prefers expanded memory for data storage; it dips into remaining conventional memory only after it runs out of expanded memory.

In fact, Allways uses more expanded memory than 1-2-3, partly because of the way 1-2-3 uses system resources. The 1-2-3 program was designed to use the entire system; it assumes it has access to all system resources, including all available memory. Allways, on the other hand, knows it is sharing memory with 1-2-3 and operates accordingly.

When Allways is invoked, it stores the expanded memory calls that describe the 1-2-3 context—how 1-2-3 is using memory, where things are stored—and substitutes its own calls. When Allways requires information from 1-2-3 or if you return to 1-2-3 mode, the original 1-2-3 memory calls are restored, then swapped out again when Allways starts up.

Figure 3.2
PC memory map

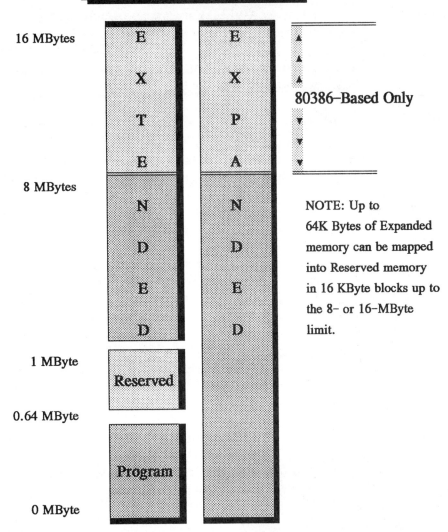

Most expanded memory users will not be aware of this flipping back and forth between 1-2-3 and Allways. However, if you use an 80286-based computer that is emulating expanded memory, you may find the operation of Allways unacceptably slow. Again, remember that if you have expanded memory, Allways will use it, regardless of how much free room you have in conventional memory. Unfortunately, some hardware emulations of expanded memory are not efficient.

If you have problems with speed, either disable your expanded memory, forcing Allways and 1-2-3 back into conventional memory, or request the

AWEMM from Funk Software. With this utility, available automatically with Allways version 1.01 and by request from Funk, you can set Allways into a conventional memory mode.

When you run AWEMM once, the program asks whether you want to enable or disable expanded memory use. Specify **disable** and Allways will not access expanded RAM, even if it is available. AWEMM modifies the Allways program so that it will not use expanded memory again until you rerun the utility and **enable** expanded memory use.

Printers

Allways is compatible with a variety of PC-based printers. Like 1-2-3, Allways requires that you install one or more printers during the installation process. Then you can specify which printer you want to use as you print Allways-formatted files. The printers listed in Figure 3.3 are supported with the initial release of Allways.

As users gain experience with Allways, it is probable that Funk Software will modify and expand this list with subsequent maintenance and upgrade releases of Allways. If your particular printer is not listed in Figure 3.3, call Funk Software technical support specialists to determine whether the appropriate driver for your printer has been added or may be available.

You can install as many printers as you need with the AWSETUP program; then, when it is time to print the Allways-formatted spreadsheet, you can select the printer you need for a given job.

As part of the **/Printer Configuration** menu you also can select the printer port that your printer will use. To use the **Serial** option on this menu, you must first issue a **MODE** command from within DOS to configure your serial port for the correct settings to interface with your printer.

A convenient way to do this is to place a **MODE** command in your AUTOEXEC.BAT file. Assuming you are using serial port number 1 (COM1:) and your printer is set up for 9600 bps communications with 8 data bits and no parity, then the following command should program your serial port properly:

MODE COM1:96,N,8,1,P

For other communications rates, substitute another value for the **96** after the COM1: entry. A 4800 bps link would be programmed with

MODE COM1:48,N,8,1,P

If your system is using a port other than COM1:, enter the correct port as part of the command. A sample command for COM2: is

MODE COM2:96,N,8,1,P

Some programs conduct this type of port setup for you. As a result, even if you enter the correct command in your AUTOEXEC.BAT file, if you then run another program that accesses the serial port with different values, you may have to reissue the MODE command to run Allways successfully. However, if the serial port/printer combination works with one program, it should work satisfactorily with Allways.

Monitors

Allways can be used with almost any PC monitor and display card combination. The best results will be obtained with a VGA-compatible display

Figure 3.3
Allways-supported printers, release 1.0.

Allways Printers

Apple LaserWriter (PostScript)	IBM Proprinter X24/XL24
Apple LaserWriter Plus/II (PostScript)	IBM Quietwriter II
Canon BJ-130 (Capsule 48/XL)	IBM Quietwriter III
Epson EX800/1000	IBM Quickwriter
Epson FX80/100	NEC P5/P6/P7/P9
Epson FX85/185	NEC P2200
Epson FX86e/286e	NEC P5200/5300
Epson FX850/1050	Okidata 192 (PROP SP: No)
Epson LQ800/1000	Okidata 192 (PROP SP: Yes)
Epson LQ850/950/1050	Okidata 292/293
Epson LQ1500	Okidata 294
Epson LQ2500	Okidata 393 (Epson LQ mode)
Epson MX80/100	Panasonic KX-P1080i/1592
Epson RX80/100	Panasonic KX-P1091
Fujitsu DL2400 (DPL24C/DPL24I mode)	Panasonic KX-P1091i/1092i/1595
HP DeskJet	Tandy DMP 130A (IBM mode)
HP LaserJet (original model)	Texas Instruments 855
HP LaserJet Plus	Texas Instruments 860XL
HP LaserJet Series II	Texas Instruments 865
HP PaintJet	Toshiba P321
HP PaintJet (transparency mode)	Toshiba P341
HP ThinkJet (Alt mode: SW5:UP)	Toshiba P351
IBM Graphics Printer	Toshiba P351SX
IBM Proprinter	Toshiba P1340
IBM Proprinter II/XL	

card and high-resolution color or monochrome monitor. If your display adapter does not support graphics, you can set Allways to text mode. In this configuration you won't be able to see the fonts, shading, and other formatting additions you make to your spreadsheets in Allways, but they'll still print correctly.

Because Allways is a near-WYSIWYG product, you get the best results with a graphics display adapter. Unless you have a color printer, the colors you see on the screen will not be reproduced on the printer, so there is no particular advantage to a color display (except that most users find a color monitor easier on the eyes and more pleasant to use).

Allways provides the highest resolution your monitor is capable of displaying, up to the VGA standard of 640 by 480 pixels. Other displays produce different results.

EGA: 640 by 350
Hercules®: 720 by 348
CGA: 640 by 200

A few companies, including IBM, produce display adapters with even higher resolution, but Allways presently does not go beyond the VGA level.

Installation

The quick-start installation described in Chapter 2, "Quick Start," may have been all the information you needed to get Allways up and running. If you had problems installing the system, or if you are merely curious about the details of installation, this section may answer your questions.

Allways is linked with 1-2-3 and cannot be executed separately from 1-2-3. You must install Allways to establish the proper link with the spreadsheet through the Add-In Manager and to set up the proper printer and display support.

The 1-2-3 Add-In Manager

The Add-In Manager is a way for third-party developers to access 1-2-3 internals so that add-in programs such as word processors, note pads, and formatters (like Allways) can run from within 1-2-3.

The Add-In Manager is installed by placing the proper codes into the 1-2-3 driver file, 1-2-3.SET, or into another file (if you have created custom driver sets). Once installed, you can invoke the manager by pressing ALT-F10 to display a 1-2-3-like menu (Figure 3.4) that you use to attach or detach an add-in program, install a program for automatic attachment, or run an attached program. If you are using release 2.2 of 1-2-3, the Add-In Manager is part of the menu structure.

Figure 3.4
The Add-In
Manager menu

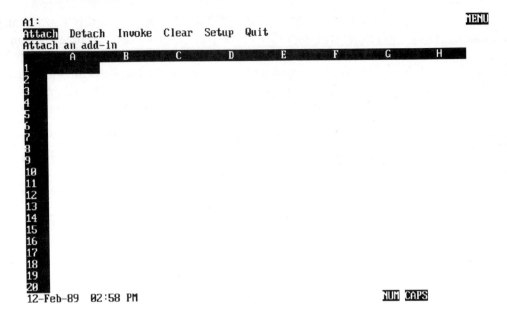

Installing the Add-In Manager

If you already are using another add-in program, the Add-In Manager is installed on your 1-2-3 disk and appears in your 1-2-3 driver file. When you install Allways and many other add-in programs, the install process automatically checks for the presence of the Add-In Manager and installs the proper files if you don't already have them.

The Add-In Manager consists of the following files:

ADD_MGR.EXE   Install program
ADD_MGR.DRV   Add-In Manager program
ADN.CFG   Add-In Manager Configuration File
DEL_MGR.EXE   Delete Add-In Manager program

You can install the Add-In Manager yourself at any time (assuming the required program files are on your disk) by typing

ADD_MGR <driver file>

Again, unless you have created custom driver files for 1-2-3, the <driver file> in this example will be 123.SET. If you forget to provide the driver set name to the Add-In Manager, an error message will be displayed and you will have to reenter the command.

NOTE: For some reason, Lotus Development's 1-2-3 INSTALL program, used to set up printer and display adapter support, among other things, removes the Add-In Manager from the driver file each time it is run.

For that reason, if you change printers, modify your display description, or use the 1-2-3 INSTALL program for any other reason, you will have to reinstall the Add-In Manager to be able to use Allways or another add-in program. You can reinstall the Add-In Manager either with the DOS-level command described earlier or by rerunning the AWSETUP program.

Removing the Add-In Manager is just as easy. Type

DEL_MGR <driver file>

You can find out which programs on your disk can be attached through the Add-In Manager by typing

DIR *.ADN

Files that end in the .ADN extension are the link files for add-in programs. There may be—in fact, there most certainly are—additional files to support the application in the 1-2-3 directory or in another directory. The *.ADN file simply provides the Add-In Manager link for the application.

If you have installed Allways, you will find the ALLWAYS.ADN file in the 1-2-3 directory. If you have installed the LEARN program to record 1-2-3 macros, you also will find the LEARN.ADN file. Other add-in programs will appear with the appropriate program name and the .ADN extension.

When you install Allways, the program is automatically set up to attach when 1-2-3 loads. This is a feature of the Add-In Manager that makes programs like Allways immediately available through the hot-key sequence as soon as 1-2-3 is read. You may not want all of your Add-In Manager applications to attach automatically, because each attached program requires some low-end memory. However, in the case of Allways, you probably will want to leave it set up for auto-attach. Without Allways attached, if you load a spreadsheet that has been formatted with Allways and make changes to that spreadsheet, you will lose some of the pointers that Allways needs to know which cells have been moved and what formatting characteristics go with each cell.

Attaching and Detaching Manager Programs

To attach a program to 1-2-3 with the Add-In Manager, use the Manager's hot key, ALT-F10, to display the **Add-In Manager** menu or select the Add-In Manager from the 1-2-3 release 2.2 menu. Select **Attach** from the menu; the Manager displays a list of programs with the .ADN extension. Select which program you want to attach either by typing in the name or by highlighting the program, using the cursor movement keys to move the highlight cursor over the name.

You can attach programs that are not in the current directory, but they will not appear on the screen. Simply include the full path name when you type the program name, and the Manager will attach it for you. You can attach up to eight applications simultaneously.

After you specify the program name, you will be asked which hot-key sequence you wish to use to invoke the program. You can select one of three key combinations—ALT-F7, ALT-F8, and ALT-F9. Specifying a hot key lets you run an attached application quickly without invoking the Add-In Manager. To run an application that is not available on one of the hot keys, call up the **Add-In Manager** menu, select **Invoke** from the menu, then choose the application from the list provided.

Once you have attached an application during the current session, it will be available, either through the specified hot-key sequence or from the **Add-In Manager** menu, but when you exit 1-2-3 the link is lost.

To make an Add-In Manager application attach automatically, select **Update** from the Manager menu to update the ADN.CFG file, which tells the Manager which files you have attached, what hot keys to use, and the like.

You may want to detach an application to free up memory for a large spreadsheet. Simply select **Detach** from the Manager menu and the specified application will be unavailable through 1-2-3 during the current session unless you reattach it. If you want to make the change permanent, select **Update** to make the change in the configuration file.

Allways Configurations

During installation you can configure Allways for your individual system and application needs, within reasonable bounds. As previously mentioned, for example, you can select one or more printers and Allways will install the appropriate drivers for them. You can tell Allways which display adapter and monitor you are using, and you can select between text and graphics display modes.

Floppy Systems

You can use Allways with a floppy-based system, although you probably will want a hard disk configuration for best results. The 1-2-3 files, at a minimum, require 400 KBytes of storage, and Allways takes up another 1.03 MBytes (1030 KBytes) or so. Fitting all this on a floppy, even if you are using 1.44-MByte diskettes, could be an exercise in frustration.

Even if you build 1-2-3 spreadsheets on a diskette-based computer, you probably will print them from a hard disk, especially if you are using Allways, because you will need access to a laser printer or other high-quality output device. If you are using a printer in the $2000-to-$5000 price range, chances are you also have a hard disk on the attached system.

You're a diehard, you say? You have a laptop machine that you plug into the laser printer and you really *must* run 1-2-3 and Allways on a floppy-based system? Well, it can be done, if you configure the system carefully. You will need at least one high-density drive, preferably 1.44-MByte capacity. These drives are appearing on some laptops and are standard issue with most PS/ 2 and other high-end desktop machines.

First, copy only the files in Figure 3.5 from your 1-2-3 system onto the floppy. Next, create a subdirectory off the root directory on the diskette called *Allways*. Copy the files in Figure 3.6 from your hard disk installed Allways directory to the diskette Allways directory.

This sample floppy configuration of 1-2-3/Allways occupies 1,177,624 bytes, barely small enough to fit on a 1.2-MByte, high-density, 5.25-inch floppy. Any data files should be stored on another diskette, which would be accessed from another drive.

An alternate configuration could put the Allways files on the B: drive; but if you do, make sure to create an **Allways** directory off the root. Allways cannot run in a root directory. By placing Allways files on the B: drive, you may have room for additional 1-2-3 drivers or Allways font files.

In addition, you could create a RAM disk in extended memory and copy your Allways files to a subdirectory in the RAM disk, remove the Allways diskette, and insert the 1-2-3 program disk.

Any of these floppy configurations are noticeably cumbersome compared with a hard disk installation, but they can permit you to do useful spreadsheet design on a laptop or on a backup system if necessary.

Figure 3.5
1-2-3 files for
floppy disk
installation

Volume in drive A is LOTUS
Directory of A:\LOTUS

.		<DIR>	8–31–87	7:13p
..		<DIR>	8–31–87	7:13p
ALLWAYS		<DIR>	12–10–88	6:44a
WK1		<DIR>	8–31–87	7:13p
123	CMP	135142	7–04–86	1:23a
123	CNF	265	1–07–89	6:57a
123	DYN	11157	8–05–86	1:23a
123	EXE	11313	12–10–88	6:23a
123	SET	57639	1–07–89	10:19a
ADN	CFG	82	1–20–89	6:19a
ALLWAYS	ADN	11877	11–02–88	
LEARN	ADN	5081	5–04–88	1:23a
SIBM1EGT	DRV	4232	5–04–88	1:23a

13 File(s)   268633 bytes free

Figure 3.6
Allways files for
floppy disk
installation

Volume in drive A is LOTUS				
Directory of C:\LOTUS\ALLWAYS				

.		<DIR>	12-10-88	6:44a
..		<DIR>	12-10-88	6:44a
ALLWAYS	ASD	3610	10-31-88	
ALLWAYS	ASF	2486	10-31-88	
ALLWAYS	CNF	67	1-07-89	11:33a
ALLWAYS	FSX	154476	11-06-88	
COUR	AFL	151216	11-01-88	
FONTSET	CNF	91	2-01-89	7:01a
HPLJII	APC	3402	10-31-88	
HPLJII	APD	4168	10-31-88	
PICA	AFL	148061	10-31-88	
TIMES	AFL	237321	10-31-88	
TRIUM	AFL	235938	10-31-88	

14 File(s)   262633 bytes free

NOTES: The specific 1-2-3 .DRV files and the Allways font and printer files you install will depend on your system configuration.

The suggested floppy configuration does not include the 1-2-3 graph print files or the **LOTUS.COM** menu program. In addition, 1-2-3 and Allways help files have been eliminated. You don't need these files for basic operation, but if you need to generate 1-2-3 graphs from the floppy system or you will require help files, you will have to redesign the configuration.

Hard Disk Systems

Hard disk configurations are easier, because you can let the respective INSTALL programs handle most of the housekeeping for you. Most hard disk installations include separate subdirectories for the 1-2-3 and Allways programs and support files, then individual directories for the spreadsheet and Allways format files.

A good way to keep individual subdirectories clean and to help you keep track of the spreadsheets you use is to create separate directories off the 1-2-3 program directory for each type of spreadsheet file. For example, databases such as mailing lists should go in one directory, billing and invoicing spreadsheets should have their own directory, and company financial figures go somewhere else.

A typical 1-2-3 and Allways directory configuration might look something like the sample in Figure 3.7. Notice that Allways created its own subdirectory off the Lotus program directory during installation. You create the individual worksheet subdirectories yourself as part of an ongoing configuration effort as you build more and more spreadsheets.

When you load or save a file with the 1-2-3 **/File Retrieve** and the **/File Save** command sequence, 1-2-3 displays possible file choices from the currently selected directory. If you will be working on several files from a directory besides the currently selected one, enter the **/File Directory** command to set a temporary save and load directory path.

You can establish a permanent path with the **/Worksheet Global Default Directory** sequence, or you can load and save files without changing the directory by pressing ESC at the file prompt. This clears the file names, leaving only the path at the top of the screen. Edit this path and enter the desired file name to load or save.

Displays

Allways is compatible with any standard display that runs successfully with 1-2-3; however, with some display adapters, you may not be able to display all of the printable file attributes. If you do not have a graphics-compatible display, for example, you will have to view Allways spreadsheets in the Text mode—just as in 1-2-3. You won't be able to see the fonts and other formatting on screen, but the enhanced attributes still will print.

Figure 3.7
Sample 1-2-3/All-ways subdirectory structure

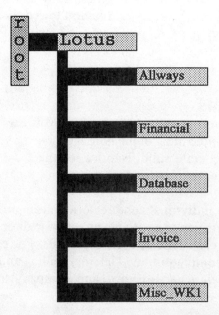

NOTE: If you use a CGA display adapter, Allways shows everything in monochrome mode to improve resolution. For this reason, you will be shown only a CGA monochrome display choice. Select this display option even if you are using a color display.

Monochrome Graphics—Monochrome graphics adapters will display Allways fonts and other attributes satisfactorily, you just won't see the on-screen color. Since most users probably will print Allways-enhanced spreadsheets on laser or other monochrome printers anyway, this is not much of a limitation.

Color Displays—A color graphics adapter and display affords the best Allways environment. If you have grown accustomed to the pseudocolor display offered by 1-2-3, you may think spreadsheets in color aren't all that great. With Allways, the opposite is true. You have a great deal of control over how Allways displays the spreadsheet on a color graphics screen, including background color, foreground color, and the color that is used for highlight.

If you like to see your computer programs in color, Allways is a good way to get a new look at your spreadsheets. Of course, CGA-, EGA-, or VGA-compatible adapters and displays work with Allways, but you get the best results with the EGA and VGA high-end adapters.

Other Allways Environments

You may be running 1-2-3 and Allways in environments that require special attention. It is not possible to test every combination of software and configuration, but this section provides some hints on a few of the more popular special installations. If you have difficulties with particular Allways configurations with other software or hardware you may be running, call Funk Software for help.

Networks

Allways is a single-user program. That means that if your system is a node on a network, you have to install your own copy of Allways, either on your local drive or in a private directory on the host, to use it. Of course, you could install a single public copy of Allways on the host, but only one user at a time could access it.

Multitasking Utilities

Allways appears to be a well-behaved program and, as such, should function well with a similarly well-behaved multitasking utility such as DoubleDOS or DESQview. We have used Allways extensively with DESQview installed on a 5 MByte Compaq 386S® computer with VGA display and have had no problems. In this environment you can use the 1-2-3/Allways combination in one window and keep word processors, databases, and other applications active in other windows.

Even though Allways uses a graphics screen display, we discovered no major problems with DESQview. When you pop up the main **DESQview** menu over the Allways screen, you will notice some degradation of the display; but when the menu is removed or when you exit and return to Allways, the display returns to normal.

One area of potential difficulty with such programs is the Allways graphics interface. Some partitioning software does not support graphics interfaces. Where information from software running in one partition spills over into the other partition, the problem will show up as a screen writethrough.

The other problem is that 1-2-3 and Allways together require at least 320 KBytes of system RAM. When you subtract the RAM overhead of the multitasking utility, there is not a lot of room left for another application.

The best rule with these types of programs is simply to experiment extensively before you commit heavily to running in that environment.

VAX VMS Compatibility

Allways functions like any other PC-based application in a VAX or other minicomputer host environment. You can use the host resources for program or data storage and for printing if you have the proper hardware link and networking software. However, Allways is a single-user product, so only one user at a time can access a given set of Allways programs.

1-2-3 to Allways and Back

Allways is a powerful program and will enhance significantly the appearance of your spreadsheets. Its biggest limitation is the fact that it operates only as a postprocessor of data. You cannot enter information directly into the spreadsheet from within the Allways graphics interface.

In addition, although you can make some physical changes to the spreadsheet inside Allways, these changes do not always appear in 1-2-3 when you switch out of Allways.

What to Save and When

There's a loose rule of thumb that has—or is supposed to have—kept computer programmers on their toes for years: The interval between file saves should be only as long as you are willing to spend time doing the work over if the system should die. Some programmers save their work every 5 or 10 minutes; others are comfortable with 15- to 20-minute intervals. Some save to two separate volumes each time—just in case. The point is, you should develop your own guidelines about data security and stick with them.

Save your spreadsheet work frequently and establish some kind of routine to ensure that the last changes got saved. This admonition is particularly important in a program like Allways.

You cannot save a file from inside Allways, you must return to 1-2-3. Because you may spend a significant amount of your overall spreadsheet preparation time in Allways rather than in 1-2-3, it is important to save the format descriptions frequently. Even though all of the spreadsheet data has been saved, if you do not issue the 1-2-3 **/File Save** command after making changes or additions to the format in Allways, anything changed or added since the last save command will be lost when you exit 1-2-3 or load another spreadsheet file.

You may become confused, particularly if you are working in the Allways Text mode, because the Allways text screen is almost identical to the 1-2-3 screen. However, you cannot save the current file from inside Allways. Unlike some programs, 1-2-3 shows no mercy when you request an end to the session. It will ask if you are sure [Yes No], but it gives no clue that the file you just spent three hours on has not been saved.

One way to make the save process easier is to include a simple save macro in each of your spreadsheets. (See Chapters 13 and 14 for more information on 1-2-3 and Allways macros.) By entering the keystrokes for a save ('/fs~r) in a little-used area of the spreadsheet, then naming the cell as \S with the **/Range Name Create** sequence, you can save the spreadsheet by pressing **ALT-S**.

Changes That Travel and Those That Don't

Allways and 1-2-3 work together to produce a formatted spreadsheet. Allways uses the data and some of the formatting information you entered in 1-2-3 to build the finished spreadsheet. However, 1-2-3 does not recognize the changes you make to the spreadsheet in Allways. It will take a little experimentation to learn precisely how the two programs complement each other and to get used to entering data in the 1-2-3 format after working with the enhanced spreadsheet in Allways.

Basically, Allways uses the data you enter in 1-2-3 directly. If you don't change the formatting for a particular cell in Allways, the format you entered in 1-2-3 will be used, though sometimes slightly differently. For example, when you first enter Allways, the cell width remains as it was in 1-2-3. You can exit Allways, modify the cell width in 1-2-3, and the change will travel to Allways, *if* you have not previously modified that setting from inside Allways.

After you make the change in Allways, the Allways version is the dominant one, even if you make another change in 1-2-3. The last width you set for that column in 1-2-3 is what you have when you exit Allways and go back to the spreadsheet. You can change the height of an Allways row, but the change does not travel to 1-2-3.

In fact, there is only one Allways format feature that travels to 1-2-3, and that is the **/Special Justify** command, which realigns the text data in a range of cells. This is the only Allways command that actually changes the spreadsheet data.

Technical Summary

This section gives you a quick reference summary of Allways technical specifications, including file names and functions, memory and storage requirements, and file format information. (See Figures 3.8 and 3.9.) The information in this section is based on Allways version 1.0. If you are using version 1.01, some of this information may be slightly different.

Allways and 1-2-3—A Symbiotic Relationship

Allways and 1-2-3 go together like jam and bread. If you like bread, you probably like it better with your favorite jam. You probably don't eat jam without the bread, however, no matter how much you like jam.

No matter how much you wish you could, you can't use Allways without 1-2-3. However, you can print an Allways-formatted spreadsheet to a disk file that will be stored complete with printer control codes and other commands. This file can then be printed, transferred, or telecommunicated as necessary

Figure 3.8
File types in
Allways

Allways File Types

File Ext.	File Type
ASD	Screen Driver
ASF	Screen Font
FSX	Main Program
APD	Printer Driver
APC	Print Cartridge Driver
API	Printer Initialization
AFL	Font Library
ALL	Format File
ALS	Library Set (Page Layout)
AFS	Font Set (User-created)
APF	Printer Font

Allways Technical Specifications

Storage

Programs	1.03 MBytes	(Varies with configuration)
Format Files	721 Bytes minimum	
	4 Bytes/Row Definition	
	4 Bytes/Start cell format	
	4 Bytes/End cell format	

Memory

Attached	~40 KBytes
Invoked	+~65 KBytes
Maximum RAM	~128 KBytes

Graphics Display Resolutions

VGA	640 x 480 pixels
EGA	640 x 350
Hercules	720 x 348
CGA	640 x 200

Versions

Version 1.0	Dec. 1988
Version 1.01	Mar. 1989
Version 2.0	Jun. 1989

Formats

Max. Fonts	8/Spreadsheet
Row Height	0->255 Points (w/fractions)
Column Width	0->240 Characters (w/fractions)
Display Colors	
Background	8
Foreground	4
Highlight	6
Print Colors	8

without using 1-2-3 or Allways. In any case, if you have 1-2-3 and if you use it even occasionally, Allways is the perfect companion for it. You will find that you can do things to your spreadsheets with Allways that you probably didn't know you needed to do.

What You *Can* Do with Allways

We will show you examples of some of the creative spreadsheets Allways can produce for you later in this book. For now, here's a short list of some of the things it can do on your spreadsheet.

≡ Add up to eight fonts at a time
≡ Draw variable-weight lines
≡ Enhance blocks with light, dark, or solid shades
≡ Create shadow boxes
≡ Draw grid lines around all cells
≡ Display in a wide variety of color combinations
≡ Merge 1-2-3 graphs with data ranges and print them
≡ Print in color with a color printer
≡ Use 1-2-3 macros for Allways functions

What You *Cannot* Do with Allways

Capable as it is, Allways does have some limitations. You cannot do the following:

≡ Enter data into the spreadsheet from within Allways
≡ Create graphs
≡ Write macros in Allways
≡ Modify the 1-2-3 spreadsheet (except justify a range)
≡ Run the program without 1-2-3
≡ Load or save a spreadsheet file

Summary

This chapter provides information on Allways technical specifications, including system requirements and details on how to install the program and how to configure it for your system. Hints are provided to help you use existing software—including RAM resident applications—with the Allways/1-2-3 combination, and for setting up Allways on a floppy and hard disk system.

In addition, this chapter provides information on enhanced and expanded memory, how Allways stores format information, and what data travels from 1-2-3 to Allways and back.

Use the information in this chapter as a reference if you need to reconfigure your Allways/1-2-3 system or when you install Allways for the first time.

The next chapters show you how to use Allways and discuss in detail each of the Allways menu commands.

Using Allways

Allways will change the way you use 1-2-3. You can use 1-2-3 for the same things you've always used it for, and you can enhance all those existing spreadsheets with Allways, but the more you work with Allways the more you are going to change how you design a spreadsheet. And you will think of other applications for 1-2-3, things you probably wouldn't even try to do in 1-2-3 without Allways.

By this point you have spent some time using the 1-2-3/Allways combination. You may have produced some spreadsheets, merged some graphs with the data, and printed a few of your forms.

This chapter and the two that follow cover some of the more subtle details of using Allways and offer some hints for making your Allways life easier.

You can use Chapters 4 through 6 as a reference section to provide direct access information about a particular operation as you work with Allways, or you can start here and read about each of the Allways commands and features.

This chapter starts with some general interest discussions, then introduces a menu-oriented structure for information that will be carried throughout the remainder of the chapter and through Chapters 5 and 6.

Each section is arranged around the Allways menu structure, a hierarchical tree that takes you deeper and deeper into the program through various branches of functionality.

First, the general information.

Getting In and Out

Once Allways is installed, you can start the program in two ways:

≡ With the hot-key combination set up during installation
≡ Through the **Add-In Manager** menu

For manual entry of Allways, that is, without using macros, the best choice is the hot-key combination. When you install any Lotus Add-In program you can select ALT-F7, ALT-F8, or ALT-F9 as the toggle to start the application.

Assuming the application is attached, you can jump directly to it by holding down the ALT key and pressing the appropriate function key.

The first time you invoke Allways with a particular spreadsheet, it may take several seconds for the screen to clear, Allways to load, and the formatted screen to be painted. Allways has to load additional code, store the 1-2-3 configuration, and start up Allways.

If you switch back to 1-2-3 to make some spreadsheet changes, then call up Allways again, the switch should be almost instantaneous if you have an 80386-based machine, a little slower with 80286- or 8088-based computers.

There may be times when you want to access Allways through the Add-In Manager. If, for example, you already have the three available hot keys assigned to other applications, you may choose to leave those assignments alone and call up Allways from the **Add-In Manager** menu. This procedure can work, but you may also find that you have memory problems with that many applications attached, and you may uncover conflicts among the various add-in programs. The best answer to the question of how many add-ins you can have attached is to try what you need. If you encounter problems, start backing out some of the programs until you hit a configuration that works.

To access the **Add-In Manager** menu, use the Add-In Manager hot key, ALT-F10, or select it from the release 2.2 menu. Select **Attach** from the menu and specify **Allways** when you are given a choice of applications to attach. (See Figure 4.1.)

After selecting **Allways**, or other add-in to attach, you will be asked which hot key you want to assign if you have available hot keys. Most Add-In

Figure 4.1
The Add-In Manager Attach display

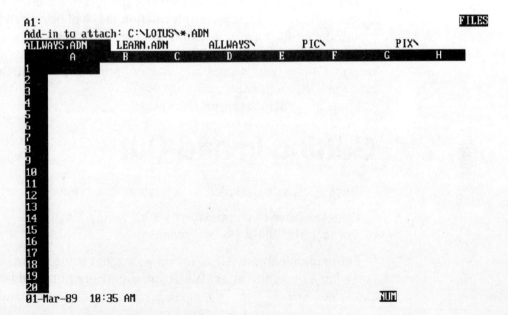

programs clear the screen at this point and display a title page while the application is attached.

You are then returned to the **Add-In Manager** menu where you can conduct other Add-In operations or select **Quit** to return to the 1-2-3 ready mode.

You also should use the Add-In Manager to call up Allways if you are using macros. If you do this, the macro will function properly, even if you should change the hot-key combination for Allways. See Chapter 14, "Macros for 1-2-3 and Allways," and Chapter 15, "Practical 1-2-3 and Allways Macros," for more information on using 1-2-3 macros with Allways.

Retrieving and Saving Work

You load and save spreadsheets for use in Allways with the **/File Retrieve** menu sequence within 1-2-3. Allways itself has no facilities for storing or retrieving worksheet files. Allways does, however, create a companion file for each formatted spreadsheet that contains the format information for that spreadsheet.

The companion Allways file is saved at the same time as the spreadsheet file. For this reason, it is important to remember to save the spreadsheet file when you exit Allways; otherwise, the formatting changes you made in Allways will be lost when you load another spreadsheet file or exit 1-2-3.

Normally this would not be a serious problem, because you probably are in the habit of saving your 1-2-3 spreadsheets regularly as you work on them. With Allways, however, you may be loading previously created spreadsheets to format them with Allways. Because this data already has been saved, you might be tempted not to save it again. Train yourself to save the 1-2-3 spreadsheet each time you exit Allways, whether to call up another spreadsheet or to modify the current one. Thus, the chances of losing spreadsheet formatting are reduced.

Label Alignments

In 1-2-3 you have three label (text) alignment prefixes. An apostrophe (') is the default prefix and causes cell labels to hug the leftmost side of the cell of origin (left alignment). You can precede a label with a quote (") to cause right alignment, or use the caret (^) to center the information in the cell of origin.

These alignment prefixes are recognized in Allways, but center and right alignments are handled slightly differently from the way they are handled in 1-2-3. The changes are positive ones and give you better control of label presentation, but you will have to get used to the differences if you are accustomed to using label alignment regularly in 1-2-3.

In 1-2-3, long labels can spill over into cells to the right of the cell of origin, but no data is permitted to hang left. If you enter a right-aligned label that is longer than the cell of origin, for example, the result is a left-aligned label that spills over into any blank cells to the right.

The same thing happens with a centered label in 1-2-3. If the label is too long to fit in the cell of origin, the information moves left to the edge of the cell, then spills to the right if adjacent cells are blank.

Allways, on the other hand, tries to carry out the label formatting instructions more literally. A centered label, for example, remains centered in the cell of origin no matter how wide the cell is. If the label is wider than the cell, text spills left and right equally into adjacent blank cells to keep the label centered.

This is a useful feature that helps you center a title over an even number of columns. Simply add a column to hold the label, set the column width to anything over zero, and the label will center around the cell of origin, placing the information in the center of the uneven range of columns.

Even if you are trying to maintain precise spacing between columns, this additional column probably will not affect the layout of your spreadsheet, because you can set the width so narrow that no noticeable space is added to your spreadsheet. As long as the cell width is greater than zero, however, the centered label will remain centered over the cell of origin.

Allways also interprets right-aligned labels as right-aligned, even if the data is too wide to fit into the cell of origin. Right-aligned labels bump up against the right edge of the cell of origin and spill left into blank adjacent cells. As in 1-2-3, however, right-aligned labels leave an extra space at the right of the label, between the last character and the edge of the cell. This convention is designed to help you align text over a column of numbers because numeric data is right-justified in a 1-2-3 cell with a right-hand space to make room for additional characters such as percent signs.

In Allways, however, you have the option of eliminating the extra space, forcing the last character in the label to fit right up against the rightmost edge of the cell of origin. If you want right alignment without the space, use a vertical bar (|) as the label prefix instead of the quote. If label data is to be centered over numeric cells that use the extra right-hand character, such as a percent sign, then you may want to do away with the right-hand space in the label.

A Speedier Allways

Although Allways uses a graphics screen display, the product offers reasonably fast response time. When you have a large spreadsheet with a lot of special formatting, then screen updates may slow down. In addition, when you have installed 1-2-3 graphs inside an Allways spreadsheet, it will take longer than normal to paint each new screen.

Some users also notice that the first time Allways is called with a new 1-2-3 spreadsheet, it takes an inordinately long time to load. There always is a slight delay when you load the program for the first time with a new spreadsheet because it must locate the Allways subdirectory, load the necessary programs and overlays, create the accompanying format file, or load an existing file.

If, however, this delay gets longer and longer, it may be because you have too many files in your 1-2-3 directory. When Allways loads it must search through the 1-2-3 files list until it finds the Allways subdirectory, then load the files it needs from there. If the list of files is long and the Allways directory happens to be at the end of it (as when you have copied an entire subdirectory with the **DOS XCOPY** command, for example), then the load time can be long.

If this seems to be the case, use one of the available disk management utilities to sort your files with the subdirectories at the top of the list. If you don't have such a utility, create a temporary subdirectory and copy all of the 1-2-3 and Allways files into it. Use **XCOPY** to get all the subdirectories: **XCOPY /S**.

Next, delete all of the files and subdirectories from the 1-2-3 directory and re-create the subdirectories at the top of the directory list, placing the Allways subdirectory at the head of the list. Finally, copy all of the files from the temporary directory back to the newly formatted 1-2-3 directory, and Allways should run considerably faster.

Also, check the entries in your system's CONFIG.SYS start-up file. If you don't already have a Buffers statement, add one to permit at least 20 buffers.

Buffers = 20

This may help speed up Allways.

The Allways Display

As soon as Allways loads, you will see an immediate difference in the appearance of your spreadsheet. Allways uses default format settings to provide a background shade or color and to select a spreadsheet-wide typeface and font size.

Allways is supplied with a default font set. With many printers the Trium-virate typeface in 10-point size is the default, but the actual default depends on which printer you have installed as the primary printer. All of the characters on your spreadsheet will be displayed in this default font the first time you load Allways. You can change this default by changing the font stored in the Number 1 position of the Allways font list.

The background color is white on a color display or light on a monochrome screen. The background color is the underlying color of the display and shows around the border. The foreground color overlays the central part of the screen, covering the background. Any characters or graphics are etched out of the central foreground, producing a reverse-video display.

Allways is a near-WYSIWYG product. That means that what you see displayed on the graphics screen is very close to what will appear on the printed page. However, there are some exceptions forced on the product by the variety of printers and printer fonts it must support and by the differences between a video display and a printer.

For many font, screen, and printer combinations, what you see will, indeed, be what you get on the printer. Sometimes, however, you may notice slight differences. One reason for the differences is that Allways has four screen fonts, whereas printers may have hundreds of font choices.

Allways displays all of the on-screen data in Pica, Courier®, Helvetica®, or Times Roman® fonts. If you specify another font for any of the cells in your spreadsheet—which you certainly will if you want to take full advantage of your flexible printer—then what you see on screen may not match what your printer produces. When a new font is specified, Allways searches its available on-screen fonts for a match that is as close as possible to the printer font you specified in point size and shape.

Most of the time the fit is pretty good. But if the Allways algorithm misses a precise match by even one pixel, there may be differences between what you see on screen and what you get on the printer.

This problem may show up, for example, when you are trying to print a date format cell. On the screen, the date may appear to fit but that cell comes out on the printer as a series of asterisks. The fix is simply to enlarge the width of the cell that contains the date by just enough to allow all of the formatted date to fit. Usually you will need to increase the size of the cell (**/Worksheet Column Set-Width**) only a little bit—maybe 0.10 character or so—to get a fit.

Specifying Ranges

Specifying ranges and moving the cursor works almost the same in Allways as it does in 1-2-3. You use ranges—which can be a single cell or any square or rectangular shape of multiple cells—to tell Allways which areas to change with a new font, shade, underline, or other attribute.

Allways has an interesting feature that is possible only because you cannot enter data from within Allways. You can set a range before you enter the menu command sequence, and Allways acts immediately on the specified range instead of asking for a range after the command is entered.

To underline the cells in the range C5..F12, for example, you can enter the **/Format Underline Single** command, then enter the range or paint the area to underline when Allways asks for it. On the other hand, you can place the highlight on cell C5, press period and paint (point to) the C5..F12 range before entering the underline command. Allways underlines the specified range immediately and returns to the ready mode. The highlighted range remains marked, but the first cursor movement key you enter after the operation clears the range setting.

The ability to specify the range before you enter the command is especially useful as you learn more about the program and start using Quick Keys and function keys. Quick Keys and function keys duplicate some of the menu options available in Allways, but they do not ask for range information. Rather, the specified operation is carried out on the current cell or the current marked range.

In the previous example on underlining, for example, you could have marked the C5..F12 range as described, then pressed the ALT-U key once for a single underline or twice for a double underline throughout the range.

Setting Fonts

One of Allways' strongest features is the support for a broad range of printers and associated hard and soft fonts. Even if the program did not support shading, underlining, and the many other features that help give spreadsheet presentations more impact, the font capability would make the program a valuable asset.

Resident and Downloaded Fonts

A font is a complete set of characters of the same point size and type style. Allways supports two kinds of font sets that the authors of the software call *printer fonts* and *soft fonts*. Other programs call these font types *resident fonts* and *downloaded fonts*. Either way, they work the same.

Every printer comes equipped with one or more fonts (character sets) programmed into it that work a little like the type balls on the old IBM Selectric typewriter. Once you select a font, everything you print appears in that font until you select another one. These built-in fonts are the resident or printer font sets. The characters are printed simply by sending the ASCII code for each character down the printer interface line from the computer. Sometimes you select the resident font you want to access by sending a special code sequence that acts like a switch to turn certain fonts on or off.

In addition to the resident fonts, some printers can accept new fonts from the host computer. If your software application wants to print characters in a font that is not part of the printer's resident font, it can download a set of characters of its own that the printer accepts and reproduces as requested. These downloaded or soft fonts expand greatly the variety of characters and symbols your printer can reproduce.

When you install one of the supported printers in Allways the program knows which fonts the printer supports as resident fonts and which fonts can be downloaded.

In operation you won't notice much difference, except that printing will be a little slower on some lines. If a required font is not available from your printer as a resident font, Allways must generate and download the required font the first time it is used.

Font Type Summary

Allways includes three typefaces as graphics-downloadable soft fonts: Courier, Triumvirate, and Times. Courier is an electronic equivalent of the standard Courier typewriter face. The other two styles are equivalent to two of the best-known and most widely used typefaces in conventional printing, Helvetica and Times Roman.

Times and Courier are called "serif fonts," because their letters include extra strokes and embellishments at the ends and corners of the letters. (The origin of the serif style is said to date from the age of the stone carvers, who found that the extra strokes at the ends of straight lines tended to help prevent the rock from crumbling.)

Serif fonts are considered to be more traditional for book work, and most experts agree that serif typefaces are easier to read in large blocks of type. The more modern "sans serif" (without serifs) fonts, such as Triumvirate/Helvetica, are commonly used in forms, in captions, and as contrasting styles for headlines and titles over serif body copy.

The term "*typeface*" refers to the design of the character. A typeface generally is part of a family of styles. Figure 4.2 shows a standard set of Helvetica PostScript® typefaces, a sans serif font. All of the type in Figure 4.2 is set in the 12-point size. Figure 4.3 shows some examples of different type sizes in serif fonts. These were created using the PostScript fonts of the QMS-PS 810 laser printer.

Each typeface can be further adjusted through control of the vertical size of the characters. In traditional printing, vertical distance is measured in points. An inch is divided into 72 points; each point, therefore, is $\frac{1}{72}$ of an inch. It's not as complicated as it might appear: the most common type sizes for text are 8 point ($\frac{1}{9}$ inch), 10 point (about $\frac{1}{7}$ inch), and 12 point ($\frac{1}{6}$ inch).

Figure 4.2
Set of Helvetica
typefaces

Helvetica	The standard style, with normal type weight and upright characters.
Helvetica Bold	**A heavier weight version, with upright characters.**
Helvetica Bold Oblique	***A heavier weight version of the standard design, with characters slanted toward the right in an "oblique" style. In serif fonts, this same style is called "italic."***
Helvetica Oblique	*A normal weight version of the standard design, slanted to the right as an oblique face.*
Helvetica Narrow	A family of more vertical style versions of the typeface design.
Helvetica Narrow Bold	
Helvetica Narrow Bold Oblique	
Helvetica Narrow Oblique	

For headlines and titles, the most common sizes are 18 point (¼ inch), 24 point (⅓ inch), and 36 point (½ inch).

On dot matrix printers, type sizes differ principally in their widths, rather than in their heights. In a term derived from typewriter technology, the width of most resident typefaces for dot matrix printers is referred to as *"pitch,"* which is a measure of characters per inch. A typical size for standard type is 10 or 12 pitch; a narrow or condensed typeface might be 17 pitch; and an extended or wide dot matrix typeface might be 5 pitch.

If you use a dot matrix printer with Allways, the printer driver you specify will give access to the resident fonts of the printer, measured in pitch, as well as the soft, or downloaded, Courier, Triumvirate, and Times fonts, supplied by Allways and measured in points.

Figure 4.3
Different sizes of
type

This is 8-point Times Roman for body copy;

This is 10-point Times Roman for body copy;

This is 12-point Times Roman for body copy.

New Century Schoolbook Bold, 18 point

New Century Schoolbook Bold, 24 point

New Century Schoolbook Bold, 36 point

The Allways Advantage

It can be difficult to program the proper command sequence for the printer attribute you want, particularly with today's laser printers. In 1-2-3 you can select a printer attribute for the entire worksheet through the **/Print Printer Options Setup** command sequence. This command sequence provides a single format line in which you enter the proper number sequence to turn on the printer attribute you want. You might enter \027\015, for example, to select a 17 character per inch (cpi) font on some dot matrix printers.

You can control individual cells or ranges during printing by entering printer control codes in a cell ahead of the range where you want the change to occur. Precede the printer control command with a vertical bar. To turn on emphasized print on many dot matrix printers, for example, you enter |\027\069 in a cell at the head of the range. If you are using a laser printer such as the Kyocera F1000A, you can enter commands from the printer's built-in command language with the vertical bar lead-in. The sequence

|!R! Font 10; Exit;

for example, specifies a 14.4-point Helvetica Bold font. The selected printer attribute remains in effect until you send another code to cancel the special font or select another one.

NOTE: The 1-2-3 printer control codes override the settings made in Allways.

Obviously, printer control from inside Allways is a lot easier than from within 1-2-3. Also, if you have used such printer control sequences in your spreadsheets, you should remove them before you format the spreadsheet in Allways or what you see definitely will *not* be what you get. Not only will the control sequences override Allways settings, but if you print a range that contains only a portion of the command, the command itself appears in your printed spreadsheet.

Function Keys

Like 1-2-3, Allways supports some special function keys. As you learn more about using the program, you may want to use these available function keys to carry out certain functions quickly without having to go through the Allways menu.

Although Allways matches 1-2-3 function key assignments fairly closely, there are some differences, partly because there are no parallels in Allways for some 1-2-3 functions. The 1-2-3 ABS function, for example, has no counterpart in Allways, nor can you zoom the display in 1-2-3. Function key F4, therefore, has a unique function in each program. Figure 4.4 is a table that shows special function keys in 1-2-3 and Allways.

The function keys in both programs can be accessed through 1-2-3 macros. Each of these keys has a name in 1-2-3, and even though the name does not always match the function in Allways, you can use this name inside Allways to conduct the function associated with that key.

When you write a macro to enter Allways and call the {Window} function key, for example, Allways will toggle between the graphics and text mode. You can use the {ABS} function in Allways to carry out the F4 (Zoom in) function, but there apparently is no way to issue the SHIFT-F4 (Zoom out) function in a macro.

Figure 4.4
Special function
keys in 1-2-3 and
Allways

1-2-3 Special Function Keys

Key	Key Name	1-2-3 Function	Allways Function
F1:	[HELP]	Displays Help	Displays Help
F2:	[EDIT]	EDIT current cell	
F3:	[NAME]	Displays range names	Displays Range Names
F4:	[ABS]	Toggles Cell address absolute	Zoom Out (Shift-F4=Zoom in)
F5:	[GOTO]	Jump to Specified Cell	Jump to Specified Cell
F6:	[WINDOW]	Jump to other window	Toggle Text/Graphics Mode
F7:	[QUERY]	Last /Data Query Command	
F8:	[TABLE]	Last /Data Table command	
F9:	[CALC]	Recalculate all formulas	
F10:	[GRAPH]	Draws current graph	Toggle Graph Display on/off

In any case, these same features are available directly from the Allways menu, and from inside a macro, the extra steps involved are insignificant. When you are entering the commands by hand, however, it is another matter. Learning to use these function keys can save you significant time when you work with complicated spreadsheets.

Quick Keys

Allways adds 13 ALT-key combinations to the basic function key list. Funk calls these *Quick Keys* and they function like 1-2-3 macros, in that you hold down the ALT key and press an associated key to issue a menu command sequence quickly.

For example, to select font 7 for a cell from the current font menu by hand, you enter the **/Format Font 7** command sequence. By using the ALT-7 Quick Key combination you install the font in position seven of the font menu immediately. You can set a font over a range of spreadsheet cells by first establishing the range in Allways. Move the cursor to the beginning of the range you want to mark, press period (.) and paint the cells you want to format with font 7, then use the ALT-7 Quick Key combination.

Other Quick Keys step through several possible choices. You can select light, dark, solid, or no shading with the ALT-S Quick Key, for example. The first time you press ALT-S the shading in the current cell or market range changes to light, the second press of the key combination changes the shading to dark, and so on.

Figure 4.5 summarizes the function of all of the Allways Quick Keys.

Figure 4.5
Allways Quick Key
summary

Allways Quick Keys

Key	Action
[Alt-B]	Boldface: Set/Clear
[Alt-G]	Show Gridlines: On/Off
[Alt-L]	Lines: Outline/All/None
[Alt-S]	Shade: Light/Dark/Solid/None
[Alt-U]	Underline: Single/Double/None
[Alt-1] – [Alt-8]	Set Font 1 through Font 8

Figure 4.6
Allways online help
sample

HELP

```
Allways Menu

To bring up the Allways menu, press / (slash). The menu contains the following
commands:

       Worksheet    Adjust column widths and row heights; set page breaks
       Format       Apply Allways formats to cells and remove them
       Graph        Add, remove, and format graphs
       Layout       Set print layout options
       Print        Define print settings and print the worksheet
       Display      Set screen display options
       Special      Copy, move, or import Allways formats; justify text
       123          Return to 1-2-3 READY mode

As in 1-2-3, you can select a command either by typing its first letter or by
highlighting it and pressing [Enter].
```

```
       Help Index
01-Mar-89  11:01 AM                                        NUM
```

You cannot use the Quick Keys from inside 1-2-3 macros because there are no named equivalents for these keys in 1-2-3, as there are for the special function keys.

Help Screens

Allways follows the 1-2-3 example for online help. However, the Allways help screens generally are easier to follow and offer somewhat better information. (See Figure 4.6.)

The Allways help file is accessed with the F1 function key from nearly any Allways screen or menu. Even if you think you understand a particular operation as you are learning your way around Allways, you probably should use the help function because frequently there is information in a help screen that you won't find in the manual. The first help screen tells you, for example, that you can return to the main menu from inside any Allways menu by pressing the slash (/) key. This is the key you use to bring up the main menu the first time; however, in 1-2-3 you cannot back out quickly this way.

NOTE: This quick return to the main menu only works from a menu. You cannot use this command from a pulldown box.

Allways help is context sensitive, which means the program knows the general area of commands you are accessing when you press help and offers immediate help on that command or group of commands. In addition, you can branch to additional areas associated with the main section with a high-lighted pointer at the bottom of the screen, or display the help index that gives you access to any help topic.

Summary

This chapter swept you into the nitty-gritty of using the 1-2-3/Allways combination. We included hints on the general features of Allways, including fonts, Quick Keys, differences between 1-2-3 and Allways, and how to get online help.

The next two chapters detail Allways menu selections and commands and help you fine-tune your use of Allways features.

5 Allways Commands and Menus—I

Allways uses a Lotus-like menu structure that pops up with the slash key (/), just as in 1-2-3. From this single-line menu you can branch into a relatively complicated tree structure through seven major headings:

≡ Worksheet
≡ Format
≡ Graph
≡ Layout
≡ Print
≡ Display
≡ Special

The final selection on the menu, **123**, returns you to the 1-2-3 Ready mode. You can accomplish the same thing by pressing ESC in the Allways Ready mode, without the menu displayed; by pressing ESC twice with the main menu displayed; and by pressing the hot-key combination you used to get into Allways from the Allways Ready mode.

For additional information on the Allways menu structure and a summary of the commands, refer to Chapter 2, "Quick Start."

Chapters 5 and 6 provide a complete and detailed reference section on Allways commands and functions. Chapter 5 covers all of the main menu commands through the **/Graph** menu tree. Everything from **/Layout** on is covered in Chapter 6, "Allways Commands and Menus—II." To find information in either of these chapters, you can refer to the table of contents, the index, or simply scan down the menu tree in Figure 5.1 for the proper sequence and find the menu entry in one of these chapters.

Each section begins with the title of the main menu selection it discusses. Under the main selection each possible submenu choice appears and the menu selections are summarized. Additional details on how to use most of the selections follow in the body of the book.

NOTES: Many submenus include **Quit** as the final selection. In all menus this selection returns you to the Allways Ready mode. You can step

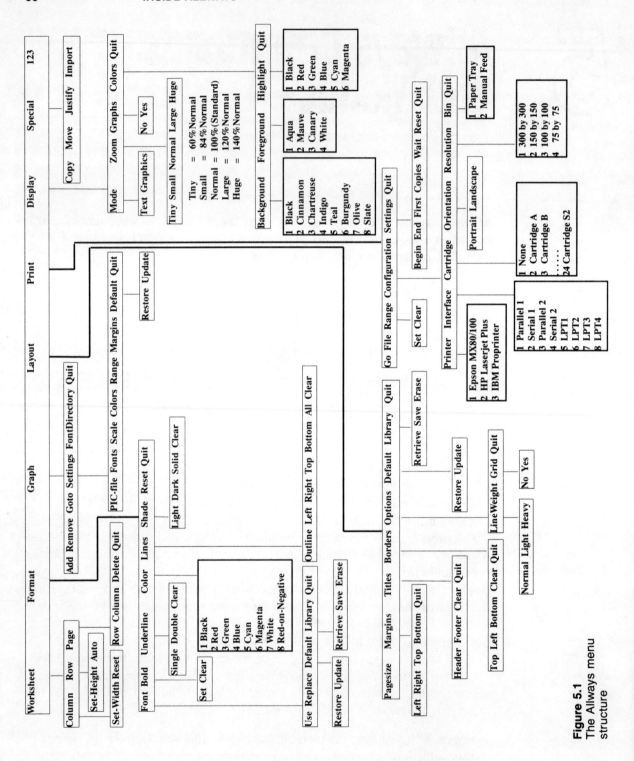

Figure 5.1
The Allways menu
structure

backwards up through the menu tree by successively pressing ESC. You can return to the main Allways menu from within any submenu by pressing the slash bar (/) (the same key that displays the main menu from the Ready mode).

Except for the **Quit** choice, all menu selections are listed in this section. Some choices are self-explanatory, however, and only the hierarchical menu option summary is provided.

If all you need is a quick reminder of what certain menu items do, read the material in the summary. If you need to study the finer details of particular information, also read the descriptive material contained in the command's discussion.

/Worksheet Column Set-Width

Sets the column (vertical range) width for the Allways display and output. Use the left or right arrow keys to move the on-screen dotted line indicator for width one character at a time; use CTRL-LEFT or CTRL-RIGHT to move the width indicator by 0.1 character.

Allways provides fine-grained control over column width down to 0.01 character. This function is similar to the 1-2-3 column width feature, with some obvious and important differences.

In 1-2-3, remember, when you set column width you can either type in a number to specify the width or use the left-right arrow keys to compress or expand the column on screen.

The Allways **/Worksheet Column Set-Width** command accepts the same kind of input, except that you can specify fractional column widths. In addition, when you use the cursor movement keys to set column width the column does not change until you press RETURN. Instead, a vertical bar moves left and right on the screen to show where the column margin will be when you press RETURN.

Each press of the cursor movement key moves the pointer line one character position and updates the top-of-screen display by one character. From the default 1-2-3 width of nine characters, one press of the left-arrow key in the Set-Width mode moves the pointer line to the 8-character position and displays

Enter column width (0..240 characters): 8

at the top of the screen.

To select fractional column widths, use the CTRL key in combination with the arrow movement keys. CTRL-LEFT or CTRL-RIGHT changes the column width by 0.1 character. The first press of the CTRL-LEFT key, for example, produces a column width of 8.9 if you start with the default of 9.0. For even finer adjustments, type in the number you want. You can set a column width of 2.31, 2.66, 0.44, or whatever you want between zero and 240 characters.

> NOTE: You can access these small column width movements from a 1-2-3 macro with the {**Bigright**} and {**Bigleft**} commands. Notice that these 1-2-3 commands have the opposite effect in Allways during these operations. Instead of moving the cursor a page at a time as in 1-2-3, these commands move the cursor 0.1 of a character width. When you use {**Bigleft**} and {**Bigright**} to move from cell-to-cell within an Allways spreadsheet, however, these functions work as they do in 1-2-3.

When you select a column width of zero you effectively hide that column. The data is still there in the 1-2-3 version, but you can't see it in Allways.

> NOTES: Until you change the column width in Allways the width set within 1-2-3 applies. When you have changed the width of a column in Allways, any further changes to the width in 1-2-3 will not appear in Allways.
>
> The column width changes in Allways do not appear in 1-2-3.

If you have experience with 1-2-3, you know how to use column width settings to change the way spreadsheet information is presented on the screen and how it prints. Although information that is wider than the cell of origin spills over into adjacent cells, usually it is better to widen the column to hold that information if you can. For one thing, data that spills over into an adjacent cell disappears from the screen and is not printed if the adjacent cell contains current data, even a space.

You can adjust columns in 1-2-3 down to 1 character wide and up to 240 characters wide to accommodate special characters, numbers, and labels. Remember that you can override these settings in Allways, and you probably will want to. However, it still is a good idea to change cell widths in 1-2-3 when you are dealing with variable width data. Such changes make it easier to read the information in 1-2-3 format and, therefore, easier to make changes you probably will require as you format the spreadsheet from within Allways.

So why would you want to make adjustments of less than one character width to the width of a column? Why would you want fractional width control? One reason is that Allways uses proportional characters, so you may want to adjust the width of a column to match precisely the space taken by a string of characters.

In addition, the shading facility in Allways provides some interesting possibilities for unusual spreadsheet design with variable width columns.

Notice Figure 5.2, for example. Here is a purchase order spreadsheet with a wide central column on which the name of the organization and the title "Purchase Order" center nicely. However, we have added two narrow columns on either side of this wide column to accomplish two goals. First, notice the closely spaced double lines that separate the Units and Price columns from the Description column. The space between each of these pairs of double rules is 0.4 character wide, providing a pleasing separation.

The second goal of thin columns is shown in Figure 5.3. Here we have used the **/Format Shade Solid** command to fill in thin columns to the right and below the box that holds the "Purchase Order" title, providing a shadow effect. We also inserted thin rows at the top and bottom of the box to heighten the effect. Each of these rows is 3 units high.

NOTE: See the section on Color in Chapter 6 for information on printing white characters on a black background.

Another useful application of narrow columns is to help you center information over an even number of spreadsheet columns. Suppose you have a spreadsheet with six columns and you want a title centered over those six columns.

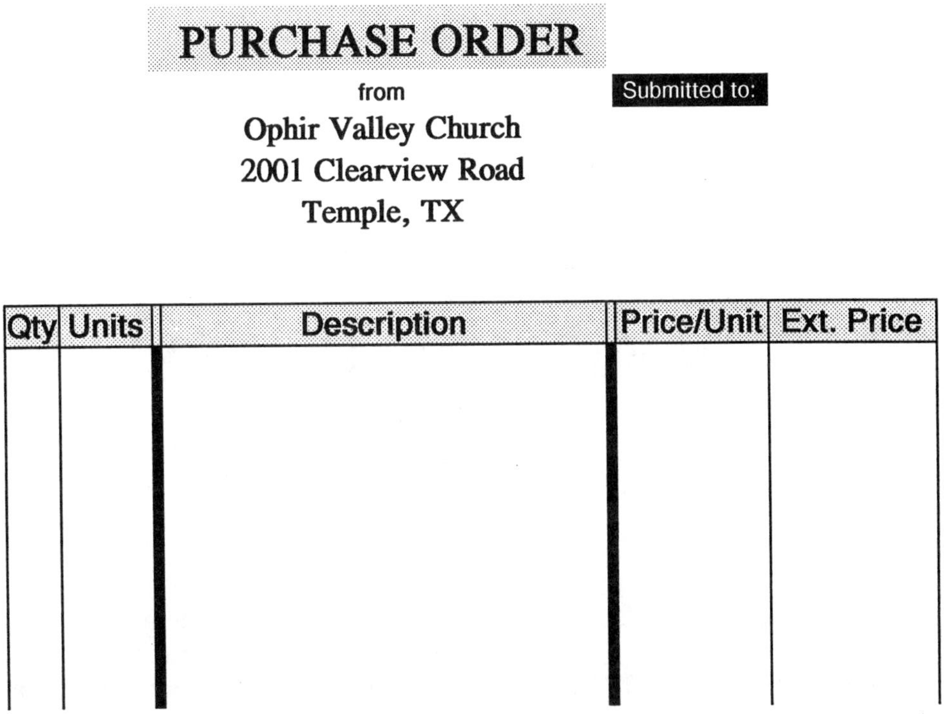

Figure 5.2
Using thin columns
for lines and
shadows

PURCHASE ORDER

from   Submitted to:

Ophir Valley Church
2001 Clearview Road
Temple, TX

Qty	Units	Description	Price/Unit	Ext. Price

The secret is to insert a seventh column in 1-2-3 between columns 3 and 4 in the range you want to print. Next, center the text for the range heading in a cell in this column with the ^ label prefix. Now enter Allways and shrink this column as much as you need to (as long as the width is greater than zero) to keep the extra column from interfering with the presentation of the data in the spreadsheet range.

Notice that Allways keeps data centered over the cell of origin, even if the information is too wide to fit in the column. Therefore, the title moves left and right from the extra column and will be centered over the six-column-wide spreadsheet range.

> NOTE: As with 1-2-3, Allways adjusts the width of a column from the top to the bottom of the spreadsheet. Any information that resides above or below the area you are formatting is affected by the changes you make.

/Worksheet Column Reset

Resets the column width to the original width specified in the 1-2-3 worksheet.

At times you may need to return a whole spreadsheet or a spreadsheet range to the way it was in 1-2-3. You can reset column widths with the **/Worksheet Column Reset** menu sequence. Use the period (.) to start a range point (paint) operation, mark the range to reset, then enter the **Reset** command. If you don't mark a range first, the **Reset** command acts only on the current column, the one where the cursor is resting.

/Worksheet Row Set-Height

Sets the row (horizontal range) height for the Allways display and output. The program displays a moving bar and a point size on screen. Use the up or down arrows to adjust the indicated point size up or down.

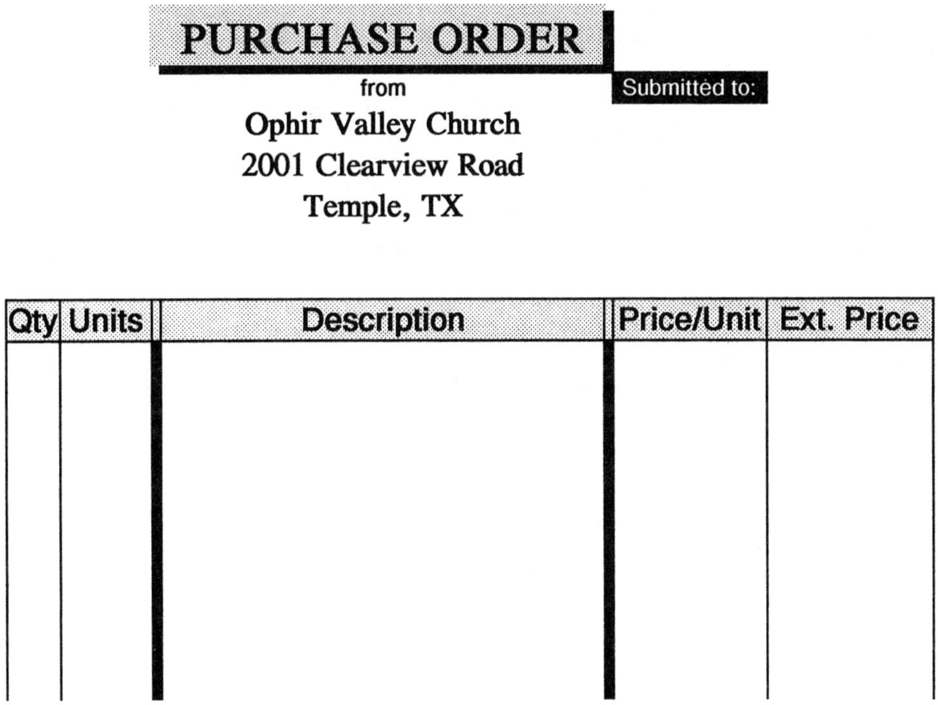

Figure 5.3
Solid shading for
shadow box

Qty	Units		Description		Price/Unit	Ext. Price

In 1-2-3 you have no control over row height. In Allways, however, you can adjust row heights from 0 to 240 units. Unlike the column width settings, row height must be set in integer amounts and there is no CTRL key movement option.

Like the column width feature, with the **/Worksheet Row Set-Height** command you either use cursor movement keys to change the height or enter a number within the allowed range to change the height immediately.

Look again at Figure 5.3. The rows at the top and bottom of the "Purchase Order" box are 3 units high in this sample spreadsheet. The narrow columns at left and right are 0.4 unit wide. When you fill in most of the bottom row and the right-hand column, you get a three-dimensional effect. This effect is increased by the white space at the upper right and lower left corners of the shadow box. This space is provided by not filling in the thin row at the top of the box or the narrow column at the left of the box.

You have some options in setting Allways row heights. If you take the default setting (see the discussion that follows under **/Worksheet Row Auto**), Allways adjusts the row height to match the height of the tallest character in a given row.

You don't have to accept these default settings, however. In fact, it often is desirable to change them. You probably will find that increasing the row height beyond the default will produce more attractive spreadsheets, if you can afford the room on the printout. This is especially true if the spreadsheet information is fairly dense. Just as an extra 0.25 incremental line spacing in a word processing document can open up the page and make the text easier to read, increasing the height of rows on a spreadsheet opens up the page and makes the data easier to read. (See Figures 5.4 and 5.5.)

Notice in the spreadsheet fragments in Figures 5.4 and 5.5 that we have used other techniques besides spacing to make the data presentation more readable. For example, instead of separating the major sections with blank rows, we have used different fonts to show the divisions. The **Personnel** heading is in 17-point type, and the subheadings **Management**, **Marketing and Sales**, and **Information Services** are in 12-point. To emphasize the beginning of each new section, the headings are outlined and shaded. Alternate columns of numbers are shaded.

> NOTE: Study these font choices carefully. It usually is a good idea to maintain a 40-percent to 50-percent or greater difference between font sizes on the same spreadsheet. However, you can change this ratio if you use bold type, boxes, shading, and so on.

In addition, the blank rows that separate each section's total from the preceding row and the next major heading in Figure 5.5 are not a full row height. Whereas the rows of numeric information are 14 points high, the

Figure 5.4
11-point rows with 10-point fonts: a closely packed spreadsheet.

Expenses (By Quarter)		1	2	3	4	5	6
Personnel	No.						
Management	Emp.						
Principals	5	50000	62500	64063	65625	67188	68750
Accounting Manager	1	35000	8750	8969	9188	9406	9625
Pers./Facilities Mgr.	1	35000	8750	8969	9188	9406	9625
Clerical	3	12000	9000	9225	9450	9675	9900
Total Management	10	132000	89000	91225	93450	95675	97900
Marketing and Sales							
Nat'l Acct Sales Reps	3	40000			31500	32250	33000
End–User Sales Mgr.	1	50000	12500	12813	13125	13438	13750
Marketing Manager	1	35000	8750	8969	9188	9406	9625
Total – Market/Sales	5	125000	21250	21781	53813	55094	56375
Information Services							
Manager	1	40000	10000	10250	10500	10750	11000
Research Associates	2	25000	12500	12813	13125	13438	13750
Clerical Super.	1	20000	5000	5125	5250	5375	5500
Clerical	4	12000	12000	12300	12600	12900	13200
Total – Info Services	8	97000	39500	40488	41475	42463	43450

Figure 5.5
14-point rows with
10-point fonts: a
more open
presentation.

Expenses (By Quarter)		1	2	3	4	5	6
Personnel	No.						
Management	Emp.						
Principals	5	50000	62500	64063	65625	67188	68750
Accounting Manager	1	35000	8750	8969	9188	9406	9625
Pers./Facilities Mgr.	1	35000	8750	8969	9188	9406	9625
Clerical	3	12000	9000	9225	9450	9675	9900
Total Management	10	132000	89000	91225	93450	95675	97900
Marketing and Sales							
Nat'l Acct Sales Reps	3	40000			31500	32250	33000
End–User Sales Mgr.	1	50000	12500	12813	13125	13438	13750
Marketing Manager	1	35000	8750	8969	9188	9406	9625
Total – Market/Sales	5	125000	21250	21781	53813	55094	56375
Information Services							
Manager	1	40000	10000	10250	10500	10750	11000
Research Associates	2	25000	12500	12813	13125	13438	13750
Clerical Super.	1	20000	5000	5125	5250	5375	5500
Clerical	4	12000	12000	12300	12600	12900	13200
Total – Info Services	8	97000	39500	40488	41475	42463	43450

separating rows are only 7 points high. So, at the same time that the information has been spread apart with slightly taller rows, the distance between sections has been compressed. This keeps the overall spreadsheet as tight as possible and, at the same time, makes individual values readable.

This technique of compressing rows also can help you get more information on a page. Compress any blank rows, such as rows between paragraphs in text data and between numeric sections. You also need fewer of these separating rows in Allways, as you can see from the examples in Figure 5.5.

When using Allways with 1-2-3 graphs, you might want to tighten up the spacing on the two-line title at the top of the graph. This is something you can't do in 1-2-3, but with Allways it produces a more finished, tighter presentation.

/Worksheet Row Auto

Sets the row height to an "automatic" calculation based on the point size of the type font in use for the specified range or ranges. Depending on the font in use, Allways generally adds one or two points to the font height.

For much of your spreadsheet work the automatic row height settings probably will do very well. Allways does a good job of adjusting row height based on the typeface selected as well as the point size of the characters. The height varies with the font, so that rows containing 20-point Triumvirate characters, for example, are set 22 points high. A 10-point Triumvirate font produces an 11-point row and a 14-point Triumvirate font automatically sets the row height at 16 points. For this reason you may notice some row height problems in one area of a worksheet, because the auto row height setting adjusts the height of the rows according to characters in portions of the spreadsheet not presently visible.

If you choose to adjust row heights manually (see the preceding discussion under **/Worksheet Row Set-Height**), you may benefit from a study of how Allways adjusts row height automatically as fonts are changed.

/Worksheet Page

/Worksheet
|
Page
|
Row   Column

Inserts a page break at the cursor position specified.

Another advantage of Allways over 1-2-3 from the user interface standpoint is its display of horizontal and vertical page breaks. When you specify a print range, a dotted line encloses the range that will be printed. In addition, if a page break occurs within the print range—if the specified range is longer or wider than the type of paper your printer is using—then another dotted line shows where Allways will break the page.

If you wish, you can force a page break horizontally or vertically with the **/Worksheet Page** menu sequence to keep certain information together on a single sheet.

First place the cursor where you want the page break to occur, then enter the menu sequence ending in **Row** for a horizontal page break or **Column** for a vertical page break. Alternately, you can enter the menu sequence, then wait for Allways to ask for the location of the page break. Either type in the discrete cell reference (C35) or move the cursor to where you want the break to occur and press RETURN.

It usually is preferable to force a page break above a column heading, if only one or two rows will fit on the page under that heading before an automatic page break. The overall effect is better with a little extra blank space at the bottom of the first page than if a major series of columns spills over onto the second page. When the columns lose their heads, the printed spreadsheet becomes more difficult to read.

/Worksheet Page Delete

/Worksheet
|
Page
|
Delete

Deletes a manually specified page break for the column or row specified by the cursor position.

Use this command to delete one or more page breaks. When you enter the **Delete** command, Allways asks what page breaks you want to delete. Move the cursor to the break you want to remove and press **RETURN**. The dotted line will be erased. You also can press period (.) and paint a range to remove more than one page break.

You also can enter a discrete cell address (C5) to erase a page break. Actually, the specific cell address is unimportant, as long as the address you enter includes the row or column that holds the page break. If you enter a cell address where two page breaks intersect, Allways deletes both page breaks. You cannot, however, enter a series of addresses (C5,C17) to delete more than one break.

/Format Font Use

/Format
|
Font
|
Use

Applies a font to a specified cell or range. (Quick Keys ALT-1 through ALT-8 select the eight available fonts on any single spreadsheet.)

With Allways you can select up to eight fonts from a popup menu and tell Allways where to use them by pointing to a range. The eight available fonts are selected from a much larger font library. If you are using a PostScript-compatible laser printer, for example, you probably have dozens—maybe even hundreds—of font combinations in the font library, but only eight of them are available at any one time.

The eight available fonts are selected by number or position in the list of currently available fonts. (See Figure 5.6.) You can change the overall appearance of an entire spreadsheet simply by replacing the font(s) in one or more positions of the font list with a new font(s).

You can select one of the eight available fonts with the **/Format Font Use** command or by pressing one of the ALT-key Quick Key combinations. ALT-1, for example, selects the font in position 1 and sets it into the current spreadsheet cell or marked range.

The font stored in the first position determines the default font for the entire spreadsheet, including the header and footer. (See the discussion of setting headers and footers under "/Layout Titles" in Chapter 6, "Allways Commands and Menus—II.") This default font also determines the effective width of spreadsheet columns and the height of rows. Normally you install the font that you want for the majority of your spreadsheet formatting in this first position and use other positions for special formats.

For headers and footers, however, you have no choice but to use position 1. If you need an extremely small or an extremely large font for header or footer text, the rest of the spreadsheet must be reformatted with another font and you must adjust the column width and row heights accordingly.

/Format Font Replace

/Format
|
Font
|
Replace

Replaces a font in the current font set.

Suppose you have formatted a number of spreadsheet cells with a Triumvirate 10 point font that is in position 6 of the current font list. The pointers inside the *.ALL file that tell Allways how to format each cell specify only position 6 of the current font list, not Triumvirate 10 point. Therefore you can change all of the Triumvirate 10 point cells to something else simply by replacing that font in position 6 of the current font list with something else from the font library.

To do this, issue the **/Format Font** sequence to call up the current font list (see Figure 5.7). Move the cursor to position 6 to highlight Triumvirate 12 point bold and choose the **Replace** option from the font menu. A list of available fonts will pop up in another window. Use the cursor movement keys to highlight the font you want and press **RETURN**.

If the font you select is a printer-resident font, the point size will be displayed in another box. You can accept the choice by pressing RETURN or move to another font selection by pressing ESC.

Figure 5.6
Allways current font
list (/Format Font)

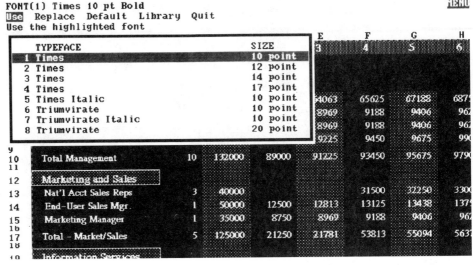

Figure 5.7
Allways available
font list (/Format
Font Replace)

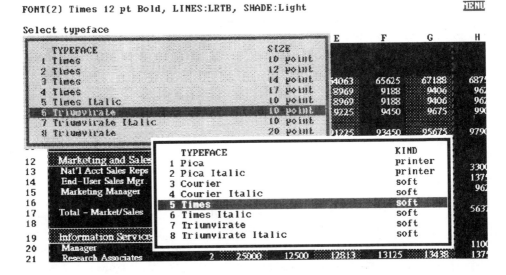

If you have chosen a soft font—a font that Allways builds and downloads
to your printer—then the last popup window (Figure 5.8) shows you a list of
possible point sizes. Use the cursor movement keys to highlight the size for
the selected font and press **RETURN**.

Allways then installs the selected font at the selected size in position six of
the current font list. This changes the way your entire spreadsheet looks because all of the cells formatted with font six, formerly Triumvirate 10 point
bold, are automatically reformatted with the new font you just installed in
position 6.

Figure 5.8
Installing Allways
font: selecting point
size

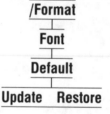

/Format Font Default

```
        /Format
           |
          Font
           |
         Default
           |
   Update    Restore
```

Updates or restores the current font set.

Until you format a spreadsheet by specifying fonts, shades, and other settings, Allways automatically sets the entire spreadsheet in the font installed in the number 1 position of the current font set, shown in Figure 5.9. When you first install Allways, eight fonts are available as the default font set. This same list of eight fonts is available each time you load a new spreadsheet.

You can change this default for the current spreadsheet easily by entering the **/Format Font Replace** command sequence, as described in the preceding section. In addition, you can establish your own default font set by first specifying the font you want in each of the font positions. When the font list is set up the way you want it, enter the **/Format Font Default Update** command. This saves the font set you specified to the default file. Each new spreadsheet then starts with these fonts as the default list instead of the one supplied with Allways.

You can restore the stored default list at any time with the **/Format Font Default Restore** command.

Figure 5.9
The Allways default
font set

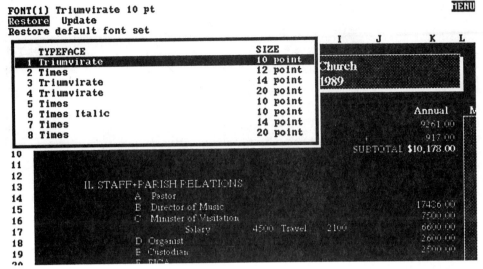

The font installed in position 1 is used for Allways headers and footers. Sometimes you may want to have the headers and footers in a different font from that of the rest of the spreadsheet. To do this, install the font you want for the headers and footers in position 1 of the font list with the **/Format Font Replace** command. This forces that font into the headers and footers. Next, install the font you want for the rest of the spreadsheet in position 2 (or any other of the seven remaining positions on the font list) and select the **Use** command on the **/Format Font** menu. When Allways asks, specify the spreadsheet range for this font.

Familiar Fonts

One of the potentially most difficult aspects of Allways formatting is learning how to select a font that is close enough to those you are used to in 1-2-3. Many users, for example, are accustomed to specifying 17 characters per inch (cpi) to print 132 columns on an 8-inch-wide printer or 260 characters, more or less, on a 14-inch-wide printer.

When you try to duplicate that selection in Allways, you won't find anything that says "characters per inch" because proportional fonts are sized in points. In addition, just selecting a point size is no guarantee that you will get precisely the cpi count you want, because each font uses space slightly differently.

However, there are some guidelines that can help you through this initial awkward stage. Assuming you still are using the printer you have always used for 17-cpi printing, you should be able to select a resident (printer) font from the Allways font list that will give you an average 16.6 or 17 cpi. If you install an Epson-compatible printer, for example, one of the printer font selections is Pica (Figure 5.10), a 17-cpi font on that printer.

Figure 5.10
Pica font selection
on Epson-
compatible printers

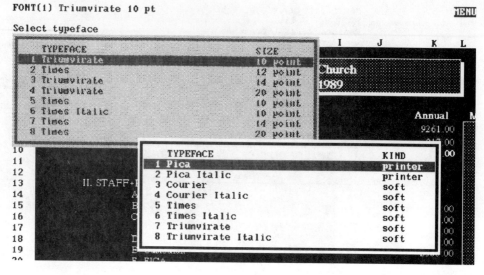

Figure 5.10
Pica font selection
on Epson-
compatible printers

Unfortunately, there is no hard and fast rule governing, or even a way to predictably guess, which fonts will produce which pitch. A single typeface, such as Helvetica, can have multiple versions, such as a 10-point plain and a 10-point narrow. Both are 10-point typefaces, but the narrow version, obviously, consumes less room on the page than the normal font.

However, remember that among the Allways features that do 1-2-3 one better is the visible page break after you have set the print range. If you don't have a pica font available, or if you want to use something more creative and variable, first do the spreadsheet formatting, next set the print range with the **/Print Range Set** command, then look for the dotted line around the outside of the range to show you the page break.

One of the problems with Allways at this point is that the dotted line that defines the print range looks the same as the dotted line that shows right margin and bottom margin page breaks. However, if there are no extra dotted lines inside the print range you specified, all of the material you specified will fit on the page. If extra lines do appear inside your specified print range, the material is too wide or too long for the page. You must either reduce the print range or select a smaller font.

By experimenting in this way, you can derive a set of fonts for your printer that will give you the print job you are seeking and are familiar with. In addition, a program such as Allways coupled with a reasonably late-model printer provides such a rich selection of printing possibilities that it should give you an incentive to break your ties to the past and try something new.

Experiment. Learn how to select fonts creatively and how to adapt your existing spreadsheets to the new features of Allways. More important, learn how to design *new* spreadsheets with the enhanced features of Allways in mind. The result will be better looking spreadsheets and a great sense of personal accomplishment.

/Format Font Library

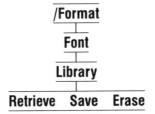

Retrieves or erases a font set from memory or saves it to memory.

In addition to the default font set and individual font sets for each spreadsheet, Allways supports a font library, a collection of eight-font sets saved in named files. When you load a spreadsheet, you can recall one of these named font sets (Figure 5.11) from the library with the **/Format Font Library Retrieve** sequence.

Allways asks for the name of the library file you want to retrieve, then places that font set into the eight numbered font positions for the current spreadsheet. When you look at the ...**Library** menu, you see that you can add a font set to the library with the **Save** command and erase a specified set of fonts with the **Erase** command.

There is no limit to the number of font combinations you can have at your fingertips, ready to load up and use for any spreadsheet. To build the library, use the **/Format Font Replace** command to establish a set of eight fonts, then use the **/Format Font Library Save** sequence to name the font set and save it to a named file.

/Format Bold

Selects or removes boldface for font in current range. (Quick Key: ALT-B toggles bold on and off.)

Figure 5.11
Allways Font
Library list

`Library to retrieve: C:\LOTUS\ALLWAYS\*.afs`
`COURIER.AFS      INVOICE.AFS      TIMES.AFS           TRIUMV.AFS`

The **Format** menu off the main Allways menu offers a rich tree of selections with which to format individual cells or spreadsheet ranges. The Fonts section earlier in this chapter discusses some of the available fonts and how to select them. Other attributes accessible from this submenu are:

≡ Bold
≡ Underline
≡ Color
≡ Lines
≡ Shade
≡ Reset

The Allways **/Format Bold Set** command is one of the program's strong features. When you consider a typeface in printing parlance, a boldface type is considered a separate font. This is true in many programs that support multiple fonts. With Allways, on the other hand, you can select up to eight separate fonts per spreadsheet, and you can set a bold attribute for any or all of these fonts. From a functional standpoint, this is equivalent to 16 individual fonts.

You can use bold, italic (a separate font with Allways), and other attributes to help differentiate information on your spreadsheets.

You can set boldface type by using the menu sequence to access the bold set command, then enter a discrete range or paint the cells you want to set in bold. Alternately, you can select the range first by pressing period (.) with the cursor in the first cell you want to set in bold, pointing to the range, and using the ALT-B Quick Key or the **/Format Bold Set** menu sequence.

Remember that ALT-B, like most of the Quick Key sequences, functions as a toggle. The first time you press ALT-B the bold attribute is set; the second time you press this key combination, boldface is removed from the current cell or marked range.

You can only set boldface for an entire label or number. If you have text that spills left or right outside cell boundaries, setting the boldface attribute for cells adjacent to the cell of origin of the text or numbers will have no effect. But you can set boldface for an entire string—even if it covers multiple cells—by setting the bold attribute only for the cell of origin.

/Format Underline

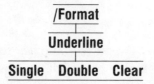

Selects or removes underlines from contents of current range.

SINGLE—Places a standard underline beneath data contained in the cell indicated.

DOUBLE—Places a double bar at the base of the full width of the indicated cell, regardless of whether or not the cell has text in it.

CLEAR—Quick Key: ALT-U toggles Single, Double, No Underline.

The **/Format Underline** (ALT-U) command adds still another font to the basic eight-font set available in any given Allways spreadsheet. You can select from single underline or double underline as a way of differentiating cell data.

Obviously, the double underline can be useful under the last cell in a column of numbers before the total. The only problem with the double underline attribute is that it covers the entire width of the specified cell, even if the cell data is not as wide as the cell. The single underline attribute, on the other hand, only draws a line under the text or numbers stored in a cell and leaves the rest of the cell blank.

If you want a single underline to cover the entire width of a cell, use the **/Format Lines Bottom** command sequence; if you only want to underline the data in a cell, use the **Underline** command.

There is a subtle difference in these two attributes. The single **Underline** attribute places a line high in the cell, directly under any data stored there. Descending character lines, or *descenders*, such as the tails on lowercase g's and p's, drop below the underline. With a line at the bottom of the cell, however, these descenders sit above the line.

The double **Underline** attribute, on the other hand, is really a double bottom line. Descenders sit above a double underline, just as they do on a bottom-of-the-cell line.

You will need to experiment with various underlining methods to get the precise effect you need for a specific application.

/Format Color

```
/Format
   |
 Color
```

Selects text colors for printing on a color-capable printer from the available choices listed. Note the "Red-on-Negative" choice, which highlights negative numbers in a spreadsheet.

1 Black
2 Red
3 Green
4 Blue
5 Cyan
6 Magenta

7   White

8   Red-on-Negative

Although the percentage of microcomputer users who have color graphics printers is relatively small, Allways offers color output support. If you have a color display, the **/Format Color** command produces colors close to what will be printed, but don't expect true WYSIWYG performance. Color presentation varies, even between different monitor/display card combinations. What you see on your screen and what your color printer produces probably will be close, but not precisely the same.

Don't confuse the **/Format Color** command with the **/Display Colors** command. The **Display** sequence sets only the color for the Allways spreadsheet display on your screen: foreground, background, and highlight colors. The **/Format Color** command selects the color for the ink on your printer.

You can specify one of seven colors by cell or range, but you can't select separate background and foreground colors. An eighth color choice, Red-on-Negative, tells Allways to print any numeric value that is less than zero in red ink.

The color printer settings affect only the primary data in a cell, the information you entered in 1-2-3. Any shading, boxes, underlining, and other attributes still appear in black.

One useful way to use this color option is to "white out" portions of an original 1-2-3 spreadsheet that you do not want to print. Many 1-2-3 users are in the habit of using \= as a cell entry to force a double line to fill the cell. By copying the original cell across the top of a range you can get a double line to separate a heading from column data.

In Allways, however, because the program uses proportional fonts, the line will appear as a dotted or broken line; it may not even fill the same space it originally did. You can solve the problem by editing the original spreadsheet and removing the lines, or you can use the **/Format Color** command to set the print attribute to White for any range that contains an unwanted line.

NOTE: This technique works on all laser and most dot matrix printers. Some dot matrix printers, however, cannot completely white out an area. The best way to find out if your printer can do this is to try it.

/Format Lines

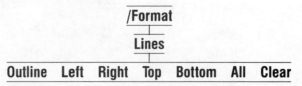

	/Format					
	Lines					
Outline	Left	Right	Top	Bottom	All	Clear

The Allways line drawing function is one of the program's most useful features. You can draw single lines on the right, left, top, or bottom of any cell or range with the **/Format Lines** sequence, or you can select **Outline** to draw a box around a cell or range.

The lines feature enables you to place 1-2-3 data close together, because lines and boxes can be used to separate information before printing the spreadsheet. Allways lines and boxes appear within the cell where they are drawn, so that additional rows and columns to hold the lines are not necessary.

The **Outline** option outlines the outer edges of an indicated range of cells.

The **Left** or **Right** option draws a line to left or right of an indicated cell, respectively.

The **Top** or **Bottom** option draws a line at top or bottom of an indicated cell.

Choosing the **All** option draws lines around edges of all cells in an indicated range. (Quick Key ALT-L toggles Outline, All, None.)

To remove all lines in an indicated range, select **Clear**.

In Figure 5.3 vertical lines were used in this sample purchase order to separate the various sections of the spreadsheet. The **Outline** function was used with **Shade** to set off the column headings and as part of the shadow box around the "Purchase Order" title.

As with other Allways format commands, you are asked for a range after the command is selected. You can enter a discrete range in number format (B1..D10) or you can paint the range by moving the highlight cursor with the cursor movement keys.

You also can set the range first by pressing period (.), then painting the range. Then, when one of the line commands is issued, it automatically applies to the marked range.

When you choose **Outline** for a spreadsheet range, the entire range is outlined, not individual cells. If you want a large box around a range of cells, mark the range, then enter the **/Format Lines Outline** sequence. A box will be drawn around the outside margins of the specified range (Figure 5.12).

To draw boxes around individual cells in a range (Figure 5.13), you must issue separate **Outline** commands for each cell, or you can draw vertical and horizontal lines through the range, effectively outlining individual cells.

/Format Shade

```
                    /Format
                       |
                     Shade
                       |
        ┌─────────┬────────┬───────┐
      Light    Dark    Solid    Clear
```

Adds a block of the indicated gray or black (solid) shading to specified range. The **Clear** option removes any shading from specified range. (Quick Key: ALT-S toggles Light, Dark, Solid, None.)

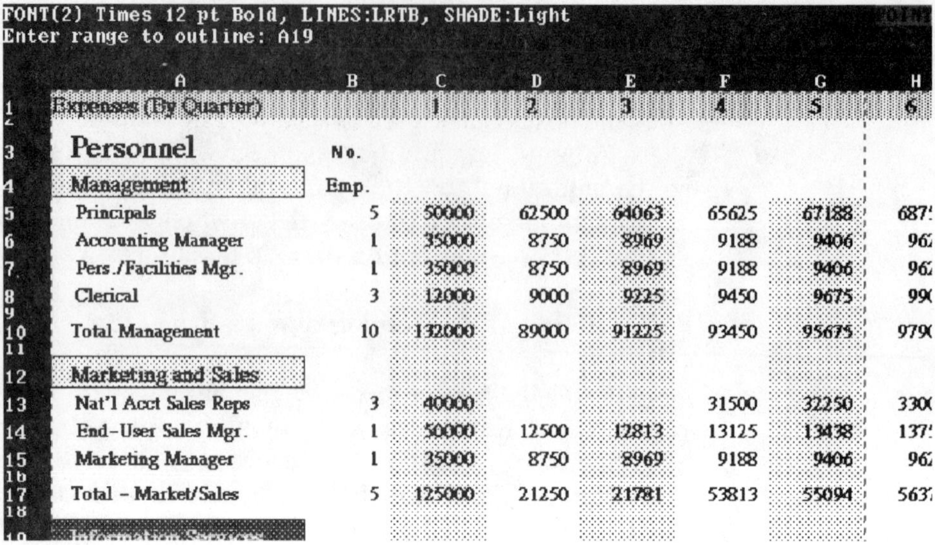

Figure 5.12
The Allways **Outline** feature used to draw a box around a range.

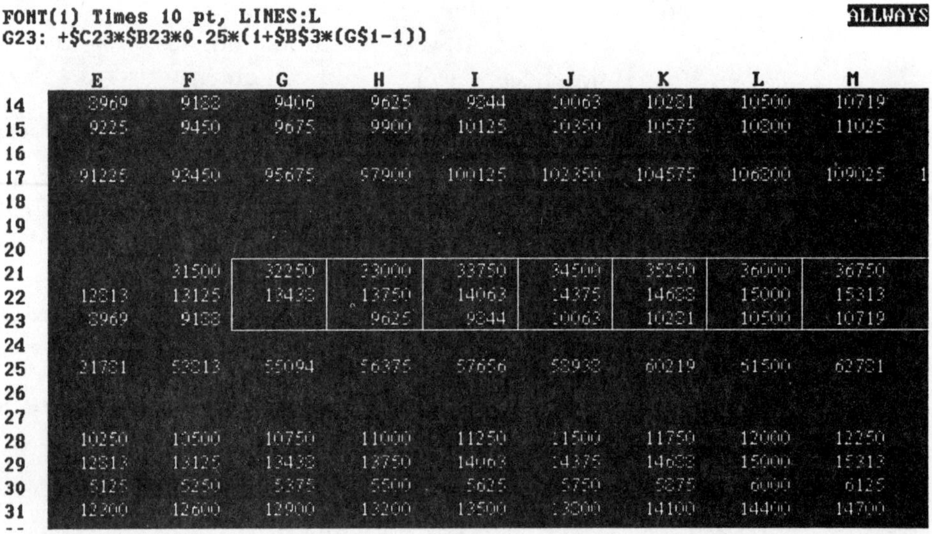

```
FONT(2) Times 12 pt Bold, LINES:LRTB, SHADE:Light
Enter range to outline: A19
```

	A	B	C	D	E	F	G	H
1	Expenses (By Quarter)		1	2	3	4	5	6
2								
3	Personnel	No.						
4	Management	Emp.						
5	Principals	5	50000	62500	64063	65625	67188	687!
6	Accounting Manager	1	35000	8750	8969	9188	9406	96:
7	Pers./Facilities Mgr.	1	35000	8750	8969	9188	9406	96:
8	Clerical	3	12000	9000	9225	9450	9675	99(
9								
10	Total Management	10	132000	89000	91225	93450	95675	979(
11								
12	Marketing and Sales							
13	Nat'l Acct Sales Reps	3	40000			31500	32250	330(
14	End–User Sales Mgr.	1	50000	12500	12813	13125	13438	137!
15	Marketing Manager	1	35000	8750	8969	9188	9406	96:
16								
17	Total – Market/Sales	5	125000	21250	21781	53813	55094	563;
18								

Figure 5.13
The Allways **Lines** feature used to draw boxes around individual cells in a range.

```
FONT(1) Times 10 pt, LINES:L                          ALLWAYS
G23: +$C23*$B23*0.25*(1+$B$3*(G$1-1))
```

	E	F	G	H	I	J	K	L	M
14	8969	9188	9406	9625	9844	10063	10281	10500	10719
15	9225	9450	9675	9900	10125	10350	10575	10800	11025
16									
17	91225	93450	95675	97900	100125	102350	104575	106800	109025
18									
19									
20									
21		31500	32250	33000	33750	34500	35250	36000	36750
22	12813	13125	13438	13750	14063	14375	14688	15000	15313
23	8969	9188		9625	9844	10063	10281	10500	10719
24									
25	21781	53813	55094	56375	57656	58938	60219	61500	62781
26									
27									
28	10250	10500	10750	11000	11250	11500	11750	12000	12250
29	12813	13125	13438	13750	14063	14375	14688	15000	15313
30	5125	5250	5375	5500	5625	5750	5875	6000	6125
31	12300	12600	12900	13200	13500	13800	14100	14400	14700

You can use the /**Format Shade** (ALT-S Quick Key) sequence to highlight a cell or range with light, dark, or solid shades. Figure 5.3 shows how shades can be used to separate column titles from column data and as part of a shadow box.

The results of shading a range may differ, depending on what printer you use and what resolution you choose for that printer. A laser printer capable of a full 300 by 300 dots per inch (dpi) resolution produces a relatively even, fine-grained shade. However, if you print the same shaded area on a printer set for, say, 75 by 75 dpi, the area will appear mottled or spotted instead of shaded (Figure 5.14).

Some printers, such as the Hewlett-Packard LaserJet (the original H-P laser printer), default to a 75 by 75 dpi graphics resolution in Allways. However, you can use the **/Print Configuration Resolution** sequence to force the higher resolution mode.

Use light or dark shades to emphasize areas of a spreadsheet or to separate columns. You can alternate light and dark shades to set off a series of columns, or you can alternate between shade and no-shade columns.

Use **Solid** shades to form shadow boxes and to produce white on black (reverse) type. To use reverse type for column headings or other special areas, use the Allways **/Format Shade Solid** command to fill in the area in which you want reversed printing. The text or numbers in the shaded range disappear from the screen.

Next, use the **/Format Color** command to select White as the printing color for the shaded range. The text or numbers in the range will reappear on the screen in white (Figure 5.15).

You can try these settings on your printer, but you may find that the printer can't reproduce the white characters. The H-P LaserJet II, for example, ignores

Figure 5.14
Shaded area printed in low resolution (75 by 75) mode.

Figure 5.15
Printing white on black for column headings. Printer: Kyocera F1000A in H-P LaserJet II emulation mode. Allways printer selection is H-P LaserJet (original) at 300 by 300 dpi.

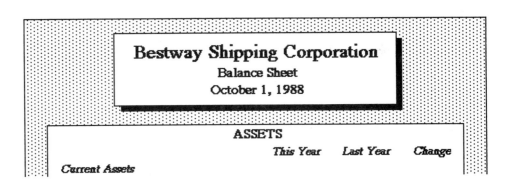

the white characters and prints the entire range in solid black. Try installing the original H-P LaserJet as another printer option. (Use the AWSETUP program supplied on Allways diskette number 1.) Use the **/Print Configuration Printer** sequence to select the original LaserJet as the active printer for the current spreadsheet. Then enter the **/Print Configuration Resolution** command to select 300 by 300 dpi resolution. (The original LaserJet defaults to 75 by 75 resolution.) Now the white on black characters should print correctly on your LaserJet II printer.

Many dot matrix printers also support the white on black printing mode correctly (Figure 5.16), but you may find that a laser printer is required for full flexibility of such settings. The quality of print on a dot matrix printer may not be as high as with a laser, as Figure 5.16 shows.

/Format Reset

/Format
|
Reset

Returns a cell or range to the current Allways default format settings: Font 1, no attributes, black background.

The **/Format Reset** command returns a specified range of the spreadsheet to the default format; that format is data displayed in Font 1 in black and all special attributes removed.

The **Reset** command can be useful to return a section of a spreadsheet to a "start over" condition. After spending some time formatting a spreadsheet range, you may decide the effect is not what you want. Sometimes you can remove one or two attributes to make the changes you want; other times it

Figure 5.16
Printing white on black for column headings. Printer: Star SR-15 in IBM emulation mode. Allways printer selection is IBM Graphics Printer.

Customer's Order Number	Phone	Date		
Name				
Address				
Date	**Description**	**Price**	**Paid**	**Due**

is easier to start over from the initial format. Use the **Reset** command to do this for you.

Either mark the range first, or issue the **Reset** command and then specify the range when Allways asks for it. Either way, any formatting you have added is removed from the specified range and that section of the spreadsheet returns to its original state.

/Graph Add

/Graph
|
Add

Adds a 1-2-3 graph, saved with a .PIC extension, to an indicated position in the Allways spreadsheet.

In 1-2-3 the spreadsheet data is a separate entity from the graph it produces. You can specify ranges of data to be used in forming a variety of graph forms, but you can only view the graph on a separate screen or print it.

With Allways you can display a 1-2-3-produced graph on the screen together with the data you used to produce it, and you can print the two entities together as if they were a single spreadsheet.

This Allways facility demonstrates an increasingly popular concept in the computer industry, "live links" between applications. Allways does not actually import the graph file you specify for the current spreadsheet. Rather, a pointer is set to link the file to the Allways spreadsheet.

Once a specified graph is tied into an Allways file, when you make changes to the data that generated the graph and save the new *.PIC file, the graph changes accordingly in Allways. This update is automatic. All you have to do is call up Allways from within the file that contains the graph and the latest version is displayed.

When you use the **/Graph Add** command in Allways, you first are asked to name the graph file you want to add. Allways displays a list of files ending in the *.PIC if you have specified a default directory containing any of these files. You can either type in a name or select from the list Allways provides.

Next you are asked to enter a range to contain the graph. You can enter almost any valid spreadsheet range, but if you enter a range that is too small, the graph is compressed and reshaped to fit the smaller space. Thus, the value of the displayed data is compromised. You can specify an area that is much larger than the original graph required, but this also can distort the meaning of the graph.

Allways enables you to paint a 1-2-3 graph into about any size area of the spreadsheet, but you should be cognizant of what is reasonable. 1-2-3 graphs are generally horizontal in orientation, and they are scaled to require no more than one screen to display. If you change the size ratio much, you may get strange results.

An interesting aspect of using graphs in Allways is that Allways displays 1-2-3 graphs in a transparent mode so that any other spreadsheet information in the same range as the graph shows through. You can devise some unusual output by overlaying the graph onto the data that produced it.

For more information on placing and using graphs in Allways refer to Chapter 10, "Using Allways for Graphs."

/Graph Remove

/Graph
|
Remove

Removes a 1-2-3 graph from its indicated position on the Allways spreadsheet.

The **/Graph Remove** command simply deletes a specified graph from the current worksheet. You are shown a list of all of the graphs linked to the current spreadsheet. You can use the cursor movement keys to select the graph to delete and press RETURN.

NOTE: Allways will not ask again. Once you press RETURN over the graph name, the graph is removed. This is not a great problem because you can relink the proper *.PIC file by simply selecting it from the **/Graph Add** list. **/Graph Remove** does not delete the original *.PIC file.

/Graph Goto

/Graph
|
Goto

Moves the cell pointer to a graph.

/Graph Goto is a useful feature when you have more than one or two graphs on a single worksheet, or when the amount of data is very large and the location of the graph or graphs is not obvious. As with the **Remove** command, the **/Graph Goto** sequence displays a list of the graphs attached to the current worksheet. (See Figure 5.17.) You select the one you want to reach by moving the cursor down to the correct name and pressing RETURN.

Figure 5.17
The /Graph Goto
display on an
Allways
spreadsheet

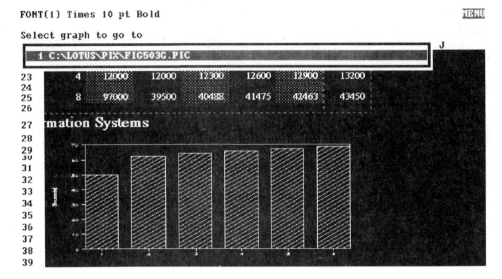

/Graph Settings PIC-file
=========================

/Graph
—
Settings
—
PIC-file

Reselects the .PIC file for the current graph, a quick way to change a displayed graph or update it without going through the extra step of removing the previous graph.

This command erases one graph display with another. It is a useful feature when you want to step through a series of graphs, for example, to determine which one best fits with the other data you are preparing on the spreadsheet.

The **/Graph Settings** command displays a pull-down box that shows the current graph settings and offers another menu for modifying these settings. (See Figure 5.18.)

You must observe a couple of cautions in using this command. First, it will replace the graph at the cursor position without asking which graph you want to replace. This actually is a strong feature, because Allways is smart enough to know which graph you are viewing currently and assumes it is the one that should receive the actions of any of the **/Graph Settings** commands. If the cursor is too far away from a graph for Allways to identify the current graph, a pull-down menu will ask you to identify which graph to work with.

Second, this command uses the spreadsheet area previously specified for another graph. If the spreadsheet range is not properly sized for the data being imported, the mcaning of the graph could change.

Figure 5.18
The **/Graph
Settings** menu and
status box

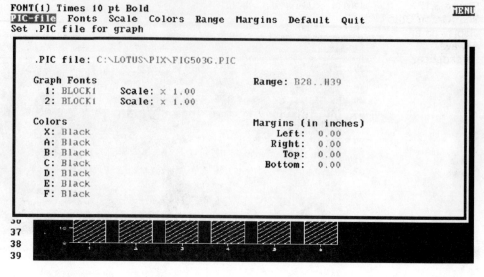

/Graph Settings Fonts

/Graph
|
Settings
|
Fonts

Selects graph font 1 (used for first title line only) and graph font 2 (used for all other text on the graph, including legends, scale numbers, and other titles).

This Allways feature closely follows the font selection feature in 1-2-3's Printgraph program. You can select from among 1-2-3's eleven fonts to change the appearance of the title line and other graph text. (See Figure 5.19.) Allways gives you a choice of two font settings, font 1 and font 2. The default setting is BLOCK1 for both fonts.

When you change the setting for font 1, the graph title line changes. When you change the setting for font 2, all other text associated with the graph changes.

It is useful to have access to this feature from inside Allways, but this facility is one of Allways' weakest ones. It offers little advantage over standard 1-2-3 and Printgraph.

You can use some of Allways' enhancement features on the title lines of graphs. You can draw a box around the title, for example, or shade it. But because of the way graphs overlay the Allways screen, you can't use Allways

Figure 5.19
Selecting a font for
an Allways graph
title

FONT(1) Times 10 pt Bold   MENU

Select graph font

.PIC file: C:\LOTUS\PIX\FIG509G.PIC

Graph Fonts   Range: B20..H39
   1: BLOCK1   Scale: x 1.00
   2: BLOCK1   Scale: x 1.00

   1 BLOCK1   Margins (in inches)
   2 BLOCK2   Left: 0.00
   3 BOLD   Right: 0.00
   4 FORUM   Top: 0.00
   5 ITALIC1   Bottom: 0.00
   6 ITALIC2
   7 LOTUS
   8 ROMAN1
   9 ROMAN2
  10 SCRIPT1
  11 SCRIPT2

37
38
39

fonts. You can change the row height around the title, but the size of the text in the title does not change. (However, see the **Scale** command, described next.)

/Graph Settings Scale

/Graph
───
Settings
───
Scale

Allows the setting of relative sizes of fonts 1 and 2 in graphs. Program will request a scale factor in a range between 0.5 and 3. The default size of 1.0 is equal to 1-2-3 PrintGraph settings.

To resize title text, use the **Scale** command and select font 1. To resize labels in other parts of the graph, use font 2. Because graphs are separate files from the 1-2-3 spreadsheet and they store data differently, the separate **Scale** command is the only way to adjust the size of text associated with graphs.

/Graph Settings Colors

/Graph
|
Settings
|
Colors

Selects colors for data ranges.

You use this sequence to select colors for individual portions of a 1-2-3 graph displayed in Allways. You can move a cursor bar among seven settings (the X range, and ranges A through F) to choose from eight colors for graph display.

/Graph Settings Range

/Graph
|
Settings
|
Range

Moves the graph to a different worksheet range or allows a change in its size.

You resize a graph with this command after the graph has been attached to the Allways spreadsheet. When you conduct a resizing operation, you also may be changing the aspect ratio. Be aware generally of what this ratio is for your graphs. Such awareness helps you spot in advance the problem of a resized graph that will be too far from the normal size to be useful.

When you enter the **/Graph Settings Range** command, Allways paints the current range of the graph near the cursor position. If the cursor is too far away from a graph position, you will be asked which graph you want to adjust when you enter the **/Graph Settings** command. You can either expand or shrink this range with the cursor movement keys. To move the graph to another area of the spreadsheet, press **ESC**, move the cursor to another area of the spreadsheet and point to a new range by pressing period (.) and using the cursor movement keys.

/Graph Settings Margins

/Graph
—
Settings
—
Margins

Sets top, bottom, right, and left margins for a graph.

The margins setting for graphs is really a way to reposition a 1-2-3 graph within the range the graph already occupies. Suppose you have a graph in the range B50..F59, including titles and legends. If you add a bottom margin of 1 from the **/Graph Settings Margins** menu, the bottom edge of the graph moves up the spreadsheet approximately one inch. The new range for the graph is B50..F53. Exactly how far the bottom margin moves up depends, in part, on the height of the spreadsheet rows within the graph range.

What you see on the screen may not be precisely what prints. In the preceding example the screen display shows a bottom margin of more than 1.25 inches, but when you print the graph the margin is one inch.

When you enter the **/Graph Settings Margins** command, the **Settings** pulldown box shows you the present graph settings and the **Margins** menu offers options to change the top, bottom, left, and right margins. You can enter any value for the margins between 0 and 9.99.

/Graph Settings Default

/Graph
—
Settings
—
Default
—
Restore   Update

Updates or restores default graph settings.

If you restore the Allways default graph settings, the fonts for graph fonts 1 and 2 are reset to BLOCK1, colors are returned to black for all graph data elements, the scale is returned to 1 for both fonts, and margins are reset to zero. Range, the other **/Graph Settings** selection, is not affected by the **Default** command.

As with other areas of Allways, you can update the graph defaults to reflect your personal preference or use patterns. Simply establish graph settings you would like to use automatically for all graphs and enter the **/Graph Settings**

Default Update command. The settings for the current graph will then become the default and will be applied to all future graphs as they are added to Allways spreadsheets.

/Graph FontDirectory

/Graph
|
FontDirectory

Specifies the location of font files and includes a subdirectory if necessary.

When you installed 1-2-3 with the PrintGraph program, you may have placed the graph font files in the same directory with the 1-2-3 files. You can, however, maintain a separate directory for the *.PIC graph files. In this case you may want to keep the graph font files in the same directory with the graph files.

Allways assumes that the font files will be in the same directory as the 1-2-3 programs. If this is not the case, you must enter the **/Graph FontDirectory** command and enter the path to the font files. If you try to add a graph without telling Allways where the font files can be found, the program displays an error message similar to

Cannot read graph font C:\LOTUS\PIC\BLOCK1.FNT

The error message shows the current path you have specified to the font files, and shows the font file the program is attempting to read for the current graph. Press **ESC** at this point and enter the correct path to the font files.

Summary

From **worksheets** to **graphs**, Allways offers rich enhancement features for 1-2-3 spreadsheets. This chapter has discussed facilities for row height and column width settings, has shown how to set page formats, how to format spreadsheets, and has offered suggestions on graph applications. Chapter 6 picks up the Allways menu tree with the **/Layout** submenus.

⑥ Allways Commands and Menus—II

Chapter 6 continues the reference section on Allways commands and functions that began in the previous chapter.

/Layout Pagesize

/Layout
|
Pagesize

Specifies the physical dimensions of the paper in use with the current printer. Allways obtains a listing of ordinary page sizes as part of the printer driver. You also can specify a nonstandard paper size with the **Custom** selection.

The **Layout** submenu includes a number of settings to change the way your spreadsheet data is presented. As soon as you enter the **Layout** section, Allways displays a pull-down box (Figure 6.1) that provides a quick-glance reference to the parameters you can set in this submenu. To change any of the items, use the cursor movement keys or the first letter of the item you want to change. Another popup box will appear to offer more choices.

When you specify the **Pagesize** option from the **Layout** menu, Allways shows you a list of standard paper sizes that are available for your printer. With most dot matrix printers you are given the choice of **Standard** (8.5 by 11), **Legal** (8.5 by 14) or **Wide** (14 by 11). With laser printers you may see other choices, including the **European A4** (8.27 by 11.69). You can select one of these or design a custom page for your application.

Custom pages can range from 0.25 inch to 99.99 inches in length and width. However, you may not be able to use some combinations of very narrow or very wide pages, depending on your printer and which fonts you are using.

/Layout Margins

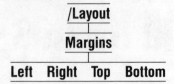

Specifies position of the printout on the page, in inches, by setting the left, right, top, and bottom margins.

You specify white space around the outside of your spreadsheet printout with the Allways margin settings. You can set the left, right, top, and bottom margins separately.

The Allways default is 1-inch margins around all sides, but you can specify margins from 0 to 99 inches. Of course, very wide margins won't work with normal paper sizes, and Allways will report an error for settings that are outside its perceived capability for your printer.

/Layout Titles

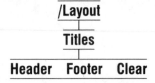

Adds or removes spreadsheet headers and footers.

Allways supports single-line headers and footers of up to 240 characters, but you probably won't be able to print this many characters with most printer/paper combinations. However, Allways has the advantage over 1-2-3 in that you can change the fonts used in the header and footer, enabling you to get more characters on a standard sheet of paper. If you specify a 5-point font in position number 1 (**/Format Font Replace**), for example, you can print more than 200 characters across an 8.5-inch-wide page.

NOTE: When you replace font 1, the entire spreadsheet will appear in this font unless you also change the font to be used for the entire spreadsheet (**/Format Font Use**). In addition, the *effective* width of all character cells in the spreadsheet changes with the replacement of the font in position 1. A 5-point font in position 1 shrinks the on-screen width of all columns, even though the numerical width of the columns remains at the default. If you specify a larger font for the rest of the spreadsheet, all of the data for a given cell will not fit unless you widen the columns. Figures 6.2–

Figure 6.1
/Layout submenu
choices with status
box

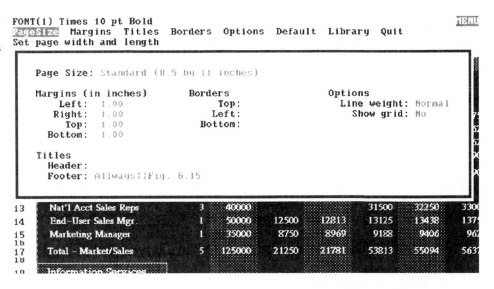

Figure 6.2
On-screen
spreadsheet with
1-2-3 default of
9-character column
width. The font in
position 1 is Times
Roman, 10 point.

6.5 show a sequence of resetting the font in position 1 and adjusting the column widths to display all characters.

Titles can include special characters, such as @ or #, which will automatically be replaced by the current date (@) or page number (#) when the spreadsheet is printed. In addition, you can use the vertical bar character (|) to separate a title into left, center, and right segments. Any header or footer characters to the left of the first vertical bar will be left-justified; data between the first and second bars will be centered; anything to the right of the second vertical bar will be right-justified. You can enter left-justified and right-justified material without anything in the center by placing two vertical bars together after the material you want on the left side of the page.

Two blank lines are left below the header and above the footer to separate header and footer text from the rest of the spreadsheet. When you enter the **Clear** command, you are given the option of removing the header, the footer, or both from the current spreadsheet.

/Layout Borders

/Layout
|
Borders

Allows specification of a range of characters or titles that can be used as a repeating border on multiple pages of a printout.

TOP, BOTTOM—Location for addition of specified row or rows as repeating border.
LEFT—Location for addition of specified column or columns as repeating border.
CLEAR—Removes specified borders.

The Allways **Border** facility works like the same feature in 1-2-3 to place a specified row or column of data at an edge of the spreadsheet. This facility is particularly valuable when you print spreadsheets or ranges that are longer or wider than the paper you are using. By setting the border range for the top

Figure 6.3
On-screen spreadsheet with 1-2-3 default of 9-character column width. The font in position 1 is Times Roman, 5 point.

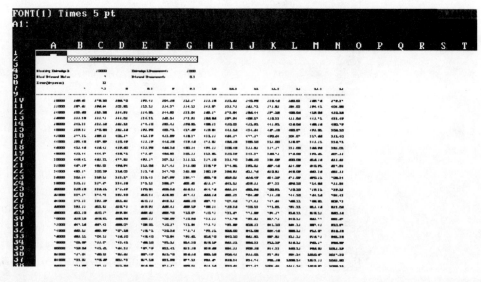

Figure 6.4
On-screen
spreadsheet with
1-2-3 default of
9-character column
width. The font in
position 2 is Times
Roman, 10 point.
The **/Format Font
Use** command was
used to specify font
2 as the font for the
body of the
spreadsheet.

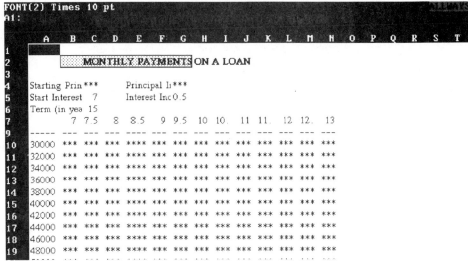

Figure 6.5
On-screen
spreadsheet with
Allways column
width of 15. The
font in position 2 is
Times Roman, 10
point. The **/Format
Font Use** command
was used to specify
font 2 as the font
for the body of the
spreadsheet.

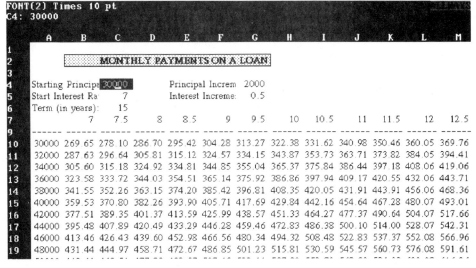

of the spreadsheet, for example, you can repeat all of the column headings on each page of the printout, making the multiple-sheet printout easier to use.

The same technique works for left or right margin borders. If your spreadsheet includes left-margin labels as row titles, simply set a border that includes the column or columns that make up the titles. The titles will repeat on each page of the printout.

When you select the **/Layout Borders** option, Allways removes the **Layout** status box and asks you to mark the range to use as a border. Use standard pointing or discrete reference techniques to mark the border range. You won't see any difference on the screen, but when the spreadsheet prints, the border cells will repeat on each page.

NOTES: When you specify the print range for this spreadsheet, *do not* include the range specified as a border inside the print range. If you do, this area of the spreadsheet will be printed twice on the first page where it appears.

1-2-3 calls the on-screen version of borders **Titles**. You can specify a range with the 1-2-3 **/Worksheet Titles** menu sequence to cause a portion of the spreadsheet display to freeze, providing on-screen titles as you move through the spreadsheet. Unfortunately, Allways does not recognize these settings, and the **Titles** feature is lost when you move into Allways.

/Layout Options LineWeight

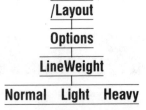

/Layout

Options

LineWeight

Normal   Light   Heavy

Allows alteration of the thickness (weight) of all lines placed on the spreadsheet using the **/Format Lines** command.

The **LineWeight** command sets the weight of *all* lines used in the spreadsheet. You cannot set different weights for different spreadsheet ranges. You will not see the differences among these settings in the screen display, only when the spreadsheet is printed. How much actual difference the settings make depends on the individual printer.

For more control over line width, you can establish narrow rows and columns and use the **/Format Shade Solid** command sequence to fill the lines. In this way you can adjust line weight in 0.01-inch increments, up to the maximum width of a cell or height of a row.

/Layout Options Grid

/Layout

Options

Grid

Adds ledger-like grid lines along the borders of every cell in the worksheet. Note that grids will follow column width and row height settings.

No—Turns grid off.
Yes—Turns grid on.

(Quick Key: ALT-G toggles grid On and Off.)

This feature is a convenience for times when you want to print spreadsheet information with each cell enclosed in a section of a grid. You have only two options with this command: turn the grid on or turn it off. The **LineWeight** option does not affect the thickness of the grid line.

The grid is a nearly transparent set of lines that outline each cell in the spreadsheet (Figure 6.6). When you change the height of a row or the width of a column the grid expands to match the change.

NOTE: The **Grid** option can be turned off and on only for the entire spreadsheet. You can produce a grid-like effect by using the **/Format Lines Outline** command around a range of cells, though the resulting lines will be darker than the **Grid** command produces.

Figure 6.6
Spreadsheet printed with **Grid** option

MONTHLY PAYMENTS ON A LOAN							
Starting Principal:	30000		Principal Increment:	2000			
Start Interest Rate:	7		Interest Increment:	0.5			
Term (in years):	15						
	7	7.5	8	8.5	9	9.5	10	10.5
30000	269.65	278.10	286.70	295.42	304.28	313.27	322.38	331.62
32000	287.63	296.64	305.81	315.12	324.57	334.15	343.87	353.73
34000	305.60	315.18	324.92	334.81	344.85	355.04	365.37	375.84
36000	323.58	333.72	344.03	354.51	365.14	375.92	386.86	397.94
38000	341.55	352.26	363.15	374.20	385.42	396.81	408.35	420.05
40000	359.53	370.80	382.26	393.90	405.71	417.69	429.84	442.16
42000	377.51	389.35	401.37	413.59	425.99	438.57	451.33	464.27
44000	395.48	407.89	420.49	433.29	446.28	459.46	472.83	486.38
46000	413.46	426.43	439.60	452.98	466.56	480.34	494.32	508.48
48000	431.44	444.97	458.71	472.67	486.85	501.23	515.81	530.59
50000	449.41	463.51	477.83	492.37	507.13	522.11	537.30	552.70
52000	467.39	482.05	496.94	512.06	527.42	543.00	558.79	574.81
54000	485.37	500.59	516.05	531.76	547.70	563.88	580.29	596.92
56000	503.34	519.13	535.17	551.45	567.99	584.77	601.78	619.02
58000	521.32	537.67	554.28	571.15	588.27	605.65	623.27	641.13
60000	539.30	556.21	573.39	590.84	608.56	626.53	644.76	663.24
62000	557.27	574.75	592.50	610.54	628.85	647.42	666.26	685.35
64000	575.25	593.29	611.62	630.23	649.13	668.30	687.75	707.46

/Layout Default

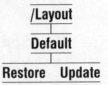

The first option, **Restore**, restores the default layout settings. The second option, **Update**, updates the default layout settings.

Allways is supplied with certain layout defaults in place. You can make your own set of defaults by establishing a series of layout criteria, then selecting the **/Layout Default Update** sequence. Allways saves your current settings as the default for all spreadsheets until you change them. The **Restore** command recalls this default—your own setting or the original shipped with Allways, depending on which one is in effect—and makes it apply to the current worksheet.

/Layout Library

Defines one or more sets of settings under library filenames that can be recalled for later use.

RETRIEVE—Loads a previously stored library file and makes it the current default layout.

SAVE—Stores the current layout settings under the file name given by the user. Files are assigned an .ALS extension.

ERASE—Deletes the specified library file name from disk storage.

The layout library is a series of separate files that contain layout settings you have designed and saved. Any time that you establish a layout scheme you want to save, you can put it away with the **/Layout Library Save** menu sequence. Allways asks for the name of the layout definition you want to save, then stores the file as part of the layout library.

Just as with the **/Layout Default Restore** command, you can apply any of these stored layout specifications to the current spreadsheet by entering the **/Layout Library Retrieve** command and entering the name of the file that contains the layout you want to use.

/Print Go

/Print
|
Go

Prints the worksheet using current printer and configuration, range, and settings.

/Print File

/Print
|
File

Prints the worksheet to a file where it is stored under the file name you give it. If you do not supply a file-name extension, Allways will use .PRN.

Printing an Allways spreadsheet to a file can be useful if you want to move the formatted file to another computer and print it, even without the Allways program. You can use the DOS **Copy** command to send the file out a printer port and, assuming the same printer is available that was specified in the **/Print Configuration** settings in Allways, the file should reproduce satisfactorily.

One caution with this technique: The Allways ∗.PRN file can become very large, because it includes all of the printer control codes and commands necessary to reproduce the Allways formats. The 1-2-3 ∗.PRN file, on the other hand, is an ASCII-compatible file that you can load into a text editor or word processor for further editing and formatting before you make a final print. The Allways ∗.PRN file is not suitable for this kind of postprocessing editing because it includes printer commands and codes in addition to output text.

One test file we used, for example, was a financial spreadsheet that required 17,538 bytes of storage in the .WK1 format. After formatting only a few cells at the top of the spreadsheet, the .PRN version required 37,683. Spreadsheets with heavy formatting, multiple fonts, shading, and the like, require 0.25 to 0.5 MByte of storage.

Once the Allways ∗.PRN file is created, however, you can transfer it to another system and print it on a compatible printer without the Allways software. Simply issue the DOS Copy *filename*.PRN command.

/Print Range

/Print
|
Range

Identifies the boundaries on the spreadsheet for printing.

Set Print Range can be set by entering cell references, or by anchoring one corner of the range and moving the cursor with the arrow keys to the other corner.

Clear clears the current print range.

After you set the Allways print range, a dotted line that shows the current range appears in the spreadsheet. If the range is larger than a printed page, a second set of dotted lines shows where page breaks will occur.

You can enter the **Range** command, then set the area you want to print. If you use a period (.) to anchor the cursor and paint the print range before entering the command, Allways will apply the print range to the marked spreadsheet range.

/Print Configuration Printer

Identifies hardware settings for printing. Selects a printer driver from among those identified to Allways as part of the installation process.

The **/Print Configuration** menu choice calls a popup window that shows all of the current settings, including the printer selected, what interface is being used, the cartridge selection (if appropriate) for your printer, the graphics resolution, and the paper bin number. You can change these settings with various menu choices under the **Configuration** submenu.

When you use the AWSETUP facility to install one or more printers, Allways copies the appropriate printer drivers to your working directory and maintains a list of the available printers. The **/Print Configuration Printer** command lists the installed printers in a popup box and enables use of the cursor movement keys to select the printer that you want to use.

If you use multiple printers and have difficulty printing at any time, check the selected printer in the **Configuration** menu. This command determines the printer that Allways will use until the setting is changed. It is not a selection for the current spreadsheet only.

/Print Configuration Interface

/Print
|
Configuration
|
Interface

Selects the output port on the computer. The default setting is Parallel 1, referred to by the system as LPT1, the primary parallel port on the PC.

Available computer ports are displayed in a popup window. You can use the cursor movement keys to select the port you want to use for the printer selected in the **Printer** section of this submenu.

/Print Configuration Cartridge

/Print
|
Configuration
|
Cartridge

On printers so equipped, selects among available font cartridges or cards.

/Print Configuration Orientation

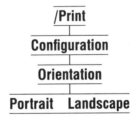

/Print
|
Configuration
|
Orientation
|
Portrait   Landscape

Selects the direction of printing on laser printers.

Portrait chooses the portrait mode (printing across the width of the paper). **Landscape** selects the landscape mode (printing across the length of the paper).

The **Configuration** menu demonstrates another nice feature of Allways. If you select a laser printer as the active printer, then the **Configuration** menu includes not only the printer and interface selections, but a choice for cartridge, orientation, and some other settings. If you specify a plain dot matrix printer, all selections except printer and interface disappear.

If your printer supports the orientation setting, you can choose to print your spreadsheet down the page (in the conventional manner) or across the

108   INSIDE ALLWAYS

sheet (sideways). (Remember the Funk software product Sideways®, with which you can rotate a spreadsheet 90 degrees before printing?) Most laser printers include what is called a Landscape mode that turns the printed material 90 degrees inside the printer before it is printed.

If you select Landscape mode, you can print wider spreadsheets because you have 11-inch-wide paper (or 14-inch or whatever you have specified) instead of 8.5-inch-wide paper. Your printouts will be shorter, however, for the same reason.

/Print Configuration Resolution

On laser printers capable of accepting this instruction, selects between various levels of resolution, measured in dots per inch (dpi), for output.

When using graphics fonts, you can determine which resolution to use on your printer. Normally you will want the maximum resolution possible, 300 by 300 dpi. However, this high resolution can slow down the output, particularly with soft fonts. If you need only a draft version of a spreadsheet, you can lower the resolution and get quicker output.

With some printers, such as the H-P LaserJet original printer, Allways sets the default resolution low to achieve relatively quick output. If your printouts don't look as good as you would like, check this setting and raise the resolution.

/Print Configuration Bin

Selects among paper feed options, including multiple bins or manual feed, on printers so equipped.

/Print Settings

Selects various printing options. (See Figure 6.7.)

Figure 6.7
The **/Print Settings** menu screen in Allways

```
FONT(2) Times 10 pt
     End  First  Copies  Wait  Reset  Quit
Set page to begin printing on
                                          F         G        H        I

              Begin printing on page:            BEGIN
               End printing on page:
            Page number of first page:      Increment:      2000
            Number of copies to print:    ncrement:         0.5
                 Wait before pages:
                                          5       9     9.5      10    10.5

9    ------- -------- -------- -------- -------- -------- -------- -------- ---
10   30000   269.65   278.10   286.70   295.42   304.28   313.27   322.38   331.62   3
11   32000            296.64   305.81   315.12   324.57   334.15   343.87   353.73   3
12   34000   305.60   315.18   324.92   334.81   344.85   355.04   365.37   375.84   3
13   36000   323.58   333.72   344.03   354.51   365.14   375.92   386.86   397.94   4
14   38000   341.55   352.26   363.15   374.20   385.42   396.81   408.35   420.05   4
15   40000   359.53   370.80   382.26   393.90   405.71   417.69   429.84   442.16   4
16   42000   377.51   389.35   401.37   413.59   425.99   438.57   451.33   464.27   4
17   44000   395.48   407.89   420.49   433.29   446.28   459.46   472.83   486.38   5
18   46000   413.46   426.43   439.60   452.98   466.56   480.34   494.32   508.48   5
19   48000   431.44   444.97   458.71   472.67   486.85   501.23   515.81   530.59   5
```

BEGIN—Sets the page number from a multiple-page spreadsheet to begin printing.

END—Sets the page number in a multiple-page spreadsheet to end printing.

FIRST—Specifies the starting page number, if page numbering has been included in a header or footer.

COPIES—Instructs the printer to make multiple copies of an output file.

WAIT—Instructs the printer to pause between printing each page; useful for manual feed of special paper stock.

RESET—Restores standard printer settings.

/Display Mode

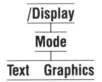

Selects Graphics or Text mode for display. In Graphics mode (available only on a graphics monitor and adapter combination), fonts, lines, shades, and other enhancements, as well as imported graphs from 1-2-3, will be displayed on screen; in Text mode, formats can be applied to a worksheet and graphs imported for printing, but neither is displayed on screen. The F6 function key toggles between Graphics and Text modes.

Allways has two display modes, Graphics and Text. Most users leave Allways in the default Graphics mode. This provides a near-WYSIWYG display, the best operating environment if your computer configuration supports it.

If your display is not capable of Graphics mode, you still can select fonts, shades, and other attributes as you can with a graphics screen; you just will not be able to see the attributes on the screen. When you print the spreadsheet from a text display, it will print the same way as it does from a graphics screen.

You may want to select the Text mode—even if you have a graphics display—during macro execution to speed up operations. Macros run faster in Text mode because it takes less time to rewrite a text screen than it does to rewrite a graphics screen.

In Text mode the Allways screen appears almost identical to the 1-2-3 display, right down to the screen colors. The only real clue to which program you are in is at the top of the screen. The word **ALLWAYS** appears in the status box at the upper right-hand corner of the screen when you are in the Allways ready mode. The cell definition line at the upper left of the screen will show the default cell formatting in either program, but in Allways you will see a typeface listed. As soon as you press the menu key (/), of course, you can tell which set of commands is available.

/Display Zoom

/Display
|
Zoom

In Graphics mode, zooms in to look at a portion of the spreadsheet in closeup, or zooms out to reduce the size of the displayed spreadsheet so that more of it can be displayed. The F4 function key zooms an image out (reduces size) in successive steps; the SHIFT-F4 function key zooms an image in (enlarges size).

TINY—Zooms out to reduce on-screen display to 60 percent of normal.
SMALL—Zooms out to reduce on-screen display to 84 percent of normal.
NORMAL—Sets on-screen display to 100 percent.
LARGE—Zooms in to enlarge on-screen display to 120 percent of normal.
HUGE—Zooms in to enlarge on-screen display to 140 percent of normal.

In addition to helping you produce creative spreadsheet printouts, Allways helps you view a spreadsheet by giving you control over the size of the display. The **/Display Zoom** command gives you access to a range of screen size settings from tiny to huge. At the tiny setting the spreadsheet is reduced to about 60 percent of normal size. At the huge setting the sheet is about 40 percent larger than normal.

At the smallest setting, you probably will not be able to read the cell entries, but you can see how sections of the spreadsheet fit together. At a 60 percent reduction, you can get almost twice as much information on the screen as at

Figure 6.8
Allways
spreadsheet in
**/Display Zoom
Normal**
presentation

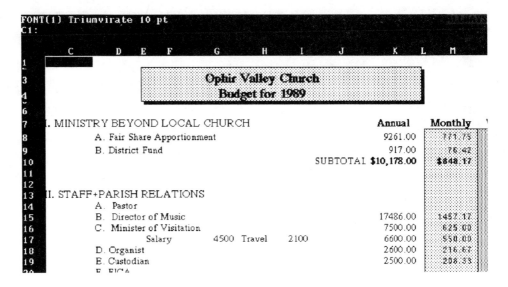

the normal size. The large and huge settings explode sections of a spreadsheet and show you fine detail that might not be visible at standard size.

Figures 6.8, 6.9, and 6.10 show how the same spreadsheet looks at normal, small, and huge settings.

/Display Graphs

/Display
|
Graphs

Controls whether graphs are displayed on screen when using a graphics-capable monitor. Displaying graphs results in slower screen painting and scrolling.

YES—Instructs the program to display graphs.
No—Suppresses the display of graphs and replaces them on-screen with a crosshatch pattern. Graphs are printed as usual.

/Display Colors

/Display
|
Colors

Select a set of colors for on-screen display on high-resolution color monitors (not including devices driven by a CGA adapter).

Figure 6.9
Allways
spreadsheet in
**/Display Zoom
Small** presentation

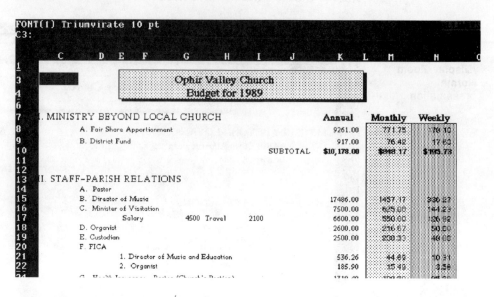

Figure 6.10
Allways
spreadsheet in
**/Display Zoom
Huge** presentation

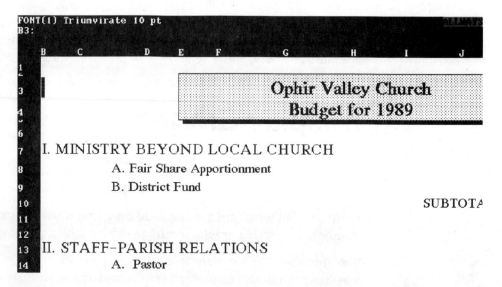

BACKGROUND—Presents a range of dark colors as alternate options. The default color for the background is black.

FOREGROUND—Presents a range of light colors as alternate options. The default color for the foreground (the worksheet area) is white.

HIGHLIGHT—Selects the color for the highlight indicator and cell pointer. The default color for highlights is blue.

The Allways default screen configuration is a pleasant one and works well with color displays and the various shades produced with a monochrome screen. However, the program also provides a broad range of custom settings. You can choose from eight background colors, four foreground colors, and six highlight colors.

Use the **/Display Colors** command sequence to display the **Background Foreground Highlight** menus. Experiment with combinations that are appropriate for your display configuration and your mood. (See Figures 6.11 through 6.13.)

Screen color settings are largely a matter of personal taste, but you also can use colors as visual tags or cues to help you remember which client or

Figure 6.11
Allways screen showing the background color choices.

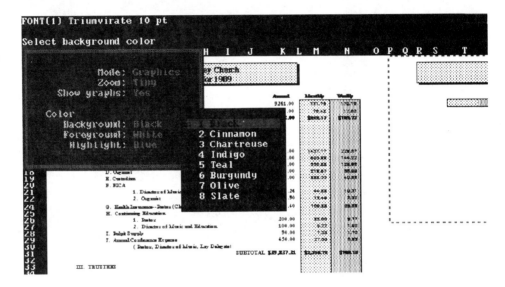

Figure 6.12
Allways screen showing the foreground color choices.

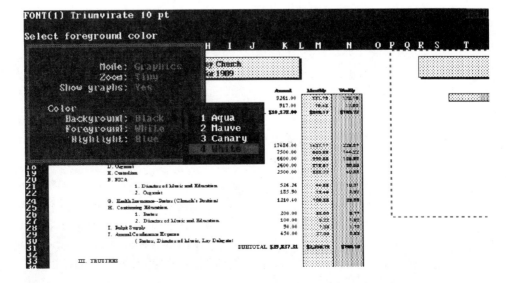

Figure 6.13
Allways screen
showing the
highlight color
choices.

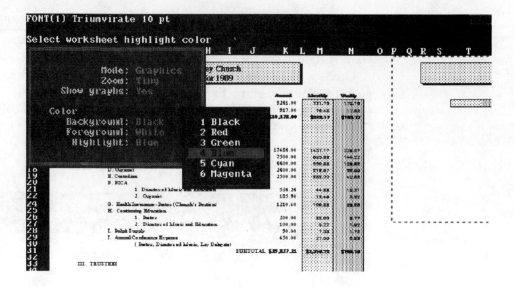

project you are working on. You could establish certain color schemes for different quarterly reports or for different users within your organization.

Don't confuse the display color settings with the print color settings. The display changes affect only the display, and the colors you see on your screen do not actually print. You can change the printed colors for output to a color printer with the **/Format Color** command sequence.

/Special Copy

/Special
|
Copy

Copies the format of one cell or a range of cells to another cell or range. Only formats are copied; data can be moved or duplicated only under 1-2-3.

Although you cannot enter, copy, or move spreadsheet data from within Allways, you can copy and move format information around the spreadsheet. This is an extremely useful feature because you can experiment with format design in a small area of the worksheet, then, when you have it set, copy the format to another area of the spreadsheet.

Suppose you have a wide spreadsheet with columns of numbers you want to shade alternately light and dark. An easy way to do that is to format the first two columns with the **/Format Shade** command. Specify **Light** for the first column and **Dark** for the second one. Next, use the Allways **/Special**

Copy command to duplicate the shading format for the first two columns in the rest of the spreadsheet.

Here's how to make this useful feature work for you. Suppose you start with the basic spreadsheet columns in Figure 6.14. You want to alternate light and dark shading, beginning with the numeric data. In this example the first numeric column is column D; the last numeric column is column W.

First, from inside Allways shade the range D2..D20 with a light shade and use a dark shade on the range E2..E20. Next, enter the **/Special Copy** command. When Allways asks for the **From:** range, enter **D2..U20**. (Notice that the From: range includes the shaded area as well as the area you want to shade with the established format in the range D2..E20.)

When Allways asks for the **To:** range, enter **F2**. Allways then copies the alternating light/dark shading throughout the D2..W20 range.

The **Copy** command installs the format from the source range into the target range and leaves the source range the way it was before the copy operation. Figure 6.15 shows a portion of the shaded spreadsheet.

/Special Move

Moves the format of the source cell or range to the target cell or range. The source cell or range then is reset to the default specifications for the worksheet.

Figure 6.14 Unformatted spreadsheet columns	Information Services						
	Manager	1	40000	10000	10250	10500	10750	11000
	Research Associates	2	25000	12500	12813	13125	13438	13750
	Clerical Super.	1	20000	5000	5125	5250	5375	5500
	Clerical	4	12000	12000	12300	12600	12900	13200
	Total – Info Services	8	97000	39500	40488	41475	42463	43450
	Management Information Systems							
	Senior Systems Analyst	1	45000	11250	11531	11813	12094	12375
	Programmer/Analysts	2	35000	17500	17938	18375	18813	19250
	Clerical	1	12000	3000	3075	3150	3225	3300
	Total MIS	4	92000	31750	32544	33338	34131	34925
	Editorial Groups	6		2	3	4	5	6
	Managing Editor	1	50000	25000	38438	52500	67188	82500
	Senior Tech. Ed.	1	40000	20000	30750	42000	53750	66000
	Editors	2	25000	12500	19219	26250	33594	41250
	Asst. Editors	2	18000	9000	13838	18900	24188	29700

Figure 6.15
Portion of the
shaded
spreadsheet

Expenses (By Quarter)	No. Emp.	1	2	3	4	5	6
Personnel							
Management							
Principals	5	50000	62500	64063	65625	67188	68750
Accounting Manager	1	35000	8750	8969	9188	9406	9625
Pers./Facilities Mgr.	1	35000	8750	8969	9188	9406	9625
Clerical	3	12000	9000	9225	9450	9675	9900
Total Management	10	132000	89000	91225	93450	95675	97900
Marketing and Sales							
Nat'l Acct Sales Reps	3	40000			31500	32250	33000
End–User Sales Mgr.	1	50000	12500	12813	13125	13438	13750
Marketing Manager	1	35000	8750	8969	9188	9406	9625
Total – Market/Sales	5	125000	21250	21781	53813	55094	56375
Information Services							
Manager	1	40000	10000	10250	10500	10750	11000
Research Associates	2	25000	12500	12813	13125	13438	13750
Clerical Super.	1	20000	5000	5125	5250	5375	5500
Clerical	4	12000	12000	12300	12600	12900	13200
Total – Info Services	8	97000	39500	40488	41475	42463	43450

You can move a format from one area of a spreadsheet to another. Suppose you have imported a format from another spreadsheet (see "Special Import") but you find that the cells and formats do not match precisely. Use the **/Special Move** command to move the format for a cell or range of cells to another spreadsheet location.

The **Move** command installs the format from the source range in the target range and resets the source range to the spreadsheet defaults. If you decide to eliminate formatting in a range of cells—or change it dramatically—and want to install that existing format in another area, use the **Move** command.

NOTE: The **Move** operation replaces existing formats in the target range (To: range) and resets the source (From: range) to the spreadsheet defaults.

/Special Justify

/Special
|
Justify

Word-wraps paragraphs of text entered into 1-2-3 as left-aligned labels. Because fonts used in Allways are not the same as those in 1-2-3, text justified under 1-2-3 will likely need rejustification in Allways. You must enter a range for justification.

/Special Import

/Special
|
Import

Allows application of the default format of one worksheet to another worksheet, as specified. Note that all formats are imported, including formats for individual cells or ranges.

The /**Special Import** function is extremely useful if you use a number of spreadsheets with the same format. Suppose you maintain a master spreadsheet for invoice entry, purchase order tracking, employee timekeeping, regular budget reports, and the like.

After you design the basic spreadsheet in 1-2-3, save an unformatted version in a separate file to serve as a master data entry spreadsheet. Next, format the master spreadsheet with all the fonts, headings, shades, and lines you want, then save it and the companion *.ALL file to an appropriate subdirectory.

When it is time to add data to the blank spreadsheet, follow these steps:

≡ Save the version with data to another file.
≡ Enter Allways.
≡ Use /**Special Import** to overlay the data master with the format from the format master spreadsheet.
≡ Print the result.
≡ Exit Allways. Do not save the formatted spreadsheet.

With this approach there is no real need to save the formatted version of the filled-out spreadsheet. You can save considerable disk space over a few months if you use a lot of repetitive spreadsheets of this type. You also can automate this load, import, print, exit procedure with a simple macro. See Chapter 14, "Practical 1-2-3 and Allways Macros," for details on how to do this.

/123

/123

Returns to 1-2-3 from Allways. This can also be accomplished by typing the hot-key combination or by pressing the ESC key in the Allways Ready mode.

7 Elements of a Graph

Like any other work of art, a chart can be realistic, representational, abstract, good, or bad. The principal difference between business graphics and art, though, is that your graphics *must* communicate to be successful. In communication there is no place for graphics for graphics' sake.

As we noted earlier in this book, you should take the time to consider the role of graphics in your business. In today's world, a picture—or a graph—is worth considerably more than a thousand words.

Remember, no matter how feature-packed the software, no matter how capable the computer, no matter how sophisticated the printer, it still is up to you to decide which type of chart will best communicate your information: a line graph, a bar chart, a pie graph, a histogram, a scatter plot, or any one of dozens of variations.

The program will not assist you much in gathering information. You have to provide answers to such questions as the following: What kind of data should I seek? How do I know if the data is valid? Is there some way to "massage" my data to enhance my message?

With the 1-2-3/Allways combination you can draw in color or use cross-hatches, shadings, different line weights, and patterns. But you'll still have to make the design choices. Which colors, shapes, designs, and other devices communicate your messages most clearly?

Designing a Graph

What is a graph? Let's take apart a basic multiple line graph for a model. Figure 7.1 is a chart of the sort that might be used to track the performance of a single stock or a group of stocks over a period of time. The chart shows the week-to-week performance of an apocryphal Dow Jones Average. It also plots a trend line that serves to smooth out the peaks and valleys and present the overall picture.

The essential elements of the graph start with the axes, labeled **A** for the horizontal X-axis, and **B** for the vertical Y-axis. The purpose of the axis, of

Figure 7.1
A basic multiline
graph

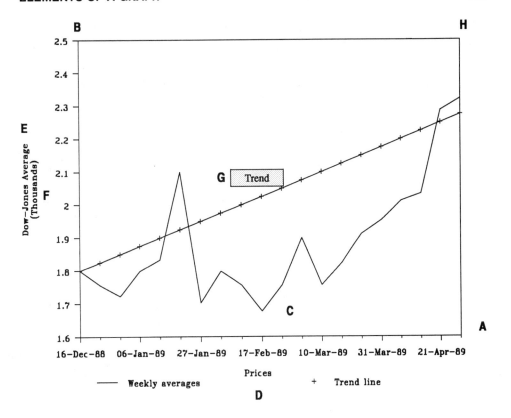

course, is to provide a scale for comparison and judgment. The horizontal
tick marks, indicated beneath the letter **C**, help the viewer identify the value
shown. They are, in effect, truncated grid lines, which, if extended, would
divide the entire graph into sections.

Other essential elements are the X- and Y-axis titles, **D** and **E**. These are
road signs for the viewer and identify the meaning of the numbers. A mul-
tiplying factor **F** may be a part of or separate from the Y-axis. In this case,
the factor tells us that a reading of 1.8 on the scale stands for 1.8 thousands,
or 1800. On the X-axis, the title might indicate specifics about the time period
(for example: measured in seconds, or figured on the basis of the 15th of one
month to the 14th of the next, or other notable differences from the ordinary).
For charts that include more than one set of data, it is necessary to have a
legend, here labeled **G**. The legend can be below the X-axis, beneath the main
title, or next to the chart's lines or bars in the form of an annotation. Another
use of annotation would be to note unusual events within the chart's time
period.

Finally, an overall title, **H**, identifies the purpose of your chart and helps
order it for presentations.

Other forms of charts—bars, histograms, pies, and so on—have similar elements, depending on the nature of the data series to be graphed.

Charting Your Charts

The lines, bars and markers of your basic charts are built on a framework created by the X- and Y-axes. The two lines, running perpendicular to each other, cross at the "0" point and, like the foul lines at a baseball park, theoretically go on for ever.

The horizontal X-axis (called the *abscissa* by mathematicians) often measures time units or intervals. The vertical Y-axis (the *ordinate*) often measures amount. Below the X-axis, the Y-axis records negative amounts; the X-axis to the left of Y can be used to describe negative values, an infrequent element of a chart.

The four open-sided areas defined by the ordinate and abscissa are referred to as *quadrants,* and are numbered as illustrated in Figure 7.2. Mathematicians call this combination of axes and quadrants the *Cartesian coordinate system,* and it is the basis for most graphs. Most of the charts in this book—and, indeed, most of the charts you will need in your professional applications—use the positive-positive values of Quadrant I and the positive-negative values of Quadrant IV.

Figure 7.2
The Cartesian coordinate system—basis for most graphs

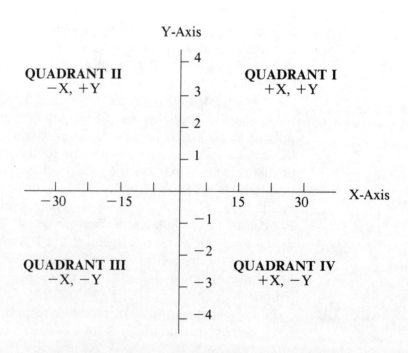

Quadrant I is most often used for time series and frequency distribution, with the horizontal (X) axis showing time units or size of intervals and the vertical (Y) axis indicating the amount. Both X and Y values are positive in such a chart.

Graphs that span Quadrants I and IV employ positive X values and both positive and negative Y values. Such a construction is often used in deviation vertical bar charts or line charts.

Deviation horizontal bar charts are generally plotted in Quadrants I and II, where Y values are positive and X values include both positive and negative values.

What Do Graphs Do?

There are, as we are about to see, dozens of types of graphs, just as there is a nearly unlimited range of sets of numbers to be plotted. But there is a single element that all graphs have in common: They exist to *compare* one or more items to another.

There are five basic types of comparisons.

≡ *Components or Parts.* Compares the relative size of individual components as they relate to the whole. A parts comparison could include a breakdown of the cost of manufacture into specific elements or a breakout of sources of income. Pie charts are most commonly used. However, segmented bar charts are valuable for showing the absolute size of an element as well as a comparison of totals. Typical forms of these charts are

Pie Chart
Segmented Bar Chart
Double Stacked Bar Chart
Surface or Area Line Chart

≡ *Items.* Compares relative sizes of individual items, showing them to be greater than, less than, or equal to each other or to a reference or index item or value. This sort of chart emphasizes direct comparisons of unrelated items at one point in time or over a period of time. Typical forms are

Bar Chart (Horizontal)
Clustered Bar Chart (Vertical)
Clustered, Paired, or Group Bar Chart (Horizontal)

≡ *Time.* Displays how an item(s) changes over time. A graph depicting the growth (or decline) of a company's revenues over time periods of, for example, months, quarters, or years would be one example of a time series. This most common use of a chart displays a single data series over a period of time to show trends. Such a chart can also be used to compare two or more series of data in the same time period. Typical forms used are

Line Charts
Vertical Column Charts
Bar-Line Combinations

≡ *Frequency.* Displays the distribution of a particular set of numbers. These graphs answer such questions as: How many or how often do items fit into specified categories? Typical forms are

Histograms
Bar Graphs

≡ *Correlation.* Examines the possible relationship between two sets of numbers. For example, the relationship between the cost of an item and the number of items sold, or the relationship between taxation levels and savings rates. These charts indicate relationships between dependent and independent variables, measured as correlations or regression analyses. A regression or correlation line can be overlaid on many charts, including

Line Charts
Scatter or XY Plots
Bubble Charts
Paired Bars

Charts used in many business presentations that do not directly involve comparative series of numbers include *word* charts (including tabular charts, organization charts, and flow charts) and *Gantt* or *PERT* charts (used for project scheduling).

With the 1-2-3/Allways combination you can create and enhance most of these charts. We'll examine examples in Chapter 11, "Creating Business Forms Using Allways."

Designing a Graph

Stop! Before you make that chart, look at the numbers.

With the aid of the microcomputer, it is all too easy to think of graphing as a strictly mechanical process, where you simply have to select a graph type from a menu, identify a range of numbers, and press the "go" button.

Look at the Numbers

To make an intelligent choice, it is important to make certain the numbers themselves are appropriate for graphing. What are some questions you should ask?

What Do the Numbers Say?

What is the most significant numerical relationship? Examine the range of numbers. Is there an obvious trend up or down? Are the numbers clustered at the high and low ends with little in the middle? Is there a single rogue number or a group of numbers that exists way above or below the others?

Do the Numbers Make Sense?

This is a most critical question that the human mind is presently better at answering than the most sophisticated computer.

The computer would merrily proceed to produce a graph about the cost of a hamburger without paying any attention to the fact that the numbers say that each burger costs $175. Your experience, though, would quickly tell you that a decimal point seems to be missing.

What is the context of the change in numbers? If we were looking at the cost of hamburgers and saw that they went from $1.25 to $2.50, we would be looking at a situation in which the price had increased by 100 percent. Looking at the cost of a Rolls Royce, we might see an increase in price from $100,000 to $115,000. The net boost of $15,000 is a lot of money; however, in terms of a ratio, it is an increase of only 15 percent.

On a more complex level, if you are handed a Lotus spreadsheet for conversion to a graph and enhancement under Allways, you should spend the time to examine the structure of the spreadsheet. Make sure that you understand how any formulas applied to the numbers. Look to see that specified ranges for formulas such as @AVG, @COUNT, @MAX, @MIN, and @SUM are appropriate. (It is fairly easy to make a mistake in a 1-2-3 spreadsheet and include a title within a range for averaging; doing so can add a value of 0 to the range, throwing off the average.)

What Sort of Scale Is Appropriate?

This question will, at least at the start, probably require a few test graphs to judge the shape and meaningfulness of the resulting curves.

If the purpose of the graph is to show the steep rise in the cost of hamburger, you could set the horizontal tick marks and grid lines farther apart than the vertical grid lines, thereby emphasizing the steepness of the curve.

In some circumstances, it may make sense to start the graph at a point above or below zero. Here it is important not to mislead the reader; such an atypical scale should be clearly labeled.

1-2-3 automatically sets the scale for a graph, almost always using zero for the graph origin. The program does, however, allow the user to manually set ranges or top or bottom limits. You'll learn more about 1-2-3's options for setting the scales for a graph later on in this book.

What Kind of Graph Should Be Used?

There are sets of seemingly rigid rules that specify particular types of charts for specific types of information. In general, they should be followed for most graphs. We'll discuss many of these rules soon.

However, after careful thought, some of these rules can be bent to accommodate graphics considerations. For example, the preferred form for a chart displaying change over time with some emphasis on individual years would be a column chart with vertical bars. If space considerations make that a difficult design to accomplish, an alternate would be a bar chart, with horizontal bars. A line chart would accent the trend, but not the years.

A Sampling of Charts from One Set of Numbers

There are (almost) a million stories in any set of numbers. Let's look at the rather ordinary financial report in Table 8.1 and see how many tales it can tell.

Table 8.1
A typical financial
report

	Ferguson Corporation Revenues			
	Storm Doors	Airline Operations	Consulting	Total
1982	$502,000	$376,435	$234,452	$1,112,887
1983	$657,432	$523,455	$245,423	$1,426,310
1984	$798,546	$756,532	$263,421	$1,818,499
1985	$976,432	$845,676	$221,234	$2,043,342
1986	$1,134,566	$746,554	$245,345	$2,126,465
1987	$1,454,324	$534,522	$254,211	$2,243,057
1988	$1,756,432	$423,452	$276,354	$2,456,238
SUM:	$7,279,732	$4,206,626	$1,740,440	$13,226,798

Figure 8.1
Four bar graphs
drawn to different
scales

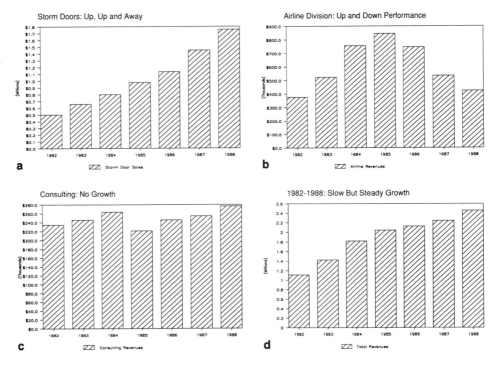

Our first graph, Figure 8.1*a*, uses a bar graph form to show the performance of one division, Storm Doors, over the years from 1982 to 1988. The story told here is one of steady growth.

The second graph, Figure 8.1*b*, uses the same form to show the performance of the second division, Airline Operations, for the same time period. The bell curve of the decline and fall of revenues in this section is apparent. Note, though, that 1-2-3's automatic selection for the Y-axis uses different, smaller numbers than those used for the Storm Door graph. If the two graphs were used together and printed the same size, most readers would probably be misled into believing that revenue levels were equivalent.

A similar problem is presented in Figure 8.1c, representing Consulting Division. A new Y-axis scale, about one-third as large as that used for the airline report and one-sixth as large as that used for storm doors, is used.

The fourth graph, Figure 8.1d, is based on total revenues for the three divisions over the seven-year period. And, yes, this uses a fourth scaling range.

Despite these problems, the three graphs do present a story—that of the various performance levels of the three divisions, although the presentation is a bit awkward.

For Figure 8.2, we've gone back into 1-2-3, redrawn all of these graphs, and placed them on the same scale. This, of course, brings up other problems, such as the fact that some of the graphs (the Consulting Division is a good example) will not show much differentiation between the numbers because of the large range for the axis. As in our other examples, all of the information is there for the reader to see, but making an intelligent appraisal of the story is a difficult task.

Figure 8.2
Four graphs on the same scale with standardized Y-axes

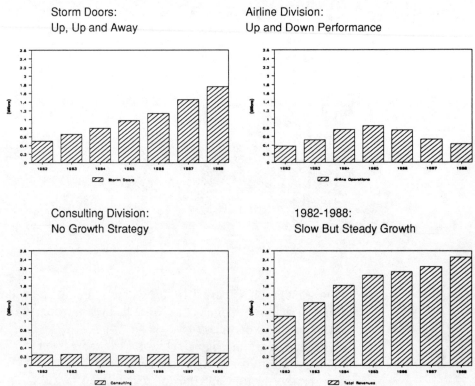

How can we best compare one division with another directly? In Figure 8.3, we've grouped the data ranges into a multiple bar graph. The apparent story of this graph: that the Storm Door Division has outperformed its sister divisions every year, drawing away from the pack from 1985 on. A bit obscured is the fact that Airline Operations have risen and fallen over the course of the plotted period. In addition, the details of the performance of the Consulting Division are obscured by the large range used for the Y-axis. Finally, there is no way to see the total revenues for each year for the entire company with this chart.

A better solution may be seen in Figure 8.4, which is drawn as a segmented bar chart—a bar graph equivalent of a pie chart. This graph shows clearly how the total revenues have grown each year, and also conveys well the story of how much of the total revenue is drawn from the Storm Door Division. It is easy for the reader to estimate the revenue contribution of the primary (Range A) set. It is difficult, though, to gauge actual amounts for the secondary (Range B) and tertiary (Range C) elements.

Probably the best graph type to show clearly both trends over time and actual amounts is the old tried-and-true line graph. In Figure 8.5, we've graphed all three ranges in a multiple line chart. The sharp growth of the Storm Door Division is obvious; the bell-curve rise and fall of Airline Operations is apparent, and the Consulting Division's boring sameness can readily be seen. Nothing is obscured here.

Figure 8.3
Example of a
multiple bar graph

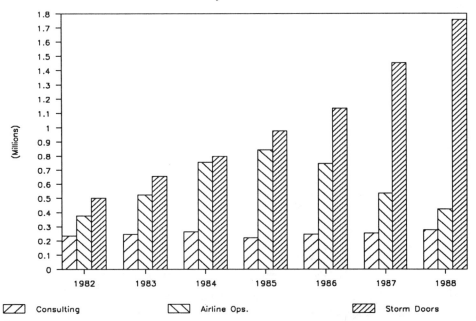

Storm Doors Pull Away From the Pack

Figure 8.4
Example of a
segmented bar
graph

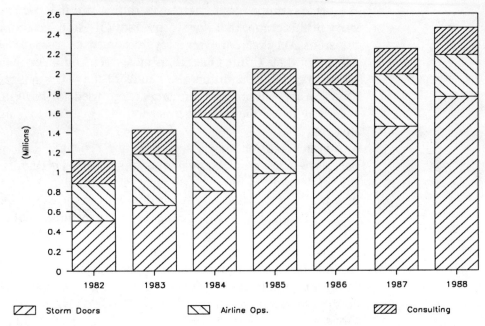

Seven Years of Good Luck: A History of Growth

Figure 8.5
Example of a
multiline graph

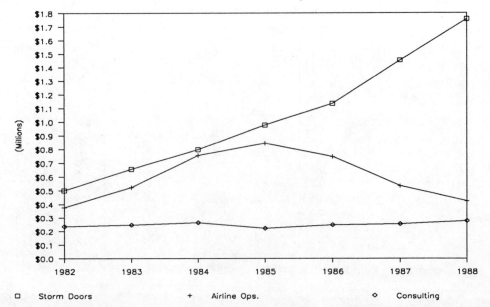

An Uneven Performance Across Departments

Finally, we've drawn one more picture from our numbers to sum up the total contributions of the three divisions over the 1982 to 1988 period. First, we added all of the numbers in each range over the time period, using the 1-2-3 @SUM function. Then, we created a pie graph, as seen in Figure 8.6.

Which graphs are "correct" for these numbers? The answer is that all of them are, although some are better than others at conveying information. My own selection would include the segmented bar, the multiline, and the pie graphs, which, among them, show

≡ The total revenues of the company each year (segmented bar).
≡ The proportional contribution of each division to total company revenues each year (segmented bar).
≡ The trends, across time, of the performance of each division, one compared against the other (multiline).
≡ The proportion of contribution to total revenues at a fixed moment in time (pie chart).

Figure 8.6
Example of a pie graph

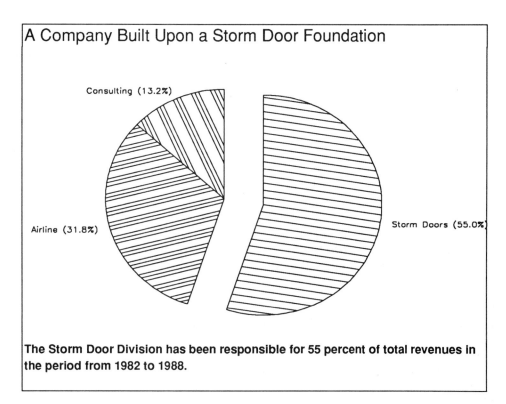

A Company Built Upon a Storm Door Foundation

Consulting (13.2%)

Airline (31.8%)

Storm Doors (55.0%)

The Storm Door Division has been responsible for 55 percent of total revenues in the period from 1982 to 1988.

Charting a Design

A basic rule of chartmaking is that the graph—including its titles, subtitles, legends, and information—should tell the whole story. Captions or explanatory text should be there to augment but not substitute for such information.

Elements of the Chart

The *main title* should be brief and to the point. It can be a formal label headline, such as "Consolidated Income Statement," or it can be used to convey a message, such as "Our Sixth Consecutive Record-setting Year."

The *subtitle* should support and expand on the main title, adding details such as dates and geographic or departmental information.

The *labels* should be used to identify plotted data. Be sure to place labels in unambiguous locations. For example, in a multiline chart keep the labels away from any intersections of trend lines.

Grids are used to help the reader to gauge the value of points on a trend line or bar chart more accurately. However, a balance has to be struck to avoid confusing the eye with too fine a grid or too many grid labels. Examples of full, horizontal, and vertical grids can be seen in Figure 8.7.

Vertical grid labels should be located directly opposite the grid points they represent. Grids should also use divisions that are easily recognized by the reader—multiples of 10 or 100; units of 1, 2, or 5; or common fractions such as fourths and halves.

Vertical scale captions should be used to identify numerals as dollars or units. Lettering should be run horizontally if possible, directly above the scale.

Horizontal grid labels should be directly beneath tick points. Grids should use divisions easily recognized by the reader—days, weeks, months, years, or quarters.

Horizontal scale captions are necessary only when horizontal grid labels are not self-evident. They should run horizontally, below the grid labels.

Figure 8.7
Three types of grids

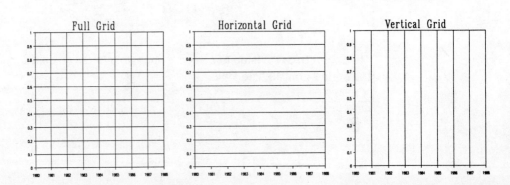

Scale unit is an important key to the reader to indicate that a kind of shorthand has been used to depict numbers. Many different styles are acceptable. Some charts use the name of the common units employed: "Thousands," "Millions," or "Billions," for example. Other tables explain that a certain number of decimal zeros have been left off: "000 omitted," to indicate thousands, or "000,000 omitted," to indicate millions. Some scale units can carry more than one bit of information: "Dollar amounts, in millions," or "Units produced, in billions." Select easily read scale units, such as tens, hundreds, thousands, millions, and billions or tons, gallons, and barrels. Avoid such unusual measures as "ten thousands" or "fifty thousands."

Notes and sources identify the origin of data or the authors of charts. This sort of extra information is not officially available when you use the 1-2-3 graphing facility, but it is quite easily added when the 1-2-3/Allways combination is employed.

Weights and Measures

Microcomputer-based graphics programs are wonderful in their ability to bring to the desktop facilities that once were the province of the highly skilled graphic artist, working with pen, ink, razor, and tape.

At the same time, microcomputer-based graphics programs present all of this power to users who most likely have little or no training in graphic design. It's great to have the ability to select from 32 different typefaces in a nearly infinite range of sizes and from three or four types of shading and line weights, but which elements should be used where?

A basic rule: Simplify. Use two or three typefaces, selected from the same family or a compatible group of families. Use two or three different type sizes, paying attention to the relative importance of the text being typeset. Use just two or three colors or shades, and make sure that your choices don't tend to distract rather than inform.

Avoid the temptation to put too much into your presentation: too many data ranges, too many typefaces, too many colors, too many shadings, unneeded grids. The whole point of using a picture instead of a thousand words is to speed up communication with a clear, simple message.

We've shown, in Figure 8.8, an example of an all-but-meaningless chart that is the result of unthinking assignment of too many of the hundreds of fonts, weights, sizes, titles, legends, and other elements of a chart available with the 1-2-3/Allways combination. It is the electronic equivalent of giving a child a large box full of crayons and asking for simplicity and moderation. Among the problems in this figure are the strange mix of sans serif, serif, and script type styles; the crowded mix of X-axis title and legends at the bottom, and the unnecessary grid. Add to all this the confusing nature of the plotted lines themselves, which all tend to come together in the middle of the chart.

Figure 8.8
A graph that
confuses by its
complexity

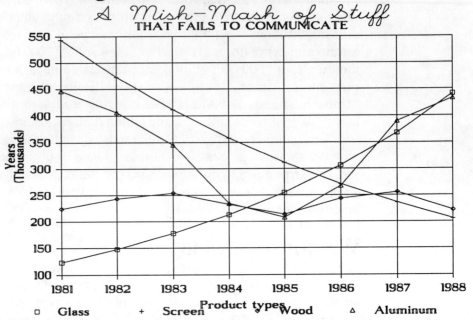

Ferguson Storm Door & Airline Co.

In Figure 8.9, we've replotted the same numbers in a more intelligible style, a stacked bar graph. This form clearly shows the individual performance of departments and also the total revenues of the company. For additional information, we've inset a summary box with actual yearly results for the entire company. The inset is accomplished by taking advantage of the fact that graphs are "transparent" when displayed within Allways and can overlay text and numbers. We created the table of figures on the 1-2-3 worksheet and then adjusted its exact location to fit into the proper position on the .PIC file enhanced under Allways.

Some Simple Rules of Design

Line weights—the weights of lines, trends, borders, grids, and other elements of the chart—are important to consider not only because of readability concerns but also as part of the effort to ensure that information is presented in a manner that does not mislead the reader. For example, bolder lines are more prominent and therefore appear more important than finer lines.

NOTE: An important consideration: Bear in mind that many charts destined for publication will be altered in size at some point in the publication process. It is, in general, a good practice to produce charts larger than they will be when reproduced. A moderate reduction will tend to make the final copy appear more sharply drawn.

Figure 8.9
The same
information,
simplified

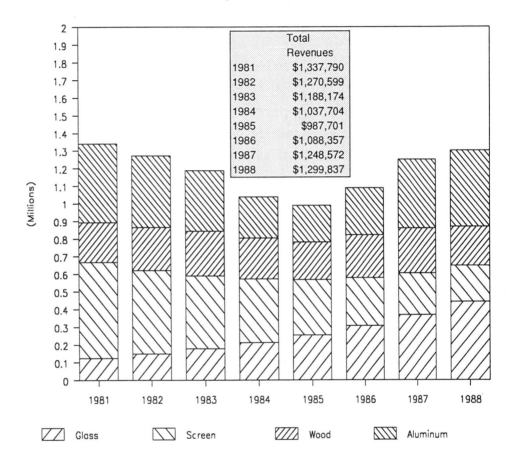

Ferguson Storm Door & Airline Co.
Total Revenues and Departmental Results: 1981-1988

	Total Revenues
1981	$1,337,790
1982	$1,270,599
1983	$1,188,174
1984	$1,037,704
1985	$987,701
1986	$1,088,357
1987	$1,248,572
1988	$1,299,837

Glass   Screen   Wood   Aluminum

The *trend lines* (curve lines) should be the most prominent lines of the chart, because they carry the information. A smooth, regularly curved line can be made heavier than a more actively changing line. In a multiline chart, a solid line will often appear to have more importance than a patterned line or one that uses symbols. One way to make the patterned and solid-line curves appear to have the same importance is to make the patterned lines slightly wider.

The best line style is solid. In a multiline chart, if the lines do not cross (or do not cross very often), it will generally be better to use all solid lines with clear labels.

Borders around charts should be made lighter in weight than trend lines. In fact, you might want to consider whether a chart should have a border at all. A chart without a border is more easily reduced or enlarged to appropriate proportions and more easily placed on a page.

The *base line grid* is used as the point of reference—the zero point on an amount chart, the 100 line on an index. It should be the heaviest of grid rulings.

When you are using *patterns and shading* remember that in our part of the world we read from left to right. Patterns with directional slopes should slant toward the right to carry the eye forward, along with the movement of the trend.

Crosshatching or shading in an area, in a multiple bar or column, or in a surface chart helps convey information easily. Conversely, white areas tend to obscure information. The only exception would be the use of a white segment between crosshatched areas.

NOTES: In selecting crosshatches, consider whether the chart will be reduced for publication. Crosshatches that appear to be quite different in full size may seem identical when reduced.

The choice of crosshatches and shading in charts can have an effect on the appearance of a trend. For example, horizontal crosshatches tend to reduce the apparent size of bars, whereas vertical hatches increase the apparent size. Stacked bar charts that mix horizontal and vertical crosshatches can also result in unusual "bowed" appearance for bars.

Columns with diagonal crosshatches slanted in opposite directions can set up "moire" patterns that confuse the eye and make the bars seem nonparallel, and the areas contained within the bars will appear distorted.

Slicing Pie Charts Too Thinly

Slicing a pie chart too thinly results in loss of communication at best and confusion at worst. In the example shown in Figure 8.10, a pie chart graphing the relative market shares of 11 hamburger restaurants is too crowded at the low end. The pie wedges for the four companies with 1 or 2 percent market shares are difficult to distinguish, and 1-2-3 also overprints the labels.

Several solutions could be used here. Probably, the best would be to group the four smallest companies in an "OTHER" category with a 6 percent share, and then insert a table with the identities and exact market shares of the four smaller companies. We can see a version of such a chart in Figure 8.11, as enhanced using Allways.

How Numbers *Do* Lie

Numbers—in black and white or otherwise—can lie or mislead. Perhaps, to put it more charitably, we should say that the way numbers are used can have as many nuances—and uses in communications—as do words.

Figure 8.10
An overcrowded pie
chart

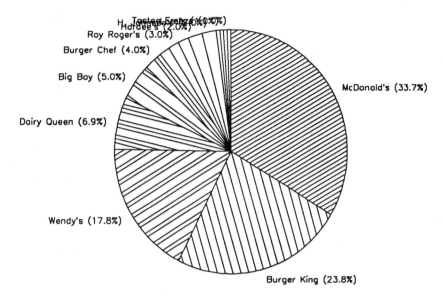

Figure 8.10
An overcrowded pie
chart

Too Many Slices of the Pie

Now, please, do not take this as an endorsement for falsification of data. Such an effort almost always backfires, with results much worse than would result from full disclosure, no matter how unflattering the numbers. There may be times when you feel tempted to apply the same sort of perceptions and images that are the stock in trade of Madison Avenue. Before you do, ask yourself this question: What would be the worst possible result of the discovery of the artifice behind your work?

One way to give a chart more movement or to exaggerate or downplay the steepness of a trend is to expand or contract one of the axes. A chart, for example, that shows a long, slow climb over a 20-year period, followed by a sudden sharp drop over the next five years, could be altered to make the curve look much less severe by graphing the first period in five-year increments and the last period in one-year ticks.

Another deception involves selective use of reporting years. For example, in Figure 8.12a, titled "A Disingenuous Performance," we see what appear to be healthy climbing sales for the years from 1930 to 1985. There is not a decline in sight. But look closely at the time scale on the X-axis: there seem to be a few five-year periods missing between 1950 and 1965 and between 1965 and 1980. Now look at the graph in Figure 8.12b, titled "The Unvarnished Truth." This graph includes those missing periods, combined with the data shown in the first graph. The beginning and end points are the same, but suddenly we see a bit of volatility, including a flat spot in one of the

Figure 8.11
One solution to an
overcrowded pie
chart

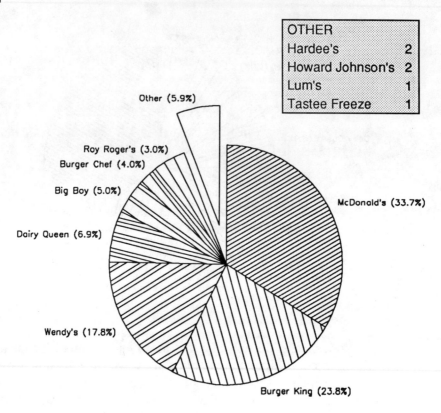

Another Way to Slice a Pie

OTHER	
Hardee's	2
Howard Johnson's	2
Lum's	1
Tastee Freeze	1

Other (5.9%)

Roy Roger's (3.0%)

Burger Chef (4.0%)

Big Boy (5.0%)

Dairy Queen (6.9%)

McDonald's (33.7%)

Wendy's (17.8%)

Burger King (23.8%)

missing periods and a precipitous decline in another. If your reader looks carefully, you will be (properly) accused of cheating.

A more subtle manipulation of the axes of a chart involves use of a broken amount scale, that is, a chart that starts at a point other than the zero baseline. Trends can be grossly exaggerated through the use of a broken scale. For example, in a bar chart, this can make small differences at the top of a bar appear to be major peaks and valleys.

In Figure 8.13 (top), the line has a steep climb (and decline) with its unusual starting point of 1200. The correctly plotted graph at the bottom of the figure is considerably less dramatic, though accurate. This is an area that should demand your attention when using 1-2-3, as well as many other microcomputer-based charting packages. There is little consistency as to automatic selection of a baseline starting point. Until you are fully comfortable with all of the assumptions of 1-2-3, make it a point to examine scaling decisions as a matter of course, and override them when they are not appropriate for the type of story you need to tell.

Figure 8.12
Falsifying data by
manipulating time

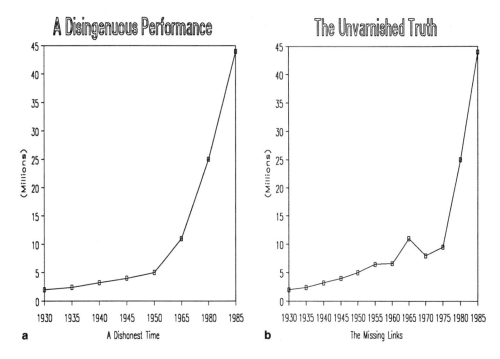

a — A Dishonest Time

b — The Missing Links

This is not to say that you will never want to start a baseline at a number other than zero. In fact, such a decision is quite common in plotting series that are entirely set in very high ranges. For example, a chart representing the Gross National Product or the national debt would present numbers that drop no lower than the tens or hundreds of billions. If such a graph were indeed started at zero, it would either have to be a couple of yards long to present a meaningful set of tick marks on the Y-axis or the differences between the amounts on that axis would have to be so great that it would be all but impossible to gain any information from the graph.

So, stop and examine the automatic selections made by the 1-2-3/Allways program and determine whether they are appropriate for the story being told. And if the baseline is set at other than zero, be sure that this information is pointed out to the reader.

A broken amount scale in a bar chart can have the effect of minimizing numbers. Using the 1-2-3 program, you cannot specify a baseline amount for bar graphs, which will keep you out of this particular trap.

A subtle manipulation of the aspect ratio of the chart, from vertical to horizontal in this instance, can be seen in Figure 8.14, based on the same information charted in the earlier Wind Shifter Sales charts in Figure 8.13. In this instance, the same data was charted in a vertical box instead of a horizontal one. The differing proportions result in an upward curve that looks

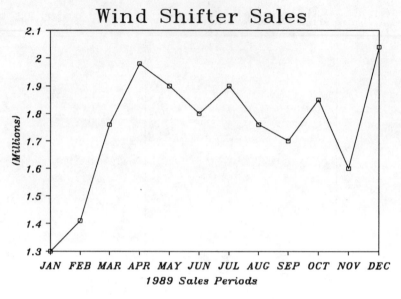

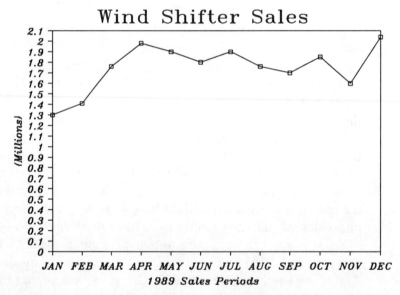

more gradual in the horizontal version; conversely, a decline can be made to look less precipitous by charting it in a box that is wider than it is tall.

You should avoid incompatible data, either in single data series charts or multiple series. In Figure 8.15, for example, the vast difference between the data for 1980 and the data for 1985 makes it all but impossible for the viewer to make a quick visual comparison.

In Figure 8.16, we see another example of a bar graph drawn with incompatible (but, in this case, real) data. The disparity between the U.S. death rate

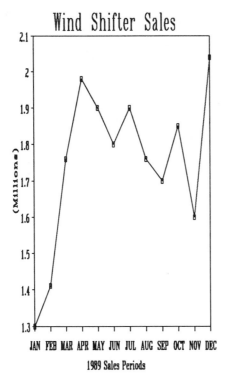

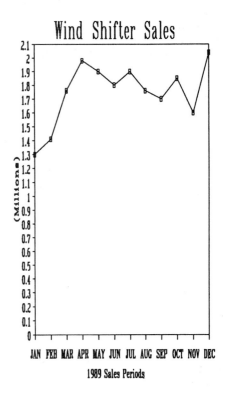

(8092) and the death rates of Canada, Britain, and Japan (in the range from 5 to 46), is too great for the graph to show if it is printed on a standard-sized page. In this case, we chose to inset into the graph a table with the actual numbers, which gives readers the information they need, as well as some comparative information on population sizes of the four countries.

An alternate way to salvage such a chart would have been to use data labels, created within 1-2-3, to give the actual figures for each of the bars. This would, though, have left a barren central space in the graph. We'll show other ways to deal with difficult numbers in some of the discussions of specific types of graphs later in this book.

NOTE: Changing the aspect ratio of a graph within Allways is quite simple—perhaps too simple. When you load a graph prepared with 1-2-3 into an Allways worksheet, you "paint" the screen to show the range for the graph (or enter coordinates to accomplish the same thing) and the image is automatically fitted to the space. You should take time to examine the imported graph to see if its aspect has been altered in a manner that misleads and resize it if necessary. In Figure 8.17, you can see how an innocent change in the aspect ratio of a bar graph from vertical to horizontal tends to reduce the apparent magnitude of numbers as well as the differences between numbers.

Figure 8.15
Example of a
graph showing
incompatible data

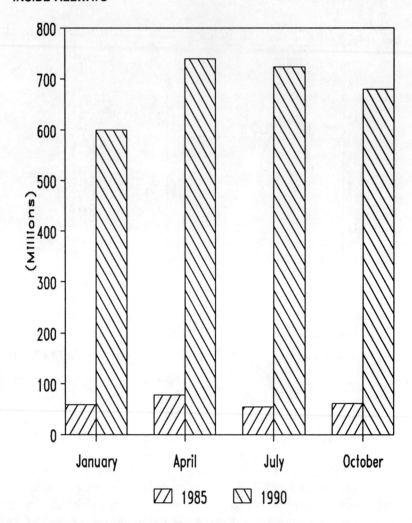

Be aware of design elements that can foster optical or perceptual illusions. Certain color combinations have greater impact than others: reds and blacks appear more significant than yellows and blues.

The perceived difference between a chart constructed in open outline and a chart with a solid fill can be significant. In 1-2-3, there is no provision for the otherwise common area graph, a line chart that emphasizes relative amounts through shading of the landscape beneath the trend line. If, however, you work with a graphic artist who will manually enhance your line graphs or with an add-on product that permits editing graphics images, you should be aware of this pitfall.

The absence or presence of a grid on a graph can change the viewer's perception of the story behind a piece of data. Be certain that your use of labels is unambiguous, too.

Figure 8.16
Graph using a
clarifying inset

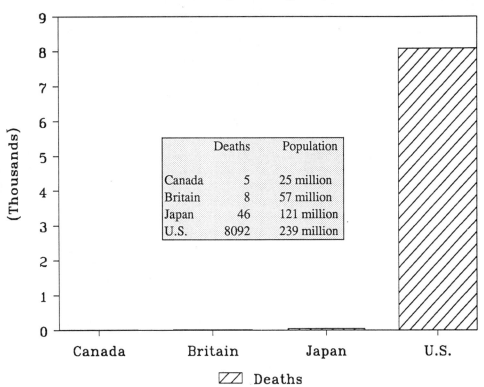

Killed by Handguns, 1985

	Deaths	Population
Canada	5	25 million
Britain	8	57 million
Japan	46	121 million
U.S.	8092	239 million

Your choice of shading can have an effect on perception. In Figure 8.18, the columns have diagonals slanting in opposite directions. This arrangement makes the columns appear distorted and nonparallel. The tired eye also has difficulty reading values. Downward pointing hatches tend to minimize; heavy hatches appear more significant than light, wide stripes.

Misrepresentation by Axis Scaling

In its default setting, 1-2-3 automatically sets scale limits, based on the data it is given for graphing. For example, in creating a graph to illustrate a range of numbers from 110 to 500, 1-2-3 automatically sets a Y-scale with a lower limit of 100 and an upper limit of 500.

There are a number of reasons why you may want to override the default settings and manually choose upper and lower limits. For example, in pre-

Figure 8.17
Effect of changing
aspect ratio of a
bar graph

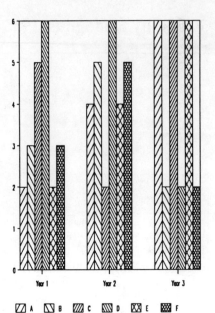

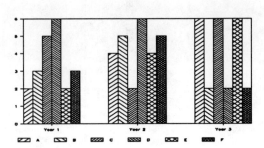

paring a set of comparative graphs with differing values, you may want all graphs to have the same lower and upper limits; or you may want to ensure that a particular graph starts at zero to avoid any unintentional bias in presentation.

X-Axis (Time or Horizontal Scale)

The tick marks along the horizontal scale must be even, each indicating the same amount of time.

In the following examples, we have two simple sets of data that represent the price of hamburgers at fast food restaurants in the period from 1940 to 1990.

The first set of data, depicted in Figure 8.19, top, has an irregular set of years. An anomalously high burger price for 1947 is included, even though most of the other data points are set at five-year intervals; in the same series, data for 1955 and 1985 are omitted. The average price for hamburgers, based on a 1-2-3 @AVG formula, is false, since it gives full weight to a 1947 reading, does not include the missing data points, and gives improper weight to other data points representing longer periods of time.

A careful reader of the table might notice the unusual 1947 date. An especially careful reader might see that the numbers jump from 1950 to 1960 and from 1980 to the 1990 projection. However, the graph produced from these numbers draws the eye to the curve, making it easy to overlook the unusual data points on the X-axis.

Figure 8.18
Poor shading
choice makes this
graph difficult to
read

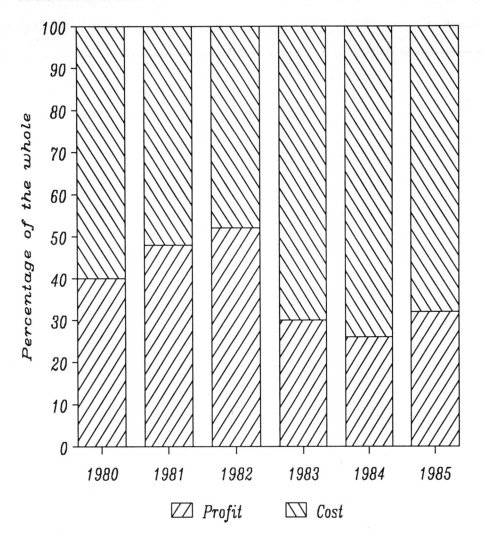

Figure 8.18
Poor shading
choice makes this
graph difficult to
read

The second set of data and the associated graph (Figure 8.19, bottom) show an orderly progression from 1940 to 1990 at five-year intervals. The shape of the graph is different, showing a steadier upward trend, and the calculated average price is different (and correct).

Y-Axis (Vertical Scale)

The two charts in Figure 8.20 are based on an identical set of values, but give the appearance of conveying dissimilar information. The difference between them comes in the selection of a Y-axis, or vertical, scale.

In Figure 8.20 (top), 1-2-3 examined the numbers it was presented and automatically set the Y-axis to run from 24 to 56. The result is a steeply

Figure 8.19
Misrepresentation
by faulty X-axis
scaling

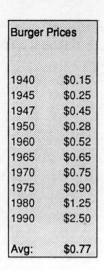

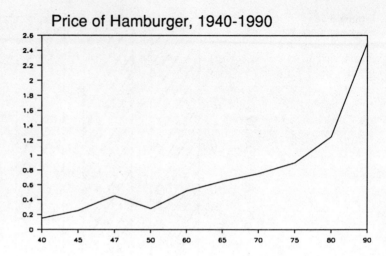

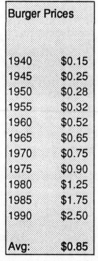

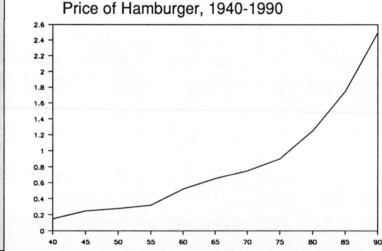

climbing curve with two sharp downward movements, one for 1945–1950 and one for 1985–1990.

The top chart clearly conveys the impression that the per capita consumption has increased steadily over the 50-year period of the graph. To a less attentive eye, though, the chart might also give the impression that consumption has grown from a base of zero over those years.

The bottom chart, based on the identical set of data points, uses a manually selected Y-axis scale, this time running from 0 to 60. This new analysis shows a much more gradual curve upward, and also flattens out the two downward movements, making them seem considerably less significant.

Figure 8.20
Effect of Y-axis
scale on data
perception

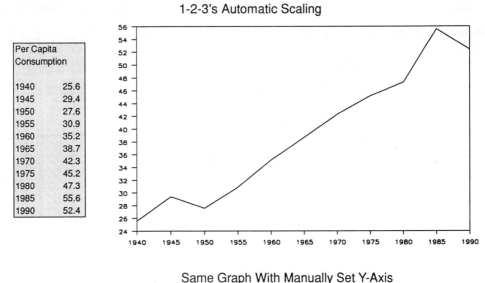

1-2-3's Automatic Scaling

Per Capita Consumption	
1940	25.6
1945	29.4
1950	27.6
1955	30.9
1960	35.2
1965	38.7
1970	42.3
1975	45.2
1980	47.3
1985	55.6
1990	52.4

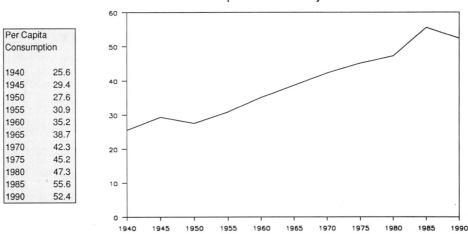

Same Graph With Manually Set Y-Axis

Per Capita Consumption	
1940	25.6
1945	29.4
1950	27.6
1955	30.9
1960	35.2
1965	38.7
1970	42.3
1975	45.2
1980	47.3
1985	55.6
1990	52.4

Which graph is "correct"? Both are—you could use either one, unless you select one type of scale over the other with the deliberate intent of misleading the reader.

Comparative Scales

In the next example, we have a progression of production figures from the period 1925 to 1990. Note how the rate of consumption of hamburgers greatly increased about 1970.

In Figure 8.21, the top graph is based on a vertical scale that goes from 0 to 40, automatically set by 1-2-3 to match the data it has been given. The more recent data, shown in the bottom graph, is graphed with a Y-axis scaled from 0 to 600.

Figure 8.21
Two graphs with
differing vertical
scales

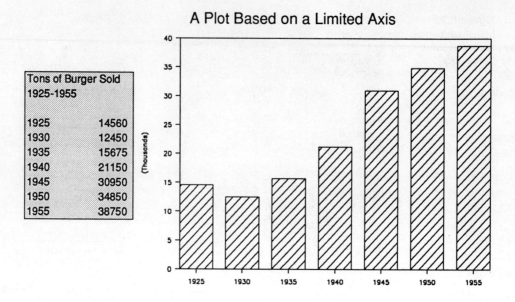

Tons of Burger Sold 1925-1955	
1925	14560
1930	12450
1935	15675
1940	21150
1945	30950
1950	34850
1955	38750

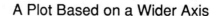

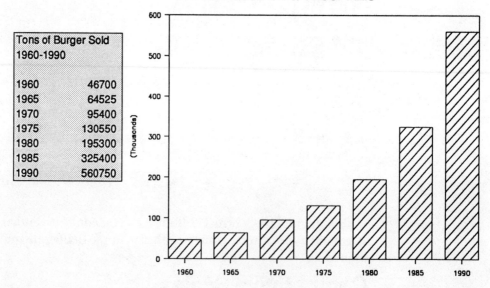

Tons of Burger Sold 1960-1990	
1960	46700
1965	64525
1970	95400
1975	130550
1980	195300
1985	325400
1990	560750

    The net result is that it is all but impossible to see the continuing trend over the entire period from 1940 to 1990, and equally difficult to compare one year in the earlier series to another year in the later series. A casual reader might even believe that hamburger consumption dropped off precipitously in 1960, exactly the opposite of what did occur.

Figure 8.22
Progression along
a common axis

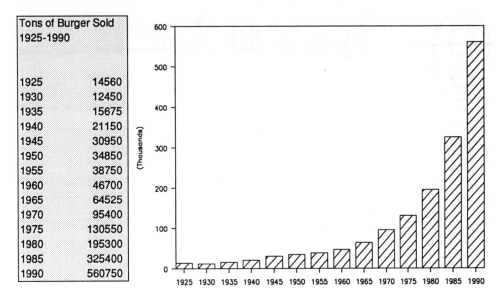

Tons of Burger Sold 1925-1990	
1925	14560
1930	12450
1935	15675
1940	21150
1945	30950
1950	34850
1955	38750
1960	46700
1965	64525
1970	95400
1975	130550
1980	195300
1985	325400
1990	560750

The third graph in this set, shown in Figure 8.22, brings all of the data together in a single graph. It is easy to see the steady progression from 1925 to the present date, and it is easy to come up with a ranking of any one time period relative to another. This chart, however, is not without problems, because it does include numbers that are at great extremes from each other (a 40:1 ratio between lowest and highest number). This chart should be printed as large as possible to allow more room at the low end.

⑨ Types of Graphs

This chapter explores the various types of graphs available to users of the 1-2-3/Allways combination. It starts with a description of the types of graphs available and then moves into a discussion of when best to use the various forms. Finally, it looks at some step-by-step operations you can use to create these graphs using 1-2-3 and Allways.

Creating Graphs with 1-2-3

Allways is useless without data fed to it from a 1-2-3 spreadsheet. This data can be text, numbers, or a combination of both. Put another way: Remember that 1-2-3 does not know that Allways exists, but Allways is entirely dependent on the data given it by 1-2-3.

It's time to write a theme song: *As you work in 1-2-3, Think Allways.*

Later, we discuss how to use some of the built-in functions of 1-2-3 to create worthy numbers for graphing, or how to create your own formulas for the purpose.

Step-by-Step: Producing a Graph Under 1-2-3

There are three basic steps in the production of a graph under 1-2-3.

1. Create a 1-2-3 spreadsheet with a meaningful set of numbers for graphing. A great deal of the work in intelligent graphing—developing meaningful numbers—must be performed long before issues of graphic design are considered. The development of those numbers comes through a process of structuring a spreadsheet properly and using appropriate mathematical and statistical formulas. These formulas can be applications of built-in 1-2-3 functions, such as @STD or @VAR, or they can be calculations entered as formulas into 1-2-3 cells.

2. Use the 1-2-3 graphing facilities to create a graph. You must
   A. Select the appropriate X range and at least one Y range. (For most types of graphs, 1-2-3 will accept as many as six Y ranges, labeling them A through F.)
   B. Choose scales, grids and tick marks.
   C. Name titles, legends and labels.
   D. Select shading and colors.
   E. Save the graph, under 1-2-3. The system will automatically store it with a .PIC filename extension, using a specialized format recognizable to 1-2-3 and other programs, including Allways.
3. Use Printgraph (a separate program within the Lotus Access System to specify type fonts, sizes and pen colors for printers).

NOTE: In 1-2-3, just as in Allways, you can create and output a graph even if you do not have a graphics card and monitor in your system. In such a case you will be working in the dark in the production of the graph, relying solely on the messages from the software about options selected. The output on a graphics capable printer under 1-2-3 and as improved by Allways, however, is the same with or without the use of a graphics card and monitor.

Improving the Graph Using Allways

Later in this book, we'll show how to enhance the graph using the facilities of Allways. We'll pick up at step 2, with the saved version of a graph. You must also bring over to Allways a spreadsheet to contain the graph. This spreadsheet can be the 1-2-3 worksheet used to produce the graph or it can be a blank worksheet.

This next effort is a substitute for the 1-2-3 step 3, using Printgraph. Therefore, let's call this step 3A.

3A. Add a graph from 1-2-3 to the Allways worksheet. When the Allways **/Graph Add** command is issued, Allways reaches into 1-2-3 and displays on screen a listing of available *.PIC files found in the default directory. You can select one of the displayed files, or press the ESC key, go to the command line, and directly enter a PIC file name from any disk or directory accessible to the system.

You can use Allways to place the graph anywhere on the worksheet, and to establish its size and shape. (Be aware that the shape of the space you choose can affect the "aspect ratio" of the resulting graph: Circular pies can become oblong; squares can become rectangles or rectangles squares. Take care not to mislead the reader.)

Now that you're using Allways, you can add a fourth step.

4.   Edit the scale, fonts, and colors of the graph using the facilities of Allways.

The 1-2-3 Family of Graphs

1-2-3 allows creation of five graphing forms:

LINE—Single or multiple lines depicting change over time.
BAR—Single or multiple *vertical* bars emphasizing differences between data items.
XY—Relationships between two sets of data, charted with symbols or lines.
PIE CHARTS—Comparison of parts to a whole.
STACKED BARS—Single or multiple *vertical* bars emphasizing differences between data items and including a comparison of parts to a whole.

To this family, we will now add the following types, made possible by the marriage of 1-2-3 and Allways:

HORIZONTAL—Single or multiple horizontal bars emphasizing differences between data items, and also emphasizing distance from zero or an index level. Created using the 1-2-3 +/− numerical format, as enhanced under Allways.
TEXT—Organization charts, forms, and enhanced spreadsheets. Created under 1-2-3 (using data either entered within that program or imported from a word processor or other text source) and enhanced using Allways.

Let's examine the various forms.

The Line or "Fever" Chart

Name: Line or Fever Chart.
Use for: Depiction of quantities, plotted over time.
Elements:
   —A rising and falling line, called a "curve," that joins together points on a grid.
   —The Y-axis, the vertical scale, which usually depicts quantities.
   —The X-axis, the horizontal scale, which usually depicts the passage of time.
Examples of good use: Stock prices, temperature readings, attendance figures.
Traps to avoid:
   —Sets of data in which there is too little variation in quantity.

—Sets of data in which there is too great a distance between the lowest and the highest data points with other clusters of data closer together.

The line chart is perhaps the most readily recognized form of chart and one of the quickest and easiest to produce—the jagged or smooth path of lines connecting marked or assumed points of data. Some designers call this form a "fever chart," drawing the allusion to a hospital's bedside graphing of a patient's temperature.

This form of chart is best used

≡ For depictions of data over a long period of time.
≡ For data that will be projected beyond known data.
≡ For the comparison of several series of data.
≡ For trends showing frequency distribution.
≡ If a multiple-amount scale is to be used.
≡ When the visual emphasis is to be on the *movement* of a trend rather than on a precise reading of a data point at a particular moment in time.

Probably the best-known example of a line chart is the daily, weekly, or monthly stock market chart. In its simplest form, this chart displays the progress of a single commodity—either a particular stock price or an index such as the Dow Jones Industrials Average—over time.

Elements of a Line Chart

The key to the line chart, of course, is the *line*, or "curve," that connects data points. These points are ordinarily plotted against the Y-axis for quantity and the X-axis for time period.

The data for a standard line chart is unaltered; in specialized charts, the *data points* may be the results of calculations intended to "smooth" the numbers so as to make trends more apparent to the reader.

At the bottom of the chart, the *horizontal scale* is labeled with *time divisions*. The divisions must be even; for example, ticks could represent the 12 months of the year, one-year periods, or five-year blocks of time. An example of an unacceptable set of time divisions would be a chart that had tick marks for a three-year period, then a five-year period, then a single year. Similarly, for an honest chart, tick marks must be included for every expected time period, even if it happens that there is no data for that period. The horizontal scale is itself part of the grid, representing 0 on the Y-axis.

The *vertical scale* is labeled with quantities or percentages.

Grid lines in the final, printed graph should be kept to the minimum number and weight needed for best communication to the reader, so as to not overwhelm the curve being plotted.

Keys are employed when there is insufficient space to individually identify each of a set of multiple lines.

Labels are the signposts for the reader. They identify the units of measure and the units of time division, and, in some cases, they include explanatory notes. For example, a label can explain, in a line chart based on a standardized index, that "1985=100." Labels can also be used to qualify numbers, for example, indicating that some or all of the data is based on estimations or projections, rather than coming from actual readings.

Notes and captions, although not actually a part of the line chart itself, can be used to explain some elements of the graph. A block of text prepared in 1-2-3 could be used as a note or caption to a graph that has been enhanced under Allways.

Line Chart Traps and Problems

The simplicity of the line chart can lead to problems if the nature or quality of the data is not appropriate or complete.

If there is too much information, the chart will have to be too large to be practical, or the divisions too small to be read.

If the data points vary greatly, from very low to very high, the chart will have huge areas without information, and the reader will find it difficult to discern a trend.

If data points do not vary much from one another, the resulting chart will be very close to flat and not convey much information.

Massaging Numbers for Line Charts

The many ways to massage the numbers to be used in a line graph to help with understanding or to aid in graphic presentation, including calculations of moving averages and the use of logarithmic scales, will be discussed later.

You can use the line chart successfully for the depiction of two (or more) series if they are comparable. Some charts attempt to compare two trends based on differing Y-axes (a sometimes dishonest maneuver). 1-2-3 does not permit this, for either honest or dishonest purposes.

In Figure 9.1, the sales from three different units are charted over the same time period, a successful illustration of three separate data series. This form of graph works well when the ranges of numbers are not widely separated and when there is not so much volatility that the eye cannot easily follow individual lines.

Step-by-Step: Creating a Line Graph in 1-2-3

As we have discussed, line graphs represent data points over time. Typical uses would include graphs of changes in sales figures, test scores, or temperatures.

Each value is indicated at a calculated height above the horizontal axis.

Ranges: A 1-2-3 line graph can have as many as six ranges for the Y- or vertical axis. The first range must be identified to the system as A, with

Figure 9.1
Example of a
multiline graph

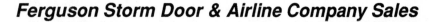

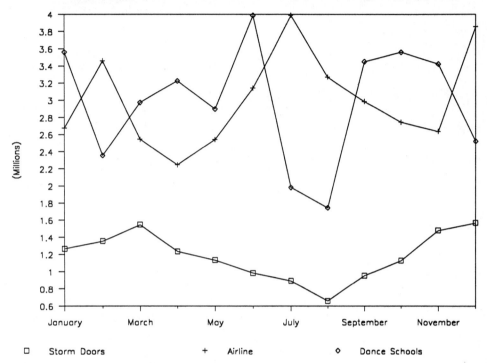

subsequent ranges named B through F. 1-2-3 automatically assigns different symbols to the various ranges. A numerical scale is automatically assigned along the Y-axis, but you can modify it.

Data ranges: These can be rows or columns. 1-2-3 identifies Y-axis ranges as A–F for most types of graphs.

Graph data ranges: In a multiple range chart, 1-2-3 matches corresponding labels or values based on relative positions within a range. Therefore, when you specify data ranges, each range must be the same size as all others.

The single X range is used to create labels along the X- or horizontal axis.

Grids: You can specify the inclusion of vertical grid lines (from the tick marks on the horizontal or X-axis) or horizontal grid lines (from the tick marks on the vertical or Y-axis), or you can call for inclusion of both horizontal and vertical grids.

Horizontal grid lines help the viewer make a precise reading of the amount represented by a particular data point. Vertical grid lines help the viewer concentrate on the critical date or time period represented by a particular point along the X-axis. In any case, you should examine the final appearance of a line graph to ensure that grid lines do not obscure the message of a chart.

The 1-2-3 command is

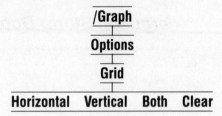

NOTE: You must specify **Both** to obtain horizontal and vertical grids. If you select **Vertical** after previously selecting **Horizontal**, the latest option will override the earlier one, and only vertical grid lines will be drawn.

Symbols: The default setting for 1-2-3 line graphs calls for use of lines connecting data points, with each data point identified with a symbol. In a single line graph, you might choose to eliminate symbols if the primary story of the graph is the shape and direction of the curve, rather than individual data points along its length. Similarly, because in 1-2-3 you cannot specify different line weights or styles (dashes or dotted lines or the like), the use of symbols is imperative in most multiline graphs. An exception might be when each of the lines is well separated from the other(s) and can be associated with a data label within the chart itself. You also can direct the system to plot a graph using only symbols.

Finally, there are some circumstances where you might want to have the system create a line graph with *neither lines nor symbols*. If you use a combination of **Neither** and the command

/Graph Options Data-Labels

you can use data values as entries on a graph.

In 1-2-3 you can tell the system what format to use for each range in a line chart. To select lines, symbols, or both for a specific range, enter the letter (A through F) representing that range. To apply options to all ranges in a graph, select **Graph** under the **Format** menu. The command structure is:

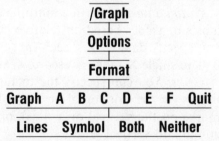

Index Charts

Name: Index chart.

Use for: Depicts quantities, plotted over time, charted against a reference point or "index" value. (See descriptions of Line and Bar Graphs for discussion of strengths and weaknesses of this form.)

Elements of a line index chart:
—A rising and falling line, called a "curve," that joins points on a grid.
—An index line, usually represented as a value of 100.
—A Y-axis, the vertical scale, that depicts quantities.
—An X-axis, the horizontal scale, that depicts the passage of time.

Elements of a bar index chart:
—A set of individual bars or columns representing an amount by the height or length shown.
—An index line, usually represented as a value of 100.
—A Y-axis, the vertical scale, that depicts quantities.
—An X-axis, the horizontal scale, that depicts points of time, or sources.

Examples of good use: Comparison of prices or other levels against a significant point in history, such as a stock-market crash or development of a new technology or a political event.

Traps to avoid: An index value that is considerably above or below the range of numbers plotted in the graph. (See discussions of Bar and Line Graphs for other traps to avoid in each form.)

The index chart is useful to show the relation of a trend to a base year or period. A common use of an index chart is to graph prices or cost-of-living trends.

Index charts are often used:

≡ To compare the relationship of two series that differ greatly in amount. For example, the cost of a postage stamp could be tracked against the Gross National Product by comparing both sets of prices against an index year.
≡ To compare the relationship of two series that use different basic units. For example, the cost of the postage stamp could be compared against the number of pieces of mail carried by the Postal Service.

1-2-3 does not officially support creation of the index chart as a graphic device. However, such a chart can be constructed using 1-2-3 and Allways. The first step involves the establishment of an index value and then the calculation of other data points in relation to that index. The resulting numbers are used to create a standard line or bar chart, which is saved within 1-2-3. The final step, and one that must be carefully done, involves taking advantage of the fact that graphs placed into an Allways worksheet are transparent.

Using Allways, the designer places a shade bar or a solid line on the worksheet, then adjusts the position of the imported 1-2-3 graph so that the line demarks the index range. The construction can be done in any order: You can draw the line first and then place the graph over it, or place the graph and then add the line.

Remember, too, that Allways has a fairly wide range of options for the weight and thickness of lines. You can select normal, light, or heavy lines that can be put into place with the **/Format Lines** command. Or you can construct lines by adjusting column or row widths or heights and filling in the columns or rows, using **/Format Shade** and selecting light, dark, or solid weights.

Figure 9.2 shows an index chart that has been created using the 1-2-3 and Allways combination.

Use care in selecting a base year for the index trend—the choice will obviously have an effect on the information communicated by the chart. Accompanying text or captions should explain why a particular base year was selected.

The base year should be a time that can be defended as normal. Selecting as a base year a period in which the data points were low will result in most of the trend line being plotted above the baseline. Selecting a base year in which data points were high will yield a trend line mostly below the baseline.

Note that Lotus 1-2-3 automatically sets the Y scale for the above-zero quadrant; manual specification is not available. This is not a problem for most viewers who are alerted to the Index Chart nature of the graph.

The index value of the base year is usually set at 100, and values for other years are plotted against that index value. For example, suppose the base year is 1983, and the actual value for 1983 is 5000 (index = 100). The year to be compared is 1981, and the actual value is 2500. The index values for 1981

Figure 9.2
Sample index chart
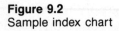

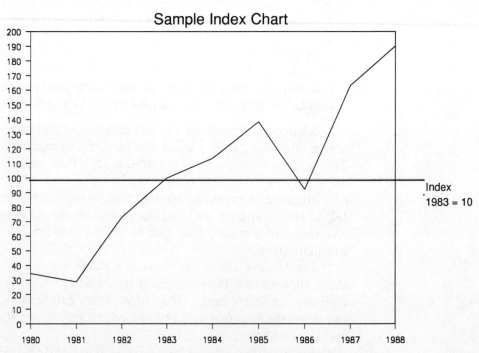

Net Income Per Share, Compared to 1983 Index Year

would be 50. (The formula, which would be applied in a Lotus spreadsheet, would be to divide the actual value of each year to be graphed by the actual value of the base year, then multiply the quotient by 100.)

It is also possible to assign a base to more than one year. For example, to use an index based on a three-year period, take the total for the three years and divide by three to obtain an average value for the base value.

For many uses, the bar chart is simpler to gauge and more readily understood than a line chart. The typical format for the bar chart is vertical, showing numerical values of a specific item over a period of time. The frozen moments of time depicted by each column of data receive primary emphasis. (Another form of bar chart that uses horizontal bars will be discussed later.) Keep in mind that bar charts tend to emphasize individual points in time at the expense of the overall flow or trend of figures.

The Bar Chart

Name: Bar chart.

Use for: Depicting quantities, either plotted over time or distributed over a series of sources. Individual figures are highlighted, rather than the overall flow. Bars can represent

1. The value of a single commodity over time.
2. The values of different commodities at the same point in time.

Multiple bar charts can plot the values of more than one commodity over time or depict single commodities over time with more than one source at each point in time.

Elements:
—A set of individual bars or columns representing an amount by the height or length shown.
—A Y-axis, the vertical scale, that depicts quantities.
—An X-axis, the horizontal scale, that depicts points of time or sources.

Examples of good use: Production graphs.

Traps to avoid:
—Sets of data in which there are too many numbers.
—Situations in which flow or trends need to be highlighted, rather than individual data points.

As in the line chart, the time intervals for the X-axis should be regular— every year or every three years or the like. It is not a proper practice to skip a period as was done in preparation of Figure 9.3. Such a chart is not a truthful representation of a trend. If data is unavailable, space can be left on the chart by entering a zero value for a particular year or years and indicating on the chart that some data is missing, as was done for Figure 9.4. The note was created as an element of the 1-2-3 worksheet, then inset using Allways.

Figure 9.3
Unexplained
missing data can
make all data
suspect

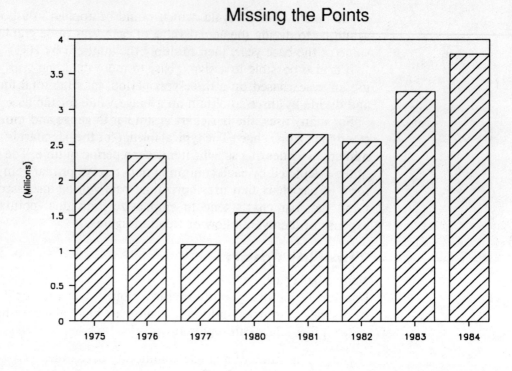

Figure 9.3
Unexplained
missing data can
make all data
suspect

Figure 9.4
One way to treat
missing data

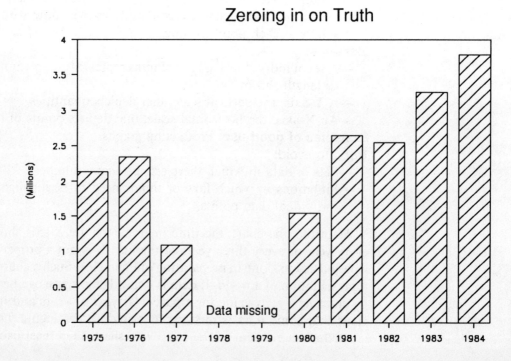

As we've previously discussed, it is generally not proper to have a broken scale for a bar chart with a Y-axis starting other than at zero. In fact, 1-2-3 blocks you from creating a limit lower than zero for a bar chart. However, if a chart contains one or two unusual points—for example, if the range of all other bits of data is from 10 to 75 and there is one column at 300—it is generally acceptable to lop off the scale at the high end if you clearly indicate what has been done. (See Figures 9.5 and 9.6.)

Another advantage of the bar chart is its applicability to comparisons of several sets of data that cover the same period of time. The practical limit is three or four sets, even though with 1-2-3 you can have as many as six. An example of a crowded, barely readable multiple-bar comparative chart can be seen in Figure 9.7. We've also taken this same chart and, using Allways, changed the aspect ratio to an extreme horizontal and an extreme vertical version. The results can be seen in Figure 9.8.

Yet another variation of the vertical bar chart is the stacked bar graph (Figure 9.9). This is a combination chart that shows a whole column's total and several subdivided elements of each column— in effect, a noncircular pie chart. This sort of device is very effective when you have an unusual story to tell. For example, if total receipts went up at the same time as profits declined (one model from an inflationary cycle), the stacked bar chart could give the whole picture.

Elements of a Bar Chart

In any bar chart, the *bars*—sometimes referred to as *columns* in a vertical graph—indicate a quantity by their length. In a vertical bar chart the bars

Figure 9.5
Out-of-balance bar graph

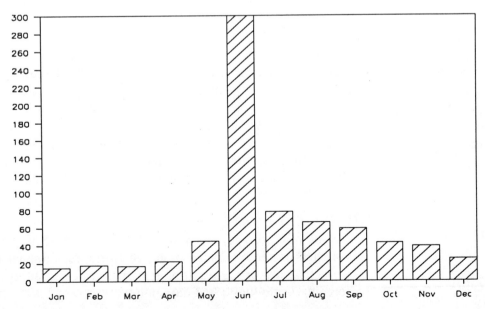

Figure 9.6
Lopped-off bar
graph

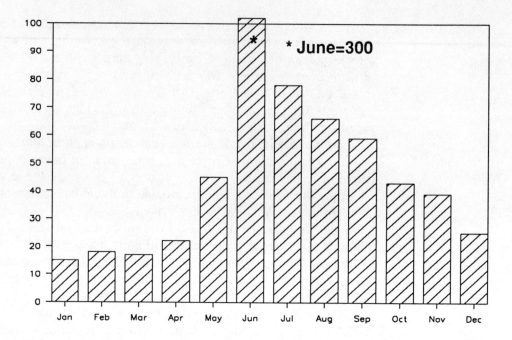

extend upward (and sometimes downward) from the X-axis. In a horizontal bar chart, the bars extend to the right from their baseline, the Y-axis.

The *data* for a standard bar chart is generally not altered, except for rounding off of numbers and conversion to easily chartable units. For example, when all numbers are in millions or billions, six zeros can be dropped and an appropriate notation added to the graph's legend.

The *horizontal scale* is labeled with time divisions or with labels for various quantities to be charted.

The *vertical scale* is labeled with quantities or percentages.

As with line charts, *grid lines* should be used sparingly—just enough to assist the reader in gaining an accurate reading of the information.

Keys are used when there is insufficient space to individually identify each of a set of multiple lines.

Labels are employed to identify units of measure or time divisions.

Notes and *captions* provide additional information and clarification of sources of data or any manipulations performed on data points.

Traps and Problems

Avoid situations in which you have too many data points to be able to show each one individually, or in which the resulting chart will be too big for practical use or the resulting bars will be too small or too close together to communicate individual data points.

Figure 9.7
An overcrowded
bar graph

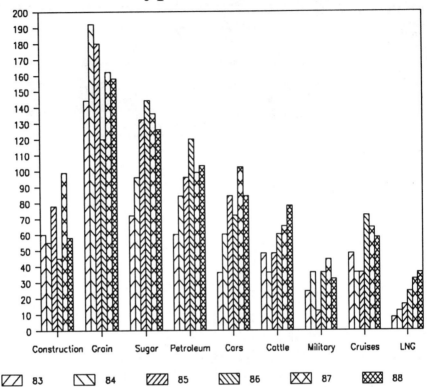

Types of Vessels

The 1-2-3 Bar Graph

A single-range bar graph compares values in one set of data to each other. A multiple-bar graph compares values from as many as six sets of data at each point along the X-axis.

In a single-range bar graph, the A range contains the range of values for each bar. In a multiple-range bar graph, the first range must be identified to the system as A, with subsequent ranges named B through F. 1-2-3 uses shadings or colors to identify each set of bars in a multiple-bar chart. A numerical scale is automatically assigned along the Y-axis, but you can modify it.

Grids: You can specify the inclusion of vertical grid lines, horizontal grid lines, or both. Horizontal grid lines are valuable because they help the viewer make a precise reading of the amount represented by a particular data point, which is important in a bar graph. Horizontal grid lines could prove distracting, however, because they are drawn through the bars. Examine the final appearance of a bar graph to ensure that grid lines do not obscure the message. Vertical grid lines in a bar chart do not ordinarily convey meaningful information.

Figure 9.8
Effect of extreme horizontal (top) and vertical (bottom) aspect ratios on graph shown in Figure 9.7

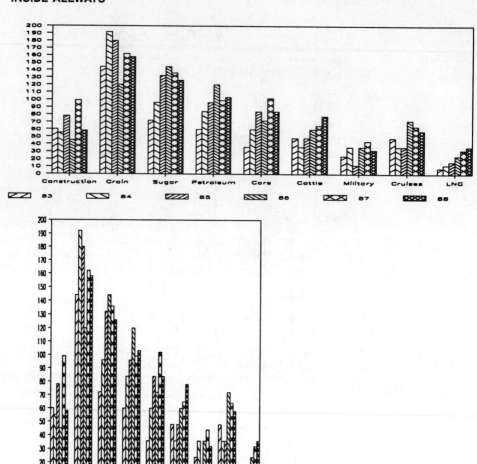

Axis titles: X- and Y-axis titles can be added to any bar chart under 1-2-3. The vertical, or Y-axis, title often indicates the unit of measure being employed, such as dollars, units sold, or number of employees. The horizontal, or X-axis, title generally identifies categories that appear as labels on the X-axis. As many as 39 characters can be used for each axis title; you will probably find shorter titles make for a better appearance.

NOTE: It is possible to include graph titles, legends, and axis titles as worksheet entries. To do so, specify the cell location for the title or legend, for example, \C32, rather than typing in a text entry. In addition to reducing the chances for error, such an approach also links the graph's titles and legends to the worksheet. In our example here, if a change is

Figure 9.9
A stacked bar
graph

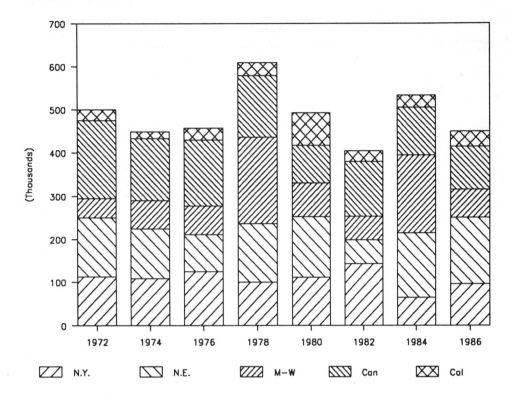

Figure 9.9 / A stacked bar graph

made to the entry at cell C32, that change will automatically be made to the *unsaved* graph when viewed. Remember, though, that Allways works only with the saved file. Changes made to the 1-2-3 worksheet or graph settings must be saved to a *.PIC file to use Allways as an enhancement tool.

X-axis labels: Labels are used to identify individual categories along an axis. For example, individual bars or groups of bars can be labeled with months or years or other categories. 1-2-3 takes its X-axis labels directly from the worksheet, using the range specified at the time of the creation of the graph.

The X-axis label must be short enough to fit in the space allotted along the length of the axis; if the labels are too long, they will overprint and be unreadable, as seen in Figure 9.10, top. (Note the addition of an index line, created by reducing the row height at the appropriate place on the Allways worksheet and using a dark shading at that location. Note also the use of the 1-2-3 **Compose** command to create a degree sign, using a LICS [Lotus International Character Set] symbol.) The labels can be rewritten in the worksheet, or the program can be instructed to use a skip factor and display only every *n*th label on the graph. Figure 9.10, bottom, shows the X-axis of the same graph, this time using a skip factor of 2. In this case, 1-2-3 lists every other

Figure 9.10
Overcrowding the
X-axis

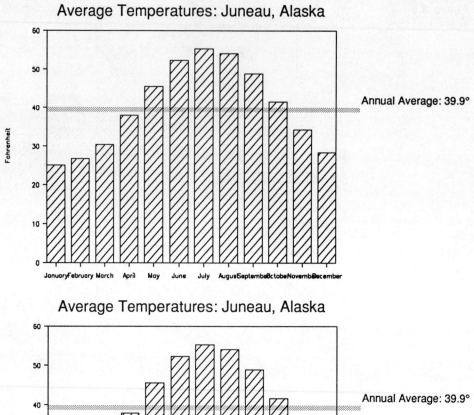

Average Temperatures: Juneau, Alaska

Annual Average: 39.9°

Average Temperatures: Juneau, Alaska

Annual Average: 39.9°

month name, and because the names of the months are well known, the reader can readily understand the graph. Be careful not to skip over labels that are not obvious.

Y-axis label: The label along the Y-, or vertical, axis is prepared automatically by 1-2-3, based on the widest spread of values used by the various Y ranges plotted.

Deviation and Paired-Bar Charts

The deviation bar chart is a quick visual means of displaying percentage or amount changes through the use of positive or negative scales. These scales can extend left and right of a common baseline in a horizontal bar chart or above and below a baseline in the vertical bar chart form. For example, in Figure 9.11 we can quickly appraise the fictitious sales performance of nine automobile manufacturers. The accepted form for entry of data is to have the positive sequence arranged in descending order, the negative sequence in ascending order. Here are the make-believe numbers illustrated in the chart.

1989 Automobile Sales in United States

Company	Percent Change from 1988
General Motors	+40.3
Nissan	+34.6
Ford	+25.3
AMC	+19.1
Chrysler	+8.9
Toyota	−0.8
Mazda	−5.6
Volkswagen	−12.8
Saab	−23.6

Figure 9.11
Vertical deviation
bar chart

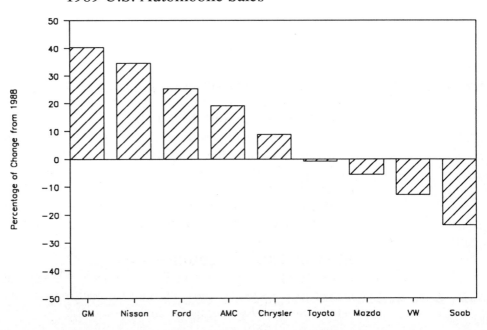

1989 U.S. Automobile Sales

The Horizontal Bar Chart

The horizontal bar chart is a single-axis device best used for comparing different items at a particular point in time. For example, a chart could be drawn showing the number of home computers sold in the United States in 1983 and 1984 by five companies. The chart, starting always from a zero point at the left, traverses a regularly spaced axis.

The horizontal bar chart can have some of the same variations of the standard vertical graph, including stacked bars and multiple bars (often representing a second time period). It is also possible to extend the bars to the left of the axis to chart negative numbers, as in a representation of profit and loss.

NOTE: 1-2-3 does not draw horizontal bar graphs within its ordinary graphing function. There is, however, an alternate form of very simple graphing with 1-2-3 called +/− graphing. And, through the special facilities of Allways, we're about to show how to enhance the +/− graph into a valuable, though limited, addition to the 1-2-3 family of graphs.

The 1-2-3 +/− Graph

1-2-3 includes the ability to create minihorizontal bar graphs within worksheets. Note that this does not involve the creation of a .PIC file. These special graphs are called +/− graphs, because of their use of the + or − symbol for drawing the bars.

The reason for the inclusion of this specialized graph form within the worksheet itself is recognition of one of the limitations of 1-2-3 versions 1 and 2 (and one of Allways' reasons for being): You cannot ordinarily include a graph within a worksheet. Instead, you must create the graph and save it as a .PIC file, then print it out using the PrintGraph program on a separate piece of paper.

According to Lotus, this simple graph form is intended to allow quick and easy communication of trends to viewers of a 1-2-3 worksheet on screen or in a printout of the worksheet itself.

Adding Allways to your arsenal does deal with the separate piece of paper issue: Allways easily allows the importation of a 1-2-3 .PIC file into an Allways worksheet. However, the +/− graph form is the only way to obtain a horizontal bar graph under 1-2-3.

We'll step you through the creation of a +/− graph under 1-2-3. Following that, we'll show you how to enhance that simple graph under Allways.

Step-by-Step: A Lotus +/− Graph

The 1-2-3 +/− graph works by substituting the + symbol for each positive integer in a range and the − symbol for each negative integer in the range. Select this form by issuing the command:

/Range Format +/−

Here are some examples of resulting ranges.

Integer	New Cell Contents
5	+++++
3	+++
1	+
−1	−
−3	−−−
−5	−−−−−

Obviously, use of this format will be limited by the specified column width. Therefore, it generally makes sense to use the +/− format as a representation of the whole number by dividing all of the integers by a set number, such as 10, 100, or 1000. (Be sure to indicate the division in a label to the graph.)

Following is an example of the use of the +/− graph form. We've chosen to chart here a bit of information from the almanac, a selection of crops produced by American farmers in 1972. Working within 1-2-3, we've entered three columns in the spreadsheet: crop names, production figures, and a third range for creation of the +/− figures.

Here are some of the numbers we're plotting:

Corn, grain	11,146,000,000
Wheat	3,089,872,000

Now, if we were to apply a +/− format to those numbers, we would have to display more than 11 *billion* pluses for corn and a bit over 3 *billion* pluses for wheat. This obviously will not work. Instead, we create a formula that makes a more reasonable scale. The formula we applied to the raw number in Cell C8, for example, was

+(C8/1000000000)

which yields a more reasonable number of 11.1.

Our next step is to apply the +/− format to the entire range that results from this formula.

In Figure 9.12, top, we can see a screen picture of the original 1-2-3 worksheet. In Figure 9.12, bottom, we can see a screen picture within Allways of the same worksheet without any enhancement except for the application of the default typeface, in this case Helvetica 10 pt. Remember, with this special form of graph, you will be working with a straight 1-2-3 text chart, not a .PIC file, and all of the Allways facilities can be used.

Enhancing the +/− Graph With Allways

We don't have to be satisfied with the ordinary output of 1-2-3. Enter Allways. Since the +/− graph is not a .PIC file but is instead a standard 1-2-3

Figure 9.12
1-2-3 (top) and
Allways (bottom)
screens of +/–
chart in progress

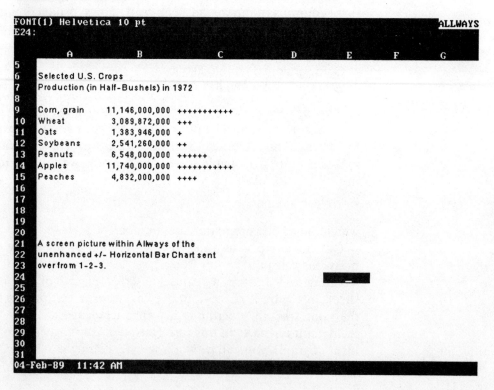

worksheet, we actually have a broader range of enhancements that can be applied to the worksheet. These include

≡ Selection of appropriate type fonts for each element of the graph.
≡ Application of shading to all or part of the graph.
≡ Addition of lines and outlines to all or part of the graph.

Figures 9.13 through 9.15 show steps in producing an enhanced version of the 1-2-3 +/− graph shown in Figure 9.12, as produced using Allways, employing all of the above facilities.

In Figure 9.13, we see a screen picture of the first step in enhancement of this graph, the application of a PostScript typeface to the text and numbers brought over from 1-2-3.

Figure 9.14 shows a screen picture of a few more of the Allways enhancements, including the drawing of outlines around each of the three elements and the application of a light shade. The top title is set in one font, the labels and numbers in a second, and the important +/− characters (in this case pluses only) in a third, larger font to emphasize the pluses. A laser printout of the finished chart can be seen in Figure 9.15.

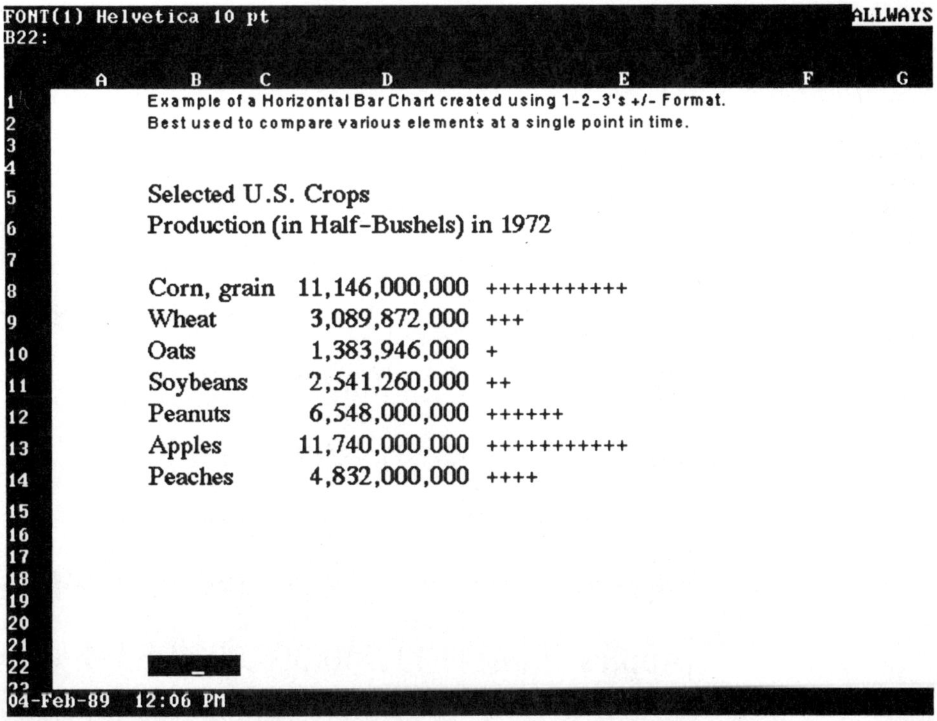

Figure 9.13
Midway through the
Allways +/−
enhancement

```
FONT(1) Helvetica 10 pt                                              ALLWAYS
B22:
          A      B      C      D                    E          F      G
1       Example of a Horizontal Bar Chart created using 1-2-3's +/- Format.
2       Best used to compare various elements at a single point in time.
3
4
5       Selected U.S. Crops
6       Production (in Half–Bushels) in 1972
7
8       Corn, grain  11,146,000,000  +++++++++++
9       Wheat         3,089,872,000  +++
10      Oats          1,383,946,000  +
11      Soybeans      2,541,260,000  ++
12      Peanuts       6,548,000,000  ++++++
13      Apples       11,740,000,000  +++++++++++++
14      Peaches       4,832,000,000  ++++
15
16
17
18
19
20
21
22
23
04-Feb-89   12:06 PM
```

Figure 9.14
Allways enhancement of +/−

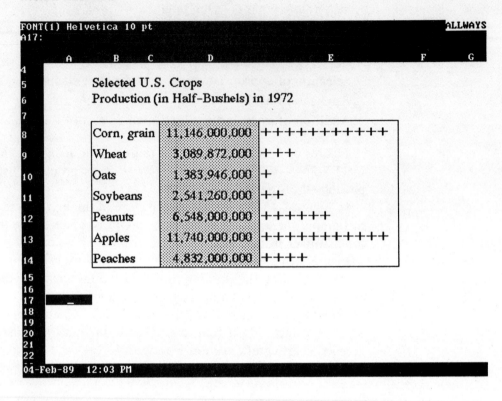

Figure 9.15
Laser printer final
output of enhanced
+/− chart

Selected U.S. Crops
Production (in Half-Bushels) in 1972

Corn, grain	11,146,000,000	++++++++++
Wheat	3,089,872,000	+++
Oats	1,383,946,000	+
Soybeans	2,541,260,000	++
Peanuts	6,548,000,000	++++++
Apples	11,740,000,000	+++++++++++
Peaches	4,832,000,000	++++

Stacked Bar Graphs

In a stacked bar graph, 1-2-3 produces bars that include as many as six components.

The single X range is used to indicate the set of labels for the horizontal axis.

The stacked bars are made up of Y ranges. The first Y range is identified to the system as range A, with subsequent ranges named B through F. 1-2-3 uses the A range as the lowest portion of each bar, with B through F successively stacked above it, in alphabetical order.

1-2-3 assigns shadings or colors to indicate the various range components of each bar. Numerical labels are automatically added along the Y-axis.

The XY Graph

Name: XY chart.

Use for: Display of correlation between two series through a comparison of individual values of the X range against a corresponding value for one or more Y ranges.

Elements:
—Data points or a line that joins data points, demonstrating correlation through the direction, slope, and curvature of the line.
—A single X range is plotted along the horizontal axis.
—From one to six Y-axes (the 1-2-3 limit) are plotted along the vertical scale.

Examples of good use: Correlation of stock prices against profit levels; sales of a product against changing price levels; sales of a product against an external event, such as temperature or rainfall.

Traps to avoid:
—Sets of data in which there is very little correlation, resulting in an unclear story.
—Sets of data in which there is too great a difference between the lowest data point and the highest, with other clusters of data in between.

In an XY graph, each value from the single X range is paired with the corresponding value from each of as many as six Y ranges. The single X range is plotted along the horizontal axis. Y ranges are plotted along the vertical axis. The first Y range is identified to the system as A, with subsequent ranges identified as B through F.

1-2-3 assigns different symbols for each XY comparison line. The program also automatically indicates numerical scales along both the X- and Y-axes.

An XY chart is used to show correlation (or lack of it) between two series. The direction, slope, and curvature of the line is an indication of relationship. Another use is to chart one set of values against another. Another name for XY graphs is "scatter diagrams."

Some examples of XY charts include:

≡ Salary charted against educational level.
≡ Beer sales charted against temperature.
≡ A price elasticity chart, indicating the expected or actual demand for a product at different price levels.

XY charts are the only type of graph where the X range is used to specify data. Values in the X series tell 1-2-3 how far along the X-axis to place a point; values in the various Y series (named A through F) tell the program how high up the Y axis to place a point.

A special use of XY type graphs is the plotting of regression data, with the X range specifying the independent variables and the Y range the dependent variables.

A scatter version of an XY graph uses only symbols. An elasticity curve typically uses only lines. Just to help keep it all clear, 1-2-3's default setting calls for the use of both lines and symbols.

Figure 9.16 presents a screen picture of a 1-2-3 worksheet for an XY graph. This is a very simplified version of a price/demand or price elasticity chart, which looks at the effect of varying price on sales. Figure 9.17 shows a finished laser printout of the XY graph, as enhanced using Allways. In this case we have inset in a box the actual numbers from the 1-2-3 worksheet, and then applied shading and PostScript fonts. The black-on-white text block is achieved by setting the text color for the block at white and then adding a solid shade

Figure 9.16
Data for XY graph
on 1-2-3 screen

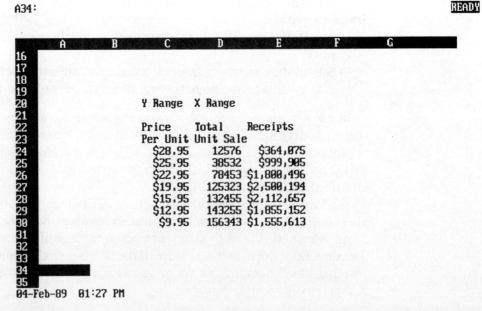

	Y Range	X Range	
	Price Per Unit	Total Unit Sale	Receipts
	$28.95	12576	$364,075
	$25.95	38532	$999,905
	$22.95	78453	$1,800,496
	$19.95	125323	$2,500,194
	$15.95	132455	$2,112,657
	$12.95	143255	$1,855,152
	$9.95	156343	$1,555,613

04-Feb-89 01:27 PM

Figure 9.17
Price/demand XY
graph

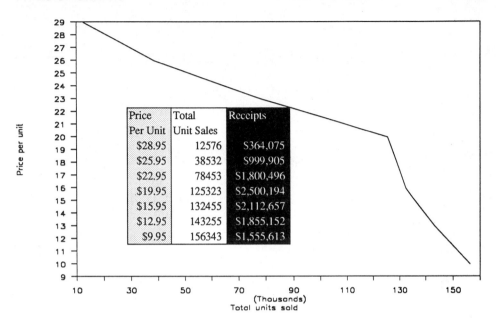

Price Per Unit	Total Unit Sales	Receipts
$28.95	12576	$364,075
$25.95	38532	$999,905
$22.95	78453	$1,800,496
$19.95	125323	$2,500,194
$15.95	132455	$2,112,657
$12.95	143255	$1,855,152
$9.95	156343	$1,555,613

to the block; such a feature will only work with certain printers, generally PostScript laser devices.

Pie chart

Name: Pie chart.

Use for: Depicting the division of a whole into its constituent components, at a fixed moment in time.

Elements:
—A circle representing the whole.
—"Pie wedges" or spokes, emanating from the center and separating the parts of the whole.

Examples of good use: Budgets, market share, explanations of cost elements of a price.

Traps to avoid: Too many divisions of the pie, resulting in wedges that are too fine. A limit of about 10 wedges for a full-sized pie is recommended.

A pie chart is a comparison of parts to the whole. The X range is used solely to provide labels for each wedge of the pie. The A range is used to indicate the set of values for each wedge. 1-2-3 automatically indicates a percentage value for each wedge of the pie. The unadorned pie chart uses range X for labels and range A for data. In the default condition, 1-2-3 draws a simple circle and subdivides it into blank wedges. A special feature of the pie chart form within 1-2-3 is the availability of shading and color for on-screen display and, later, printing. To give the wedges some definition, create a range B that is equal in size to range A, the data for the graph.

As many as seven different shades or colors, plus an empty or unshaded wedge, can be indicated. The various shades are assigned by using values from 1 through 7; zero or 8 indicates an unshaded wedge.

NOTE: Make sure to have a B range of the same size as the A range being graphed.

Pie charts can emphasize one or more specific wedges of the pie. To accomplish this, add 100 to the values in range B for the wedge or wedges to be "exploded."

Figure 9.18 is a screen picture of a 1-2-3 worksheet with the simple data set for a pie graph. The components of revenue in cells B8 through B15 are used for the X range; the dollar amounts in cells D8 through D15 are the A range. Figure 9.19 shows a screen display of an unenhanced pie graph as seen from within 1-2-3.

A B range is added next to assign shadings to the pie wedges. Figure 9.20 is a screen picture of a 1-2-3 worksheet with shading values set from zero through 7. Figure 9.21 shows a screen shot of the still unenhanced 1-2-3 pie graph, with the wedge shadings added.

NOTE: The appearance of the various crosshatches available within 1-2-3 will vary slightly, based on the graphics card and monitor you use to display an image and the capabilities of the printer used for hard copy.

Display images used in this chapter were produced using a CompuAdd 386/20 computer using a VGA adapter and monitor; printouts were made using the QMS-PS 810 PostScript laser printer.

Figure 9.18
1-2-3 screen with
pie chart data

G20:   READY

	A	B	C	D	E	F	G
1							
2		Pie Charts					
3							
4		Revenue Analysis					
5							
6		TOTAL REVENUES:		$8,234,455			
7							
8		R&D		$988,135			
9		Sales		$1,193,996			
10		Advertising		$1,235,168			
11		Administration		$988,135			
12		Raw Materials		$658,756			
13		Manufacturing		$2,058,614			
14		Shipping		$411,723			
15		Profit		$699,929			
16							
17							
18							
19							
20							

05-Feb-89   08:15 AM

Figure 9.19
1-2-3 screen picture
of unenhanced pie
chart

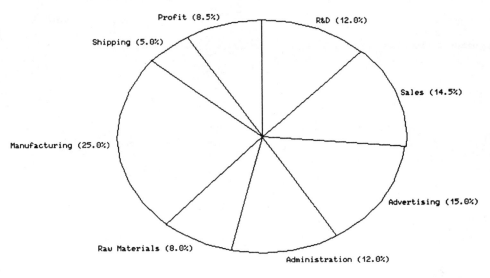

Figure 9.20
1-2-3 screen
showing shadings
range

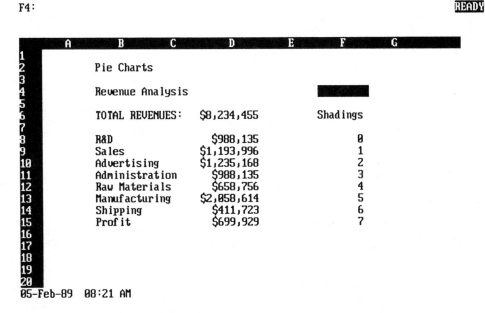

Figure 9.22 is a chart showing the wedge crosshatches available using the system described above. Take some time to experiment with the various shadings available through your system.

Now let's look at the way you can explode a pie wedge by adding a value of 100 to the shading value in Range B. Figure 9.23 shows a 1-2-3 screen picture with the Japan value set at 101, which will pull out that wedge and use shading number 1. Figure 9.24 shows a screen picture of the Allways

Figure 9.21
1-2-3 screen
showing shadings
on pie chart

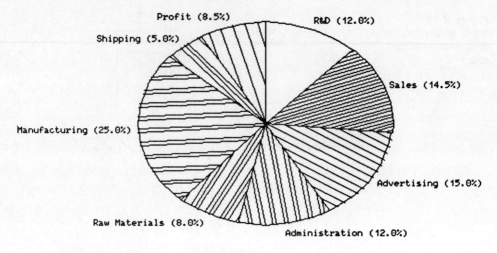

Figure 9.22
Available
crosshatches for
1-2-3 pie charts

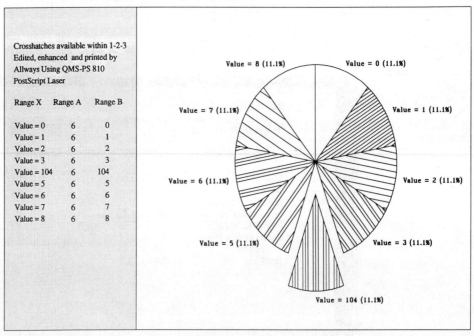

display of the resulting pie chart from these figures. A laser printer hard copy of the same pie chart is shown in Figure 9.25.

Finally, let's look at a pie chart that uses multiple exploded wedges (Figure 9.26). In this case, a value of 100 was added to the B range specifications for three wedges.

Figure 9.23
Exploding a pie
chart wedge (1-2-3
screen)

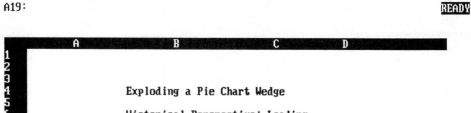

A19:   READY

	A	B	C	D
1				
2				
3				
4		Exploding a Pie Chart Wedge		
5				
6		Historical Perspective: Leading		
7		U.S. Trading Partners in 1973		
8				
9		Canada	$15,073,000,000	0
10		Japan	$8,312,000,000	101
11		W. Germany	$3,756,000,000	2
12		United Kingdom	$3,564,000,000	3
13		Mexico	$7,708,000,000	4
14		Netherlands	$2,860,000,000	5
15		France	$2,263,000,000	6
16		Italy	$2,119,000,000	7
17				
18				
19				
20				

05-Feb-89 09:28 AM

Figure 9.24
Exploded pie
wedge (Allways
screen)

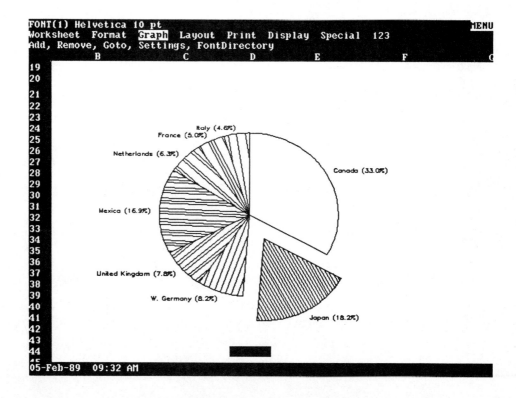

FONT(1) Helvetica 10 pt   MENU
Worksheet Format **Graph** Layout Print Display Special 123
Add, Remove, Goto, Settings, FontDirectory

05-Feb-89 09:32 AM

Figure 9.25
Printout of pie chart
with exploded
wedge

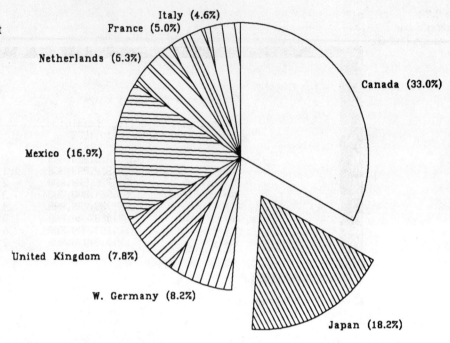

Figure 9.26
Multiple exploded
pie wedges

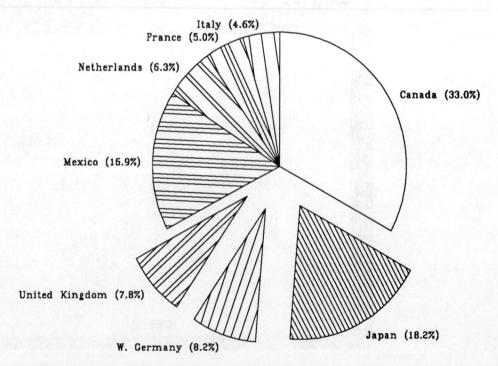

Why a Pie?

If your aim is to show how the various elements make up a whole, the best form is probably the pie chart. This type of device is useful when there are a small number of components—perhaps 8 or 10 at the most.

The standard pie chart represents 100 percent. Each data point is computed as a percentage of the whole and then converted to its appropriate segment of a 360-degree circle. Lotus 1-2-3 will do all of the calculations for you—you just feed in the data.

Most smaller pie charts should be limited to no more than six wedges. If the chart is larger, a few more might be acceptable. Further, extremely small segments—three degrees or less—should generally be merged together into an "Other" category to present a meaningful chart. (See Figures 8.10 and 8.11.)

A good use of pie charts is in combination with a stacked bar or multiline chart. You can depict trends and whole numbers with the bar or line chart, and show the makeup of the whole with the pie.

Elements of a Pie Chart

The standard pie chart has just two basic elements, the *circle* or *pie* and the *slices*. The whole pie represents 100 percent, with the slices representing proportionate segments.

Critical to communication with a pie chart are *labels* or *keys* to identify the names of and percentages represented by the various pie slices as well as the identity of the whole represented by the pie.

Notes and *captions* provide additional information and clarification of sources of data or any manipulations performed on data points.

Traps and Problems

Pies with more than eight or ten divisions will become too difficult for the reader to distinguish. Similarly, if there is too great a disparity between the largest data point and the smallest, then one or more of the divisions may become too tiny to be used.

You will need to pay attention to variations in aspect ratios in all types of graphs. In pie graphs, however, it is quite easy for the viewer to notice that a circle has gone out of round. In Figure 9.27, you can see three views of the same graph. If you were to calculate the relative areas of equivalent pie wedges in the normal, vertical, and horizontal pies, they would be about proportional and therefore theoretically not misleading. However, the human brain is easily fooled here.

The Text Chart

Name: Text chart.
Use for: Display of numbers, words, or concepts.

Figure 9.27
Effect of change in
aspect ratios

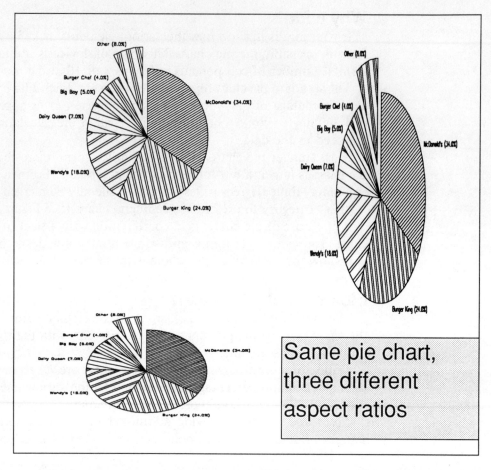

Same pie chart,
three different
aspect ratios

Elements:
—The text.
—A frame or grid, and accompanying graphics elements.
Examples of good use: Tables of organization, flow charts, timetables.
Traps to avoid:
—Using text where a graph or graphic would communicate better.
—Overusing fonts, shades, lines, and other graphic elements to the distraction of the reader.

The text chart is a presentation of numbers or words without a mathematical relationship. In this book, we will consider a text chart to be a piece of work originally produced with a Lotus 1-2-3 spreadsheet and then enhanced under Allways.

The principal elements of a text chart, of course, are the words and numbers themselves. Optional design elements include lines and rules, different fonts, and type sizes and weights. In specialized text charts such as a table of organization, boxes or grids are employed.

Some types of information are by definition text charts, including calendars, timetables, tables of organization, and the like.

The freeform nature of the text chart can be used as a strength to offset some of the weaknesses of other forms of graphs. The best uses of a text chart include:

≡ Situations in which there is too much information or too many different types of information to be meaningfully conveyed in a graph with a mathematical basis.

≡ Situations in which it is important to convey the exact amounts of particular values, rather than the relative representations shown in a graph.

≡ Situations in which there is great variation between the high and low ends of a series of data.

Good examples of text charts can be found in annual financial reports, where it is the numbers themselves that are most closely studied.

Figure 9.28 shows a small portion of a 1-2-3 worksheet prepared by Funk Software, Inc., as a demonstration file for Allways. Figure 9.29 shows a screen picture of the same worksheet displayed under Allways, and Figure 9.30 shows a laser printer output of the text chart.

Finally, Figure 9.31 shows an Allways-enhanced text chart intended as a promotional handout. The outline boxes and shadings exist only in the Allways worksheet.

Figure 9.28
1-2-3 screen of
balance sheet

A22: [W1]   READY

	AB C D E	F G H I J
3		Bestway Shipping Corporation
4		Balance Sheet
5		October 1, 1988
6		
7		
8		
9		ASSETS
10		This Year Last Year
11	Current Assets	
12	Cash	247,886 126,473
13	Accounts receivable	863,652 524,570
14	Inventory	79,071 53,790
15	Prepaid expenses	9,257 11,718
16	Investments	108,577 31,934
17	Total Current Assets	1,308,443 748,485
18		
19	Fixed Assets	
20	Machinery and equipment	209,906 158,730
21	Vehicles	429,505 243,793
22	Office furniture	50,240 36,406

05-Feb-89 11:09 AM

Figure 9.29
Allways display of
balance sheet

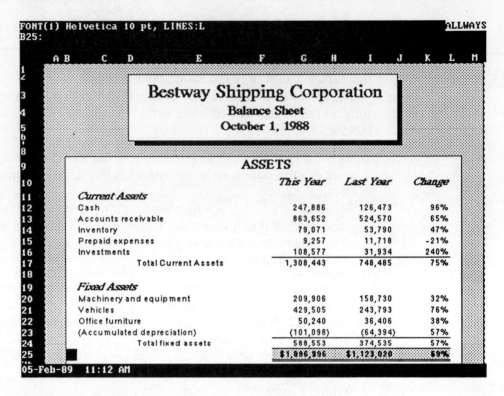

Some additional text charts will be found in this book in Chapter 11, "Creating Business Forms."

Important 1-2-3 Graphing Options

The /**Graph Options** submenu of 1-2-3 is the gateway to a number of limited but still valuable special facilities, including customization of titles, legends, symbols, and colors. These elements are part of the .PIC file that is brought into Allways for enhancement; they are not directly available to Allways itself.

Graph Labels

With 1-2-3 you can add four types of labels to graphs:

≡ Graph titles, the general headings for graphs.
≡ Axis titles, used to identify the kinds of data displayed along each axis.
≡ Data labels, to identify each value directly.
≡ Legends, to explain symbols, shading patterns, or colors used as identifiers in graphs.

Figure 9.30
Laser printout of
balance sheet

Bestway Shipping Corporation
Balance Sheet
October 1, 1988

ASSETS

	This Year	Last Year	Change
Current Assets			
Cash	247,886	126,473	96%
Accounts receivable	863,652	524,570	65%
Inventory	79,071	53,790	47%
Prepaid expenses	9,257	11,718	-21%
Investments	108,577	31,934	240%
Total Current Assets	1,308,443	748,485	75%
Fixed Assets			
Machinery and equipment	209,906	158,730	32%
Vehicles	429,505	243,793	76%
Office furniture	50,240	36,406	38%
(Accumulated depreciation)	(101,098)	(64,394)	57%
Total fixed assets	588,553	374,535	57%
	$1,896,996	$1,123,020	69%

LIABILITIES AND SHAREHOLDERS' EQUITY

	This Year	Last Year	Change
Current Liabilities			
Accounts payable trade	426,041	332,845	28%
Notes payable	45,327	23,486	93%
Accrued liabilities	34,614	26,026	33%
Income taxes payable	88,645	51,840	71%
Total Current Liabilities	594,627	434,197	37%
Noncurrent Liabilities			
Long-term debt	488,822	349,253	40%
Deferred federal tax	147,844	92,101	61%
Total Noncurrent Liabilities	636,666	441,354	44%
Shareholders' equity			
Common stock	1,000	1,000	0%
Opening retained earnings	246,469	82,531	199%
Profit (loss) for the period	418,234	163,938	155%
Total Shareholders' Equity	665,703	247,469	169%
	$1,896,996	$1,123,020	69%

We'll examine first the options available for creation of titles under 1-2-3. The command is

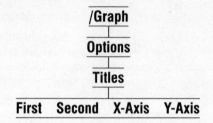

The first and second lines of the title, up to 39 characters in length each, are centered at the top of the graph. The first line is set at full size (100 percent) and the second line at half size (50 percent). When you bring the same graph up under Allways, you will be able to adjust the relative sizes of the two fonts brought over from 1-2-3.

The X-axis and Y-axis settings identify titles that go below the X-axis or to the left of the Y-axis on line, bar, stacked bar, and XY graphs. These titles also can be up to 39 characters long.

Graphing Formats

Using 1-2-3, in XY and line graphs, you can instruct the system to connect the data points with lines, to identify the data points with symbols, or both.

Going without lines creates a scatter graph. Inserting lines in an XY graph can result in a meaningless jumble if the 1-2-3 data has not been placed in an ascending or a descending order before graphing.

The command for graphing options under 1-2-3 is

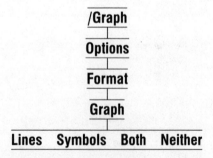

These commands are valid for line and XY graphs.

Used to instruct the system to display data points using lines, symbols, a combination of both, or data labels.

With the 1-2-3 system you also can insert data labels in a graph. These can be points of information associated with a particular piece of data or they can, in special instances, be used instead of symbols.

Figure 9.31
A promotional text chart

CAPABILITY	VENDOR				
	Digital	Apple	Sun	IBM	Apollo
Designs, Manufactures and Markets Terminals	▨	☐	☐	▨	☐
Designs, Manufactures and Markets PCs	▨	▨	☐	▨	☐
Designs, Manufactures and Markets Workstations	▨	☐	▨	▨	▨
Designs, Manufactures and Markets Minicomputers	▨	☐	☐	▨	☐
Designs, Manufactures and Markets Printers	▨	▨	☐	▨	☐
Supports OSI	▨	▨	▨	☐	☐

The command for data labels under 1-2-3 is

/Graph
|
Options
|
Data-Labels

These commands are valid for line, XY, bar, and stacked bar graphs.

Data labels are named in a range of cells and identified to the system. If a data label cell contains a formula, the program will display the cell's value as a label in the graph.

You also have control over the location for the data labels in many 1-2-3 graph types:

≡ In line and XY graphs, you can instruct the system to align labels center, left, above, right, or below data points.

≡ In bar and stacked bar graphs, data labels are automatically centered above positive bars and below negative bars.

Grid Lines

Grid lines can be added to any 1-2-3 graph, with the exception of pie charts. The 1-2-3 command is

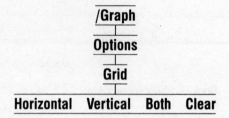

This command is valid for line, XY, bar, and stacked bar graphs.

The command is used to add or remove grid lines from the graph display. You can choose horizontal, vertical, or both types of grid lines, or you can clear previously set grids from the graph. Some users may want to use the grids only during the creation of the graph on screen. If the command is left in place when the graph is saved as a .PIC file, the graph itself will bear gridlines that will appear on the printout, whether done through Printgraph under 1-2-3 or as part of an Allways worksheet.

Shading and Color Options

In multiple bar and line charts, and in all pie charts, 1-2-3 adds crosshatch shading or colors to the various segments. This setting allows addition of a set of explanatory legends for each of the data ranges, A through F, used in the chart.

In Figure 9.32, you see the automatic assignment of crosshatches to a 1-2-3 bar graph and the associated assignment of the same crosshatches to legends.

Figure 9.33 shows the assignment of crosshatches to a 1-2-3 pie graph, based on the values 0 through 9 listed in a user-specified Range B.

Color Choices

You can instruct the system to display data range bars, graph lines, and symbols in contrasting colors on a color-capable monitor. Bars and stacked bars are drawn solid.

The command under 1-2-3 is

If monochrome (B&W) is specified, data range bars are displayed in contrasting monochrome crosshatches. When creating a pie chart, a B range can be created to specify wedge shadings.

Either setting, B & W or color, refers only to on-screen display. Color printing on a color output device is controlled by Printgraph or the Allways program.

Figure 9.32
1-2-3 bar graph
crosshatches

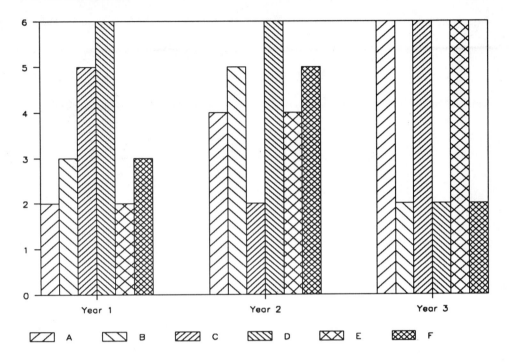

Setting Scales in 1-2-3

The command under 1-2-3 to set axis scaling is

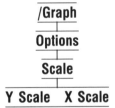

This is available for line, XY, bar, and stacked bar graphs.

You must work on the X and Y scales individually. This command also allows specification of the skip factor for X-axis labels, as in

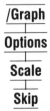

This is available for line, bar, and stacked bar graphs.

This command instructs the system to set a skip factor for display of labels on the X-axis. 1-2-3 will display the *n*th entry on the horizontal axis. For

Figure 9.33
1-2-3 pie graph
crosshatches

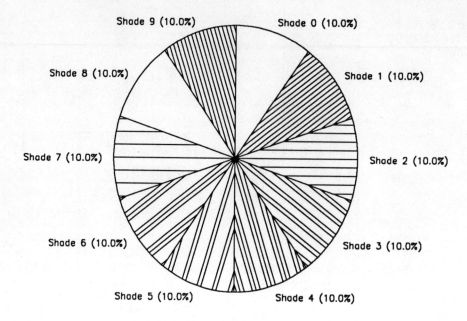

example, if the skip factor is set at 2, the X-axis will have tick marks and data points for all data, but will display only every second data label.

One level down, you can choose automatic or manual scaling, a lower and an upper scale limit, a numerical format for scale labels, and whether or not a scale indicator is to be displayed when a graph is viewed.

The command choices are displayed as

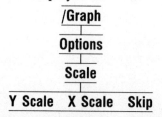

```
            /Graph
              |
           Options
              |
            Scale
              |
   Y Scale   X Scale   Skip
```

From either the **Y Scale** or **X Scale** commands you have the following scaling options. **Automatic**, the default scaling option, has 1-2-3 display all data points, using round-number scale limits that have the graph fill the screen.

The **Manual** setting displays only those data points that fall within the specified limits. Once the manual setting command has been issued, you must specify both Upper and Lower limits. The default limit for both upper and lower values is zero. Using manually set scales can result in the elimination of some data points that fall below the lower limit, or the truncation (in a bar graph) or elimination (in an XY or line graph) of data points that are greater than the specified upper limit.

The **Format** setting controls the format or style for numbers used in the graph scale. Options here are

Fixed	Constant decimal places
Scientific	Scientific notation
Currency	Monetary notation
, (Comma)	Separators between thousands
Genrl	Standard settings
+/–	Horizontal bar graph
Percent	Percentage, specified places
Date	Five choices of date style
Time	Four choices of time style
Text	Displays formulas, not values
Hidden	Specified range hidden

The **Indicator** setting tells the system whether to display scale indicators or not. The default setting is **Yes**.

Saving a Graph File

All of your work done in 1-2-3 to this point does not produce a file that can be printed—within either 1-2-3 or Allways. The graph settings must be saved, and 1-2-3 uses a special file format called .PIC files for this purpose. .PIC files can be printed with the 1-2-3 Printgraph program or uploaded to an Allways worksheet and enhanced there.

To create a .PIC file, use the **/Graph Save** command. Remember that this command saves the graph for printing purposes only. The saved graph cannot be brought back to the screen for editing. (You can, though, create a new graph using new or saved settings and store it, using the same name as the earlier .PIC file, thereby updating the graph file.) Bear in mind also that any changes you may have made to the 1-2-3 worksheet in the course of preparing the graph have not been saved until the **/File Save** command is issued.

1-2-3 will store .PIC files in the current directory, unless a different directory is specified as part of the file name.

NOTES: If you change the graph type, the previously specified data ranges are still available to the system. Thus, you can cycle through appropriate graph types to see which best displays your data.

When you save your worksheet, the most recently specified graph type and data ranges are saved along with the data.

If you want to create more than one graph from the data in a single worksheet, it may make sense to use the **/Graph Name Create** command. This saves the settings for each graph under a name and stores the settings with the worksheet. Each named setting can later be called up and displayed and edited. Note that these named graphs have not been saved as *.PIC files, though. They cannot be printed using the Printgraph program or enhanced using Allways. Related commands are **/Graph Name Use** to retrieve a previously saved graph setting file; **/Graph Name Delete** to remove an earlier graph setting file; and **/Graph Name Reset** to delete all named graphs associated with the current worksheet.

10 Using Allways with Graphs

One of the strengths of Allways is its ability to enhance the limited presentation graphics offered by 1-2-3 in versions 1 and 2.

Now, Allways does not add any graph types to 1-2-3's limited repertoire (with the single exception of its ability to enhance the 1-2-3 +/– numerical format to create a version of a horizontal bar graph). Instead, Allways adds the graphic finishing touches—in construction terms, you might say that 1-2-3 builds the house, whereas Allways does the landscaping.

Here are some of the most valuable procedures you can do with 1-2-3 graphs, using Allways.

≡ Import a 1-2-3 graph, saved as a .PIC file, into a 1-2-3 worksheet under Allways.
≡ Set the size and aspect ratio of the imported graph within an Allways-enhanced 1-2-3 worksheet, or as a standalone graphic.
≡ Change the type styles and proportional size of the graph's titles, legends, and labels, choosing from the 1-2-3 Printgraph soft fonts.
≡ Add titles, notes, and captions to graphs, choosing type styles and precise type sizes from the available selection of Allways soft fonts or the resident fonts of your printer.
≡ Inset captions and text blocks into graphs.
≡ Draw rules and outlines or add shading to graphs.

PICing Up Where 1-2-3 Stops

The 1-2-3 program treats graphs in a significantly different manner from the way it treats worksheets. Worksheets are live within 1-2-3, with changes quickly reflected; this is, after all, the reason for being of the "what if" spreadsheet product. And, although the contents of worksheet files loaded into Allways cannot be changed within Allways, it is a simple matter to press the ESC key or the Allways hot key to return to the 1-2-3 screen for quick editing. From there it is, once again, just a single hot-keystroke back into Allways.

However, 1-2-3 draws a sharp distinction between the text files of a work-sheet and the graphic file of a graph. Essentially, it splits the program into three elements:

1. The 1-2-3 worksheet, a text display and associated file structure used to prepare the numbers for plotting. Worksheet files in release 2.0 and later (the versions that will work with Allways) are stored in a special Lotus file structure that is assigned a file name extension of .WK1.

2. The graphing on-screen display, a subset of commands within 1-2-3 that enable selection of graph type and ranges, as well as a large number of customization features for labels, titles, legends, axis markings, grids, and axis scales (but still limited in comparison with full-featured presentation graphics programs).

   The graphing commands enable the 1-2-3 user to preview the appearance of a graph on screen, if a graphics-capable monitor is in use; if the monitor is a text-only device, the program will allow specification of graph elements but will not display the image on screen.

   The final product of the graph section within 1-2-3 is a graphics file. This file, which is linked to the worksheet but not actually a part of it, is stored with a file name extension of .PIC. Once the graph has been created, you must save the file using the 1-2-3 command

   /Graph Save

   NOTES: For organizational purposes, you might find it valuable to assign your graph files the same name as the worksheet file. Because they have different file name extensions, the system will be able to deal with two files with the same file name. If multiple graphs are associated with a single worksheet, you can add a number to the file name and increment it for each successive graphic image. For example, a worksheet named FISH.WK1 could have graph files called FISH1.PIC, FISH2.PIC, FISH3.PIC, and so on.

   Allways uses the most recent copy of any graph file. If you have made changes in a 1-2-3 worksheet after the creation of a graph, you will have to update the separate graph file and then save it for Allways to work with the current data.

3. The third element of the graphing facility within 1-2-3 is Printgraph, a separate program within the 1-2-3 package. If you don't own a copy of Allways or one of a handful of other 1-2-3 enhancement programs, the Printgraph program is the only way to make a hard-copy printout of your 1-2-3 .PIC file.

   When you use Allways, you will be able to do without the Printgraph program, although any titles, legends, and labels added to your graph under 1-2-3 must use one of the soft fonts that are included within Printgraph. Make sure that your 1-2-3 directory, or an associated subdirectory, contains the 1-2-3 fonts, which carry a .FNT file name extension. Files include BLOCK1.FNT, LOTUS.FNT, SCRIPT1.FNT, and so on. These are copied to your working directory from the Lotus Printgraph diskette.

If you have stored the *.FNT files in a subdirectory, you will need to let Allways know where to find them. This is done by issuing the command

/Graph FontDirectory

and then specifying the full path name of the directory where the font files are located, such as C:\123\FONTS.

Note that the Allways program uses the Lotus graphing fonts (*.FNT) from the Printgraph program but otherwise replaces that facility with its own printing instructions. The *.FNT files must be available to Allways, but there is no reason for an Allways user to enter into the Lotus Printgraph program. In fact, if disk storage space is a concern, the Printgraph files can be removed from your hard disk for a net savings of about 74 KBytes. (Be sure to keep the original copies of the program on your 1-2-3 distribution diskette and on any backup copies of the program.) Keep all files with the *.FNT extension, and remove from the hard disk the following Lotus version 2.0 files: PGRAPH.EXE; PGRAPH.CNF, and PGRAPH.HLP.

The Limitations of Printgraph

As capable as Allways is as an enhancement tool for graphs and worksheets, it is nevertheless seriously handicapped when it comes to improving the appearance of graphs. These limitations are almost exclusively the result of the choices Lotus has made in its design of the specification of the .PIC format.

1-2-3 makes all of the decisions about the location and orientation of titles, labels, and legends—the only decisions you can make involve whether to include these text elements at all. 1-2-3 will also assign the default typeface (BLOCK1) to all text elements.

Remember, too, that the choices available to you under 1-2-3 must be made before the graph file is saved as a .PIC file. Once the **/Graph Save** command is issued and a name assigned to the file, there are no other options available that will change the contents of the file.

Allways is unable to change any of these definitions, because it merely picks up the .PIC file, along with 1-2-3's limitations. These include the requirement that the text elements of the graph be constructed from one of the relatively crude soft fonts that are part of the Printgraph program.

BLOCK1—A lightweight, undistinguished sans serif face.
BLOCK2—A medium-weight version.

Lotus—A medium-weight sans serif italic font.

Bold—A heavy, Gothic-like undistinguished sans serif face.

Roman1—A medium-weight serif font somewhat similar to the classic Times Roman face, but not as finished.

Roman2—A heavier-weight version of the same face.

Forum—A bold and wide serif font.

Italic1—A lightweight serif font in italics.

Italic2—A medium-weight serif font in italics.

Script1—A forgettable lightweight script font that does not display very good penmanship.

Script2—A medium-weight script font with a bit more character than Script1, but still not appropriate for many business presentation uses.

The Italic and Script fonts are designed primarily for use with plotters, which are better than raster output devices, such as dot matrix printers, at drawing neat, straight lines. Lotus recommends use of the Block fonts with dot matrix printers.

A laser printer should be able to reproduce any of the 1-2-3 Printgraph fonts well, although you will likely discover that the 1-2-3 Printgraph soft fonts are less finished than the available internal typefaces or downloaded typefaces created especially for laser printing. The quality of those faces, plus the other limitations of Printgraph, are the reasons why you should take advantage of Allways to add as many type elements as possible on the work-sheet, rather than on the graph itself. Use Allways for titles, notes, and inset boxes wherever possible.

You should conduct some experiments with the various fonts to find the ones that work best with your printer.

Another limitation of the 1-2-3 program—some might call it a bug—involves the manner in which it deals with legends for multiple bar, stacked bar, and multiline graphs. Although the on-screen display of the 1-2-3 graph in progress will show the legends properly typeset and spaced neatly in a tight group beneath the X-axis, a printed version of the same graph will show the legends spread across the entire width of the graph—beyond both the beginning and the end of the axis. And 1-2-3 limits the number of characters it will print in the legend boxes, truncating some of the legends completely when it runs out of room.

Figure 10.1 shows a screen picture of a 1-2-3 display of a stacked bar graph in progress. On the screen picture, at this point, all six legends are neatly grouped beneath the X-axis, and all of the text associated with the legend boxes is displayed. However, when this file is saved as a .PIC file and then printed using 1-2-3's Printgraph program, the legends are chopped off at the left and the right. In Figure 10.2, you see a printout generated by **Printgraph**, using the QMS-PS 810.[1]

---

[1] For variety's sake, this graph was printed on the QMS-PS 810 laser printer switched to emulate an HP LaserJet rather than set in its standard mode as a PostScript printer.

Figure 10.1
1-2-3 Screen
display of stacked
bars with legends

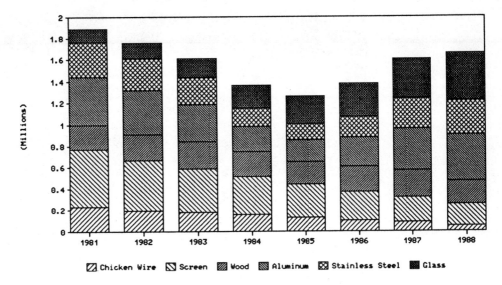

Figure 10.2
Laser printout of
.PIC file with
legends

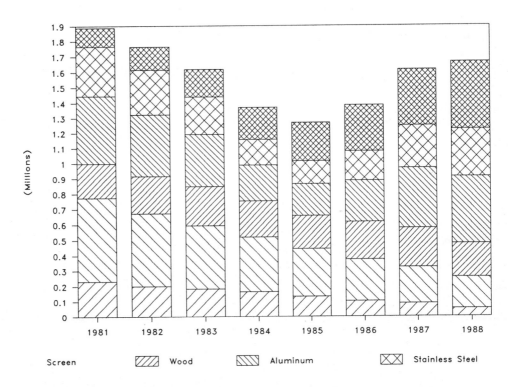

If you shift into Allways at this point and load the saved .PIC file into the worksheet, you will see the same chopped legend display (Figure 10.3).

One solution to this problem is to shorten the legend text severely. An associated caption can explain what the legends mean. Another solution is

Figure 10.3
Allways screen
display of bar chart
with legends

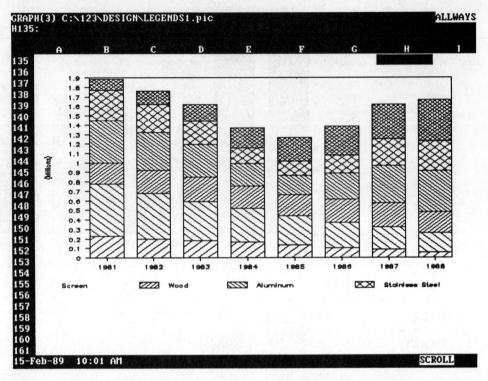

to use an inset box (Figure 10.4) by taking advantage of Allways' treatment of a .PIC file as a transparent object that can be laid over text from a 1-2-3 worksheet.

What Can Allways Do to Help?

Allways includes a number of specialized features aimed at enhancing the appearance, readability, and utility of a graph created under 1-2-3.

Before we go into the enhancement features, it is worth noting that the principal advantage Allways brings to the 1-2-3 graphmaker is the ability to integrate graphs into worksheets. This is a feature that 1-2-3 lacks, a true shortcoming when that product is measured against some of its competitors. For many users, this integration alone is sufficient to justify purchase and use of Allways.

As many as twenty 1-2-3 .PIC file graphs can be inserted in a single Allways worksheet, probably more than most users will need. These graphs can be positioned anywhere on the worksheet, including side-by-side.

NOTE: If there are more than 20 graphs to be published, the best solution may be to split up the worksheet into several pieces, each of which can have 20 graphs attached.

Figure 10.4
Laser printout of
Allways-enhanced
bar chart with
shortened legends

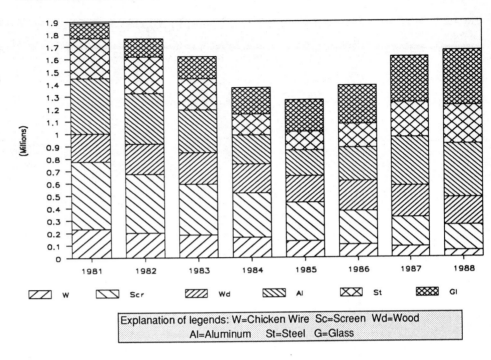

Adding a Graph

To insert a graph into an Allways worksheet, issue the command **/Graph Add**.

The program then offers a directory of .PIC files from the same 1-2-3 directory where the worksheet (WK1 file) was found. You can select a .PIC file by moving the cursor to highlight the graph you want to add; alternately, you can specify a file by typing in its name. If you manually enter the file name you can also specify a file located in a different directory or subdirectory.

You can place the graph wherever you like on your Allways worksheet, either by highlighting the range where you want the graph to appear and then pressing RETURN or by typing the cell range you want to use. In either case, the range for the graph can later be adjusted within the graph settings sheet. When you add a .PIC file to your worksheet, Allways creates an associated "settings" sheet with information about the graph (Figure 10.5).

The graph settings include:

≡ The name of the .PIC file, including the path to its storage place. You can change this file name to substitute another graph, an easy way to update or change a worksheet without altering its other settings and structure.

≡ The range on the Allways worksheet where the graph has been placed. You can alter the range for a graph already in place by selecting this setting and highlighting a new range or typing in the cell names for the new range.

Figure 10.5
Allways screen
picture of settings
menu

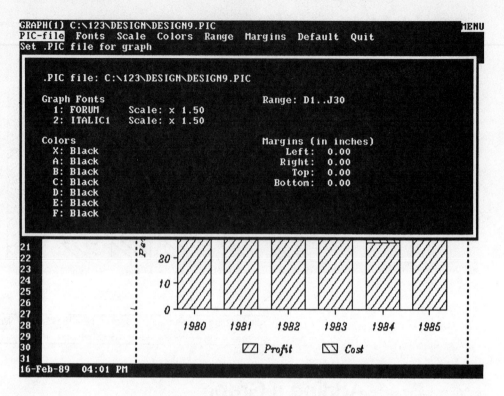

≡ The fonts that have been selected for label, legends, and the two types of titles put into the .PIC file by 1-2-3. As previously noted, you are limited to the Lotus-supplied fonts that are part of Printgraph, and only two fonts can be used per graph. By default, all .PIC graphs will arrive in Allways with both graph fonts 1 and 2 set to BLOCK1.

≡ The scaling assigned to each of the two fonts, in the range from 0.5 to 3.0. The scaling values relate to the standard font size that would be produced using 1-2-3's Printgraph. A value of 1.0 is equal to the Printgraph standard; a value of 0.5 produces characters half as large, whereas a value of 2.0 yields characters twice as large.

NOTE: The 1-2-3 Printgraph setting was designed to prevent various elements of the graph from overprinting one another. You should be able to increase the size of .PIC file text elements in an uncrowded graph. It will almost certainly be worth your while to examine an adjusted setting on the screen before it is printed to see if the new settings will work properly.

≡ The margins, in inches, that the graph is to be inset from the left, right, top, and bottom edges of the specified range. This setting is useful in adjusting the placement of a graph within a range. Insets from the edges are entered in decimal values.

≡ Colors selected for the X and Y (A through F) ranges. The availability of colors, of course, depends on the capabilities of your printer.

NOTE: If you want to eliminate the display of one range in an imported .PIC file, you can set the color for that range to white. This trick can be used, for example, in certain types of graphs in which the X-axis is not important or if you want to overlay the X-axis with rules and text created as a 1-2-3 file, enhanced under Allways.

You can also experiment with overlaying one graph on another; in such a case you will want to eliminate the display of one of the X-axes.

Whenever a graph is added to the worksheet, its initial settings are taken from the default graph settings. You can alter this default file to one that more closely matches your own standard settings by selecting **/Default Update** from the **/Graph Settings** menu.

You can remove any changes made to a graph's settings and return the settings to the default values by selecting **/Default Restore** from the **/Graph Settings** menu.

Removing a Graph

A .PIC file can be removed from the Allways worksheet in one of two ways. The most direct route is to issue the **/Graph Remove** command, which displays a list of all graphs presently placed on the worksheet. You can highlight the graph to be removed, using the cursor keys, and then press the RETURN key to delete the .PIC image from the worksheet or you can type in the name of the graph to be removed.

An alternate means of removing a graph is available if you want to substitute one graph for another. Bring the cursor into the cell space occupied by the graph you want to change, then enter the **/Graph Settings** sheet and choose the .PIC-file menu offering. The current .PIC file will be displayed; enter the name of the graph you want to substitute, then press the RETURN key.

When you use this substitution routine, you can save all of the settings that were applied to the earlier graph, including its range, margins, graph fonts, font scaling, and colors.

A Transparent Solution

You've seen how you can change the fonts and relative sizes of text elements of the graph, size the graph to a particular range, and even adjust the aspect ratio of the graph under Allways.

One other area of enhancement, which requires some creativity, offers some interesting additional facilities. This involves insetting text, rules, and shadings into or onto the graphs.

The key to this facility is the "transparency" of .PIC files added to an Allways worksheet. On most printers, text, rules, or shadings on an Allways worksheet can be seen through the clear areas of a 1-2-3 .PIC file placed in the same area. Obviously, a large black block in a bar graph or pie chart will obscure text behind it. The trick to using the transparency feature is to combine some intelligent preplanning with a bit of adjustment back and forth between 1-2-3 and Allways screens.

Let's step through the enhancement of a simple pie chart. Your goals will be to inset a table of numbers into a blank wedge of the pie and to add a title.

In Figure 10.6, you see a screen picture of a simple 1-2-3 worksheet. As a prime candidate for a pie chart, the numbers here show pieces of a whole, which in this case is a breakdown of a typical working day. Staying within 1-2-3, enter the GRAPH program, select Pie as the type of graph, and identify the X range as cells B7..B12 and the Y range as cells D7..D12. If you tell 1-2-3 to let you view the graph, you will see an image on screen like that depicted in Figure 10.7, a screen picture of a 1-2-3 display. You need to save this graph image. 1-2-3 will store the file using the .PIC specification.

Your next step is across the border into the Allways program. You'll see a text display of the 1-2-3 worksheet on the screen. You must now add the .PIC file to the Allways worksheet, using the **/Graph Add** command and selecting the appropriate graph file from the resulting directory. Figure 10.8 shows a screen picture of an Allways display that incorporates both the 1-2-3 worksheet's text and the 1-2-3 .PIC file of the pie graph.

Figure 10.6
1-2-3 screen display of worksheet for pie chart

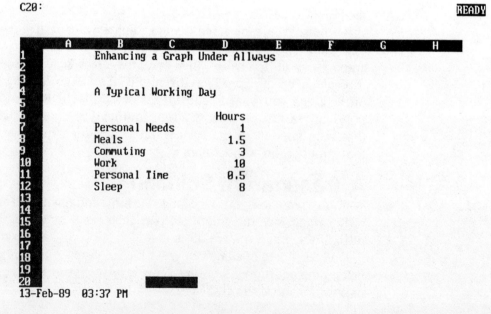

C20:   READY

	A	B	C	D	E	F	G	H
1		Enhancing a Graph Under Allways						
2								
3								
4		A Typical Working Day						
5								
6				Hours				
7		Personal Needs		1				
8		Meals		1.5				
9		Commuting		3				
10		Work		10				
11		Personal Time		0.5				
12		Sleep		8				

13-Feb-89 03:37 PM

Figure 10.7
1-2-3 screen
display of pie chart

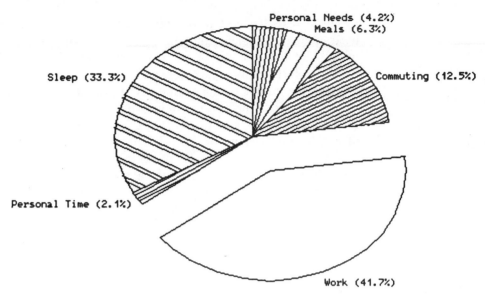

Figure 10.8
Allways screen
picture of .PIC file
with worksheet

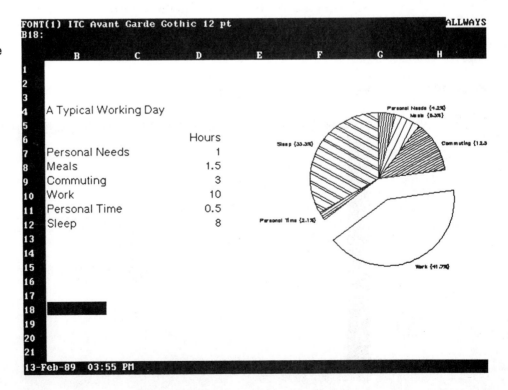

The text to be inset into a pie wedge is the block of numbers originally used to create the pie graph. One of the tricks employed here takes advantage of the fact that the cursor stays in the same cell location when you toggle back and forth between Allways and 1-2-3.

Place the cursor inside the empty pie wedge of the chart as displayed in Allways, then use the ESC key to return to 1-2-3. Note the cursor's cell location, then either enter new text, using the 1-2-3 worksheet facilities, or move a block of text from elsewhere in the 1-2-3 file to this cursor location.

Figure 10.9 shows the block of text in 1-2-3. When you shift back to Allways, the text is now inset—at the same cursor location—in the Allways worksheet, as shown in Figure 10.10.

You can use the same procedure to enter a title in the appropriate cell location of the 1-2-3 worksheet and allow it to display through a clear area of the Allways graph. Why go this route instead of merely entering a title as part of the 1-2-3 .PIC file? There are three important reasons to take advantage of Allways' facilities.

1. The title can be placed where you desire, rather than at the preset location determined by 1-2-3.
2. The title can be composed using any available font of your printer, rather than the comparatively crude fonts available as part of the 1-2-3 Printgraph program.
3. The title can be further enhanced, using boxes, lines, and shading.

In the example in Figure 10.11, as seen in a QMS-PS 810 printout, we placed a title in the lower left corner, using one of the laser printer's native

Figure 10.9
Cursor in 1-2-3
Cell H42

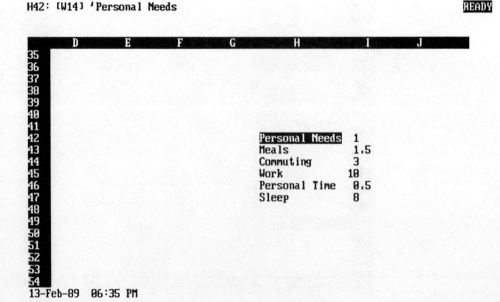

H42: [W14] 'Personal Needs   READY

Personal Needs   1
Meals   1.5
Commuting   3
Work   10
Personal Time   0.5
Sleep   8

13-Feb-89   06:35 PM

Figure 10.10
Cursor in Allways
Cell H42

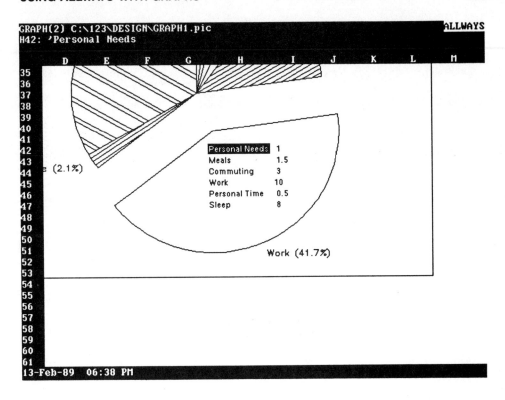

fonts. We also took advantage of a feature of some printers, including PostScript, some other laser, and some dot matrix printers, and reversed the text so that it appears as white on black. (Note that the H-P LaserJet II will not support such print reversal; the original LaserJet will.)

In this example, we enhanced the graph by putting a light shading behind part of the inset text block, and we encased the entire graph in a simple outline box.

Overlaying One Graph on Another

The transparency feature can be used, in most instances, to combine one graph with another. A simple example can be seen in Figure 10.12, in which a line graph tracing the tops of a set of stacked bars has been added to emphasize the annual totals plotted.

The process began with the creation of the stacked bar graph. A screen picture of the Allways display of the graph is shown in Figure 10.13. The next step was the creation of the line graph, using the same X- and Y-axes that were used in the stacked bar graph (Figure 10.14).

The two .PIC files are now merged into the identical range in the Allways program. This can be done by adding them both to the same range, or by adjusting the range using the **/Graph Settings** command.

Figure 10.11
Allways version of
the finished graph

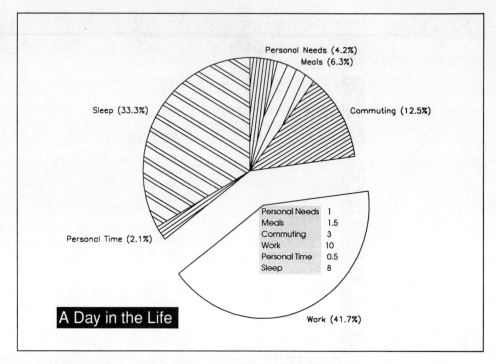

NOTE: If you use the **/Graph Settings** option in Allways to adjust locations of multiple graphs in an overlay, you should be offered a choice between the two .PIC files before you enter the settings screen. Such a choice is not offered if you began the process with the cursor lying outside the graph range or if only one of the .PIC files has been placed.

Take care not to specify titles, legends, or labels that occupy the same space in the two graphs so that one set of axis labels or titles will overprint the other. In the example, a problem arises because 1-2-3 centers the X-axis labels for stacked bar graphs, but places line-chart X-axis labels flush left. The solution is to make one of the sets of X-axis labels "invisible" by printing it in white, in this case, the line chart's labels.

Figure 10.15 shows a screen picture of the color selection menu that is part of the **Graph Settings** menu of Allways. One step before this picture was made, the X range was selected for a color change. The inverse video cursor bar shows that white is applied as a color for this range.

In Figure 10.16, you see an overlay graph in progress. The inset bar graph is acceptable, but its labels are unreadable. The trial-and-error solution involves expanding the pie chart as much as possible to allow an increase in the size of the bar graph and an adjustment of the scale for its labels. Another option involves the use of large letters or numbers instead of labels in the bar graph and using a caption to explain the meaning of the labels.

Figure 10.12
Stacked bar and
line graphs (X-axis
of line graph set to
print white)

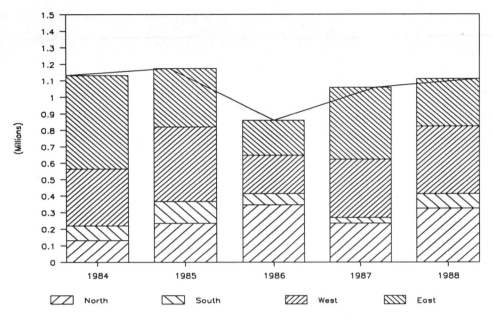

Figure 10.13
Stacked bar graph

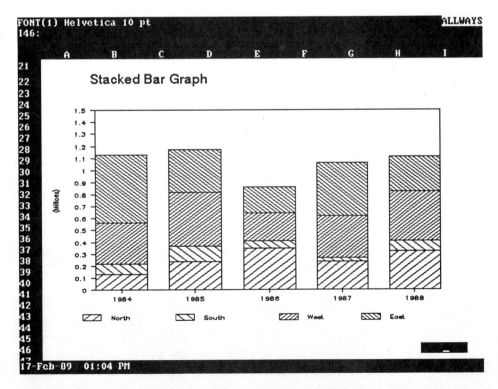

Figure 10.14
Line graph with
same axis scaling

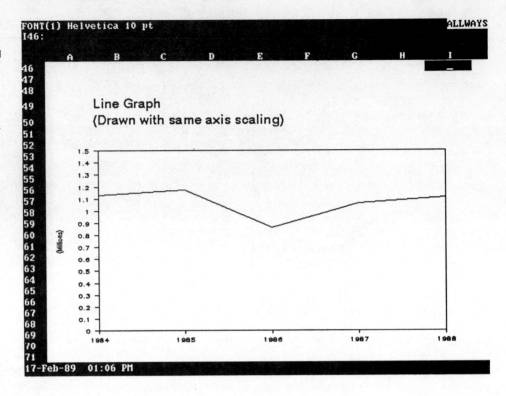

The combination of graphs using Allways and 1-2-3 is more an art than a science. You almost certainly will have to experiment with various placements of graphs to obtain the best results from your printer. You can use Allways' **/Graph Settings Margin** command to adjust the location of an inset graph within its range, and you can make some adjustments to the location of elements by changing column widths and row heights.

Be aware also that the otherwise extremely capable PostScript page definition language may block certain overlay attempts because of the way in which it constructs an image. Experiment with the order in which various elements of an overlaid graph are added within Allways to obtain the best results.

Can't This Thing Go Any Faster?

Sooner or later you will discover that Allways (like other graphics-based programs) takes a long time to scroll up or down through a graphics display. You will probably note the sluggish response if you are moving an anchored cursor down a graphics display as you set a print range or apply a font or other such range command. You also may find that you resent the seconds

Figure 10.15
Allways color menu
for ranges

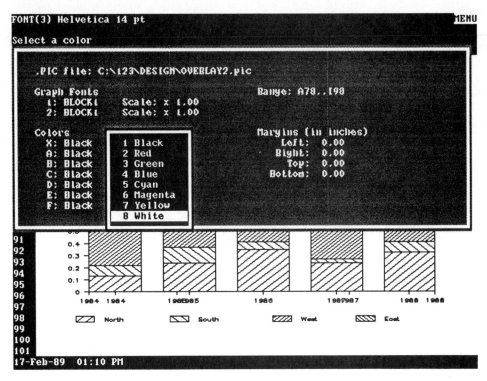

that elapse between the time you hit the hot key from within a 1-2-3 worksheet and the display of the Allways worksheet.

The speed of the loading of the program and the movement through the graphic will differ, depending on the hardware configuration you have in place and on several software decisions you may have made.

In the disk storage world, you should examine the speed of the hard disk drive and associated controller you are using on your system. Disk drive speeds are measured in a number of ways, but one benchmark to look for is the average access time; this number will tell you how long, on average, it takes the controller to locate a particular bit of information and get it into the pipeline to the microprocessor. Any particular bit may be either quickly or slowly available, depending on the location of the disk drive head at the moment the instruction is issued. The faster disk drives in use with PCs these days are in the 18-millisecond to 28-millisecond range; "slow" disk drives run 70 milliseconds or more.

In the realm of the microprocessor itself, the speediest response is likely to come from a PC based on the state-of-the-art Intel 80386 chip running at a high clock speed of 20 or 25 MHz; some Intel 80286-based systems can also run at similar high clock speeds, with similar pickups in throughput. Slower response can be expected from ordinary PC-AT models (80286-based

Figure 10.16
Bar graph inserted
in a pie graph

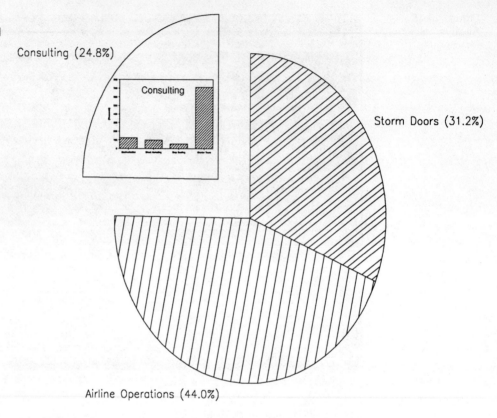

Consulting (24.8%)

Storm Doors (31.2%)

Airline Operations (44.0%)

at 7 to 10 MHz clock speeds). The slowest response is from the relatively ancient PC-XT models that use the Intel 8088 microprocessor at speeds as slow as 4.77 MHz.

Some microcomputers use various hardware tricks to eke out even more speed. These devices include the relocation of system BIOS (the Basic Input-Output System instructions of a computer) from the comparatively slow memory of a ROM chip to a faster bank of RAM; the relocation of video RAM from an adapter card into computer memory that is more closely linked to the system bus; and the use of a "memory cache" as a storage place for frequently used instructions.

Your choice of a video display card can also affect the speed of updates to the screen. The current speed demons of the video market for business users are VGA adapters that plug directly into 16-bit slots on PC-AT class machines (based on 80286 or 80386 microprocessors).

A hardware/software solution that will shave milliseconds to seconds off much of your work is the use of a *RAM disk* (also called an *electronic disk*). This option is generally limited to users of 80286- and 80386-based machines with more than 640 KBytes of available RAM. Through the use of a software program available from memory card makers and other sources (PC-DOS® and MS-DOS® versions 3.0 and above include a program called VDISK, for Virtual Disk), a block of memory is cordoned off within the machine and the operating system is instructed to treat that memory as if it were a physical disk drive.

If you were to load 1-2-3 and Allways into that electronic disk, access to both program's files would be made at the speed of the RAM chips, measured in nanoseconds (billionths of a second), rather than in the milliseconds (thousandths of a second) of a disk drive.

Remember, your program will be executing in standard memory, just as it would if the program files had been loaded from a disk drive. Your pickup in speed comes from the fact that when the computer has to go back to the program for overlays or additional subroutines, they will be available within nanosecond reach.

NOTE: If you go the route of a RAM disk, the safest way to go is to use the RAM disk solely for storage of program files and to use a physical disk drive for the storage of data and graph files. This does give up some of the speed advantages of the RAM disk, of course, but it does guard against the accidental loss of your data because of computer lockup, electrical fault, or a forgetful exit from the program before files are stored. Remember, once a computer is shut off or a RAM disk is erased, the information is forever gone. The method here is to use the 1-2-3 command:

/File Directory

to set one of your physical disk drives as the location for the data files.

To Display or Not to Display

Allways offers a program setting that disables the display of graphics. The command to shut off the image is

/Display Graphs No

Select **Yes** to turn the display back on. (The F10 function key also toggles between the two states.)

If graph display has been turned off, the box where the graph is placed will be filled with a crosshatch. (The program is still in the graphics mode, but when it comes to a .PIC file, it will save time by drawing crosshatches instead of the graph.) Of course, you need to verify that you have the correct graph in the correct position and that the various enhancements applied using Allways will accomplish your goals. However, once this has been done and you are ready to move on to other portions of the worksheet—perhaps to devote attention to enhancing the fonts and design of the text portion of the work-sheet—turning off the display will speed up your work considerably on most hardware configurations. Just remember to examine the graph at some point before you finish your work.

NOTE: Be aware that the crosshatches will fill the entire space that has been set aside for the graph, not merely the actual area *within* that space that will be occupied by the graph.

Turning off the display of graphs is different from selecting a text-only mode in Allways. You will still be able to see the effects of graphic enhancements to text using the **/Display Graphs No** command.

Figure 10.17 shows the screen picture within Allways of a graphics-capable adapter and monitor, with the display of graphs disabled. This figure shows a portion of the worksheet where two graphs have been placed one above the other, with a caption between them. The space containing the graph is filled with crosshatches. At the moment when the screen picture was made, the Allways cursor was in Cell B97. In this mode, you can see beneath the cross-hatches an underlying title, "Storm Doors: Up, Up and Away," added to the graph outside the .PIC file by enhancing text from the 1-2-3 worksheet. Both

Figure 10.17
Allways screen with graph display disabled

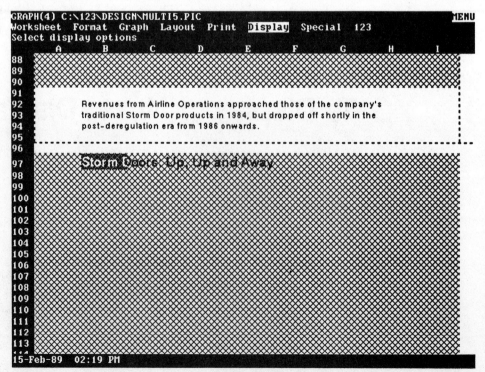

the title and the caption material are shown in approximations of their graphic character form.

When you look at the topmost line of the screen display, you see the following information:

GRAPH(4) C:\123\DESIGN\MULTI5.PIC

This line tells you that the cursor is presently located inside the box for **Graph 4** of the current Allways worksheet. This graph physically resides on disk drive **C:** in the subdirectory **\123\DESIGN** and is called **MULTI5**. Like all other graphs generated by 1-2-3, it has been stored using the **.PIC** file specification.

Working with Graphs on a Text-Only Screen

Figure 10.18 shows the same file as in Figure 10.17, but in this case Allways was instructed to operate in a text-only mode, as if our monitor and display adapter were not capable of displaying graphics.

The display of graphs has been replaced by a space full of **G**'s. On the screen, the cursor's location is noted by the fact that the **G** characters have been placed in reverse video.

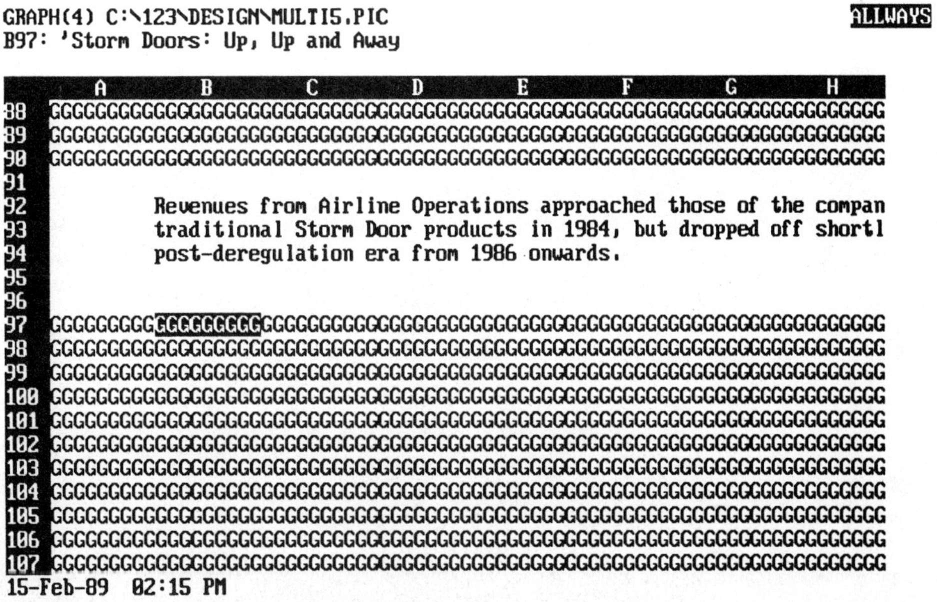

Figure 10.18
Allways screen in
text-only mode

```
GRAPH(4) C:\123\DESIGN\MULTI5.PIC                                    ALLWAYS
B97: 'Storm Doors: Up, Up and Away
        A       B       C       D       E       F       G       H
88  GGGGGGGGGGGGGGGGGGGGGGGGGGGGGGGGGGGGGGGGGGGGGGGGGGGGGGGGGGGGGGGGGG
89  GGGGGGGGGGGGGGGGGGGGGGGGGGGGGGGGGGGGGGGGGGGGGGGGGGGGGGGGGGGGGGGGGG
90  GGGGGGGGGGGGGGGGGGGGGGGGGGGGGGGGGGGGGGGGGGGGGGGGGGGGGGGGGGGGGGGGGG
91
92          Revenues from Airline Operations approached those of the compan
93          traditional Storm Door products in 1984, but dropped off shortl
94          post-deregulation era from 1986 onwards.
95
96
97  GGGGGGGGGGGGGGGGGGGGGGGGGGGGGGGGGGGGGGGGGGGGGGGGGGGGGGGGGGGGGGGGGG
98  GGGGGGGGGGGGGGGGGGGGGGGGGGGGGGGGGGGGGGGGGGGGGGGGGGGGGGGGGGGGGGGGGG
99  GGGGGGGGGGGGGGGGGGGGGGGGGGGGGGGGGGGGGGGGGGGGGGGGGGGGGGGGGGGGGGGGGG
100 GGGGGGGGGGGGGGGGGGGGGGGGGGGGGGGGGGGGGGGGGGGGGGGGGGGGGGGGGGGGGGGGGG
101 GGGGGGGGGGGGGGGGGGGGGGGGGGGGGGGGGGGGGGGGGGGGGGGGGGGGGGGGGGGGGGGGGG
102 GGGGGGGGGGGGGGGGGGGGGGGGGGGGGGGGGGGGGGGGGGGGGGGGGGGGGGGGGGGGGGGGGG
103 GGGGGGGGGGGGGGGGGGGGGGGGGGGGGGGGGGGGGGGGGGGGGGGGGGGGGGGGGGGGGGGGGG
104 GGGGGGGGGGGGGGGGGGGGGGGGGGGGGGGGGGGGGGGGGGGGGGGGGGGGGGGGGGGGGGGGGG
105 GGGGGGGGGGGGGGGGGGGGGGGGGGGGGGGGGGGGGGGGGGGGGGGGGGGGGGGGGGGGGGGGGG
106 GGGGGGGGGGGGGGGGGGGGGGGGGGGGGGGGGGGGGGGGGGGGGGGGGGGGGGGGGGGGGGGGGG
107 GGGGGGGGGGGGGGGGGGGGGGGGGGGGGGGGGGGGGGGGGGGGGGGGGGGGGGGGGGGGGGGGGG
15-Feb-89  02:15 PM
```

In this mode, the **G** characters are *not* transparent. Thus, they hide the title from the 1-2-3 worksheet. If you look up at the command line, you will note that Allways is telling you that there is a line of text, **Storm Doors: Up, Up and Away**, at that cell location.

NOTE: The Allways screen in the text-only mode is nearly identical to the 1-2-3 screen, and it is easy to become confused about which program is currently active. Allways displays the word **ALLWAYS** in the upper right-hand corner of the screen when you are viewing a file; that label, though, is obscured when the menu bar has been selected so that a command may be issued.

11 Creating Business Forms

How many preprinted forms purchased from office supply vendors do you have around your office or plant? You know the kind: the ones that are almost, but not exactly, what you need. They're the ones on which the salespeople use a pencil and a ruler to add a fourth column for quantity discount; the ones to which the service department glues a disclaimer message each time they're used; the ones on which the dimensions are listed in inches, even though your company converted to the metric system in 1972.

You can, of course, design your own forms and give them to a printer to produce. But converting your hand-drawn or typed form design to a typeset version is one of the most labor-intensive and costly services offered by most conventional printing houses. Even when you've done that, think of how many office closets are full of unusable printed forms, outdated by changing procedures and products.

One of the true powers of desktop publishing is the ability it offers users to regain full control of their business printing. Allways bills itself as "The Spreadsheet Publisher," and most users will think in terms of enhancing the appearance of Lotus 1-2-3 tables and charts. But don't stop there: Broaden your concept of "spreadsheet" to include business forms and documents.

Building a Business Form, Step-by-Step

You already know that with Allways you have a wide range of text, shading, and line capabilities, all within the powerful structure of the 1-2-3 spreadsheet program. You can apply some of these powers to the creation of office forms.

Your first project is the design and output of a customized "While you were out" phone memo form. (The standardized forms available from office supply houses are acceptable, but they do not include a few special elements that are important at your hypothetical company.) First let's list the standard elements of the phone memo form.

1. A title, "Phone Memo," "While You Were Out," or whatever
2. The name of the person for whom the call was intended—the TO line
3. The name of the person who called—the FROM line
4. The name of the caller's company—the OF line
5. The telephone number, with area code and extension, of the caller
6. The date of the call
7. The time of the call
8. A message block, plus a checklist to simplify message-taking, including Phoned, Came in, Returned Call, Wants to See You, Call Back, Will Call Again, Urgent
9. The name of the person taking the message

To these standard elements, we want to add a couple of custom features.

10. A set of check boxes to help the receptionist properly divide incoming calls between the two divisions of our company:
    Storm Door Division
    Airline Division
11. Our company name, Ferguson Storm Door and Airline Company

As with all work performed by Allways, you start with the creation of a 1-2-3 worksheet.

Before you start work, you might want to sketch a rough outline of the form on a piece of graph paper. (By the way, you could use Allways to make your own customized Forms Planning Graph Paper—we'll show you a version of that later on in this chapter.) Or you can adapt with your custom information to an existing printed form.

And remember: As you work in 1-2-3, *think Allways.*

In the case of this phone memo form, you decide to place the standard checklist (Phoned, Came In, and so on) across the bottom of the form. And, because there are seven options, you'll make your form seven columns wide, A through G.

Your first step begins within 1-2-3. Enter the Title at the top, using the ^ symbol of 1-2-3 to center the text within the column. By so doing, you take advantage of the Allways structure, which spills centered text left and right of a column too narrow for printing. Below that, enter the company name in the same manner.

Next, make the major form entries, using the leftmost column, A, for the TO, FROM, and OF categories and the center column, D, for the telephone area code, number, and extension entries.

Skip down five rows and enter the text for the operator's name; then, one row down and make your entries for the first checklist. Place the seven items in columns A through G, one item per column. Below that, make the two additional check boxes for the two divisions of the company.

Figure 11.1 shows a screen picture of the unadorned 1-2-3 spreadsheet. (For purposes of this figure, we've taken out a few rows in the message area to allow the whole worksheet to be included.) Obviously, this worksheet does not present a very attractive product. The checklist entries also run together in some of the columns.

Switching over to Allways, you see a slightly improved version of the same worksheet (Figure 11.2). Note that some of the lines of text overprint each other.

Before you set about enhancing this barren worksheet into a finished form, remember the basic rule: As you work in 1-2-3, *think Allways.*

So, go back into 1-2-3 and make a few additions to the worksheet that will allow Allways to show its stuff. First, add a row at the top of the page and a row at the leftmost edge so you can add an outline rule around the form under Allways. Now add blank columns between each of the columns that hold text. You can adjust those new columns either within 1-2-3 or within Allways; for this worksheet, we'll set the width of the new blank columns at 2 characters.

In 1-2-3, you now see a screen picture of the altered, but still ordinary worksheet (Figure 11.3). Switching over to Allways (Figure 11.4), you see the slightly improved but still almost blank canvas for enhancement.

Now it's time to pick type fonts and sizes. Allways uses the default font set, in this case Helvetica 10 point, on the attached QMS-PS 810 laser printer for all of the text in the form. The first thing you'll want to do will be to

Figure 11.1
1-2-3 screen of unenhanced phone message text

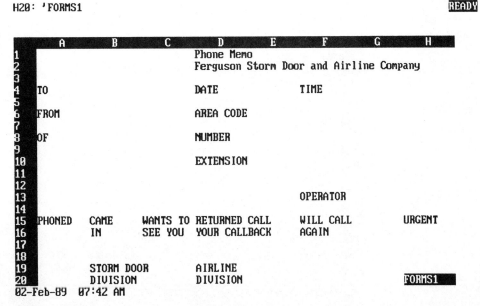

Figure 11.2
Allways screen of
the same phone
message text,
unenhanced

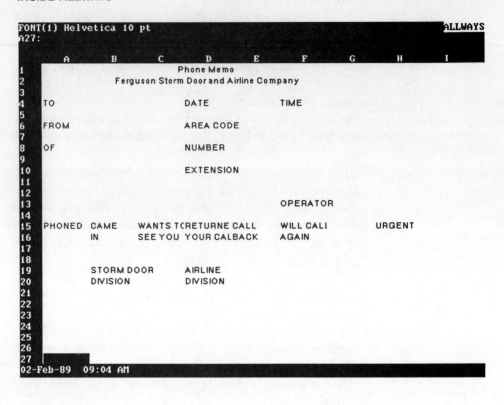

Figure 11.3
Formatted 1-2-3
phone message
text

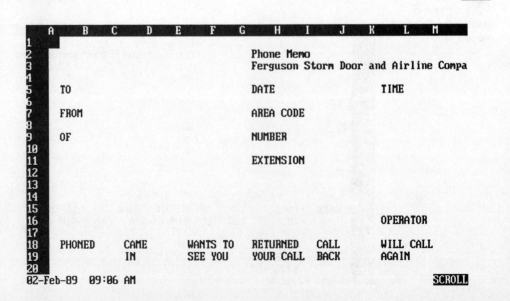

Figure 11.4
Always display of
formatted phone
message text

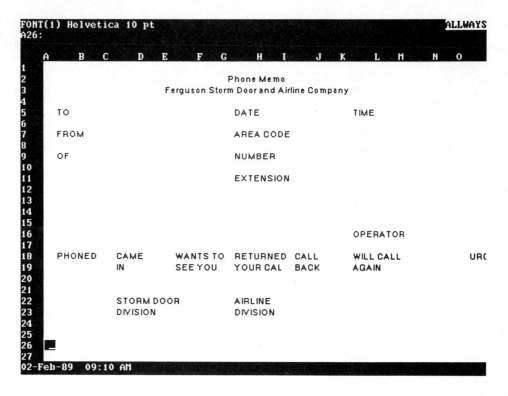

change some of the point sizes and type weights, in this case staying within the Helvetica family.

Figure 11.5 shows some new type fonts and sizes, added within Allways, for your chart. The top titles have been enlarged to 14- and 12-point Helvetica Bold and Italic, respectively. The form categories have been specified for Helvetica 8 point. Some lines and shading also have been added. The entire form has been outlined, and some breaker lines have been added between sections, using the **/Format Lines Bottom** or **/Format Lines Right** commands. The top title section and the all-important telephone number section have been given a light shading.

In preparing for the screen picture, the Allways cursor has been left in cell P16, which happens to be the top right corner of the Operator box. As a result, you see displayed across the top of the Allways screen the characteristics of that cell.

Font (1) Helvetica 8 pt, LINES:RT, Shade:LIGHT

Translated, this tells you that cell P16 uses "Helvetica typeface, in 8-point size, which is also called Font 1 of the library of fonts associated with this worksheet." Other instructions to the software order "Lines drawn to the right and top of this cell, and a light shade applied to the cell."

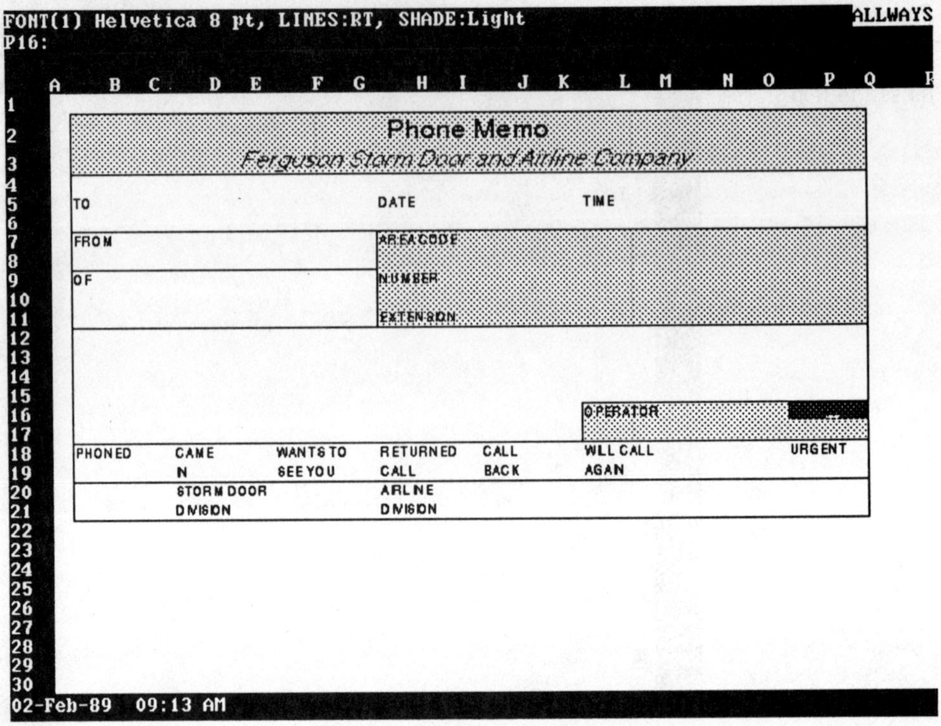

Figure 11.5
Allways display of
enhanced phone
message text

FONT(1) Helvetica 8 pt, LINES:RT, SHADE:Light   ALLWAYS
P16:

| | A | B | C | D | E | F | G | H | I | J | K | L | M | N | O | P | Q | R |

```
1
2                            Phone Memo
3              Ferguson Storm Door and Airline Company
4
5    TO                        DATE              TIME
6
7    FROM                      AREA CODE
8
9    OF                        NUMBER
10
11                             EXTENSION
12
13
14
15
16                                          OPERATOR
17
18   PHONED   CAME      WANTS TO   RETURNED   CALL      WILL CALL         URGENT
19            N         SEE YOU    CALL       BACK      AGAIN
20            STORM DOOR           AIRLINE
21            DIVISION             DIVISION
22
23
24
25
26
27
28
29
30
```
02-Feb-89   09:13 AM

Now you can put to use those 2-character columns you added to the 1-2-3 worksheet. Note that a ballot box or other symbol is missing from the checklist area at the bottom of the form. You have several options here, depending on the capabilities of your printer. For example, if your printer includes a symbol or "dingbat" font, you can use one of its symbols. If you do not have such a font, you can create your own boxlike symbol, using a pair of square brackets: [ ]. A third solution is to outline the tiny cell you created when you added those empty 2-character columns. Figure 11.6 shows a screen picture of the finished form within Allways, with the check boxes created by outlining the small cells at the bottom right of each entry. Once again, the cursor has been left in an interesting cell. Note that the **LINES** indicator here is **LRTB**, which stands for Left, Right, Top, Bottom. **LRTB** is the computer's way of specifying an outline around the cell.

Finally, Figure 11.7 shows the final printout of our form, as delivered by the QMS-PS 810 laser printer.

Sources for Forms

The best way for you, as a nonprofessional, to learn to execute forms using Allways is probably to use as templates some of the existing business docu-

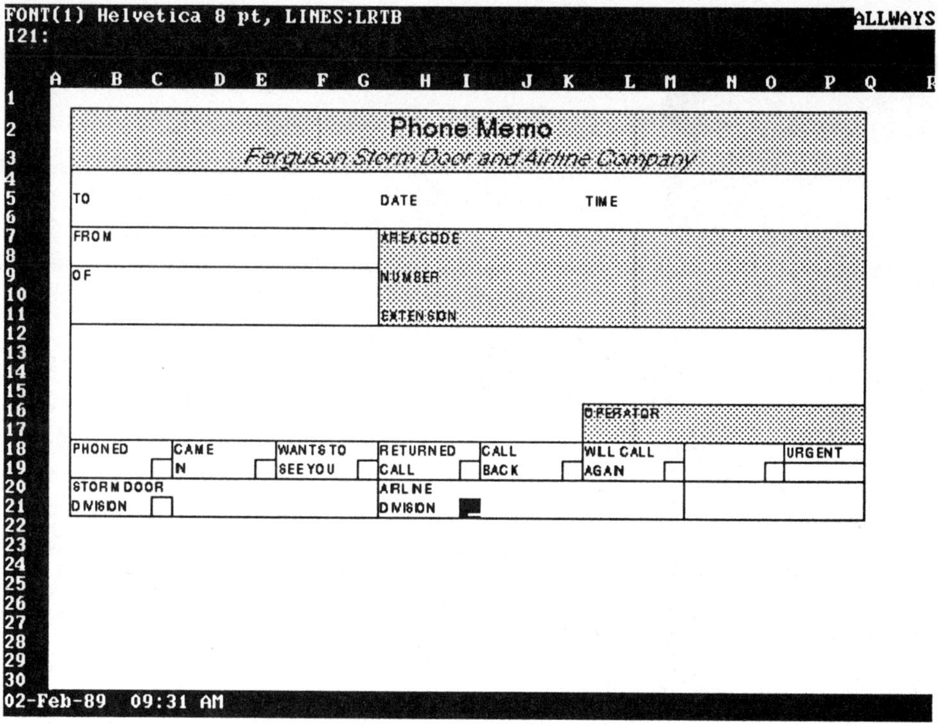

Figure 11.6
Allways screen of
enhanced text with
ballot boxes

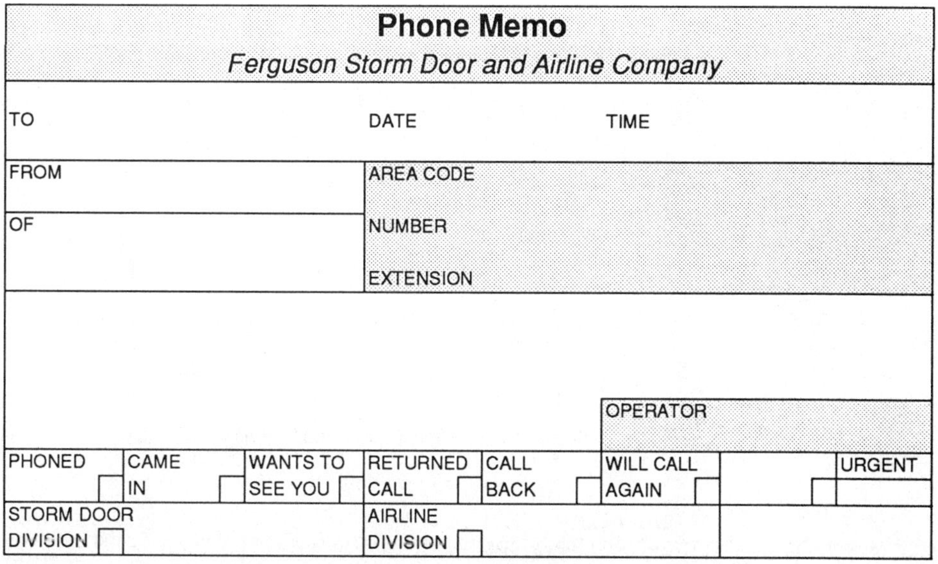

```
FONT(1) Helvetica 8 pt, LINES:LRTB                                    ALLWAYS
I21:
      A     B    C    D    E    F  G    H  I    J    K    L  M    N    O    P    Q    R
1
2                              Phone Memo
3                    Ferguson Storm Door and Airline Company
4
5     TO                         DATE          TIME
6
7     FROM                       AREA CODE
8
9     OF                         NUMBER
10
11                              EXTENSION
12
13
14
15
16                                            OPERATOR
17
18    PHONED     CAME      WANTS TO   RETURNED  CALL      WILL CALL           URGENT
19               IN        SEE YOU    CALL      BACK      AGAIN
20    STORM DOOR                      AIRLINE
21    DIVISION                        DIVISION
22
23
24
25
26
27
28
29
30
02-Feb-89   09:31 AM
```

Figure 11.7
Laser output of
completed phone
message form

Phone Memo		
Ferguson Storm Door and Airline Company		
TO	DATE	TIME
FROM	AREA CODE	
OF	NUMBER	
	EXTENSION	
	OPERATOR	

PHONED	CAME IN	WANTS TO SEE YOU	RETURNED CALL	CALL BACK	WILL CALL AGAIN		URGENT
STORM DOOR DIVISION			AIRLINE DIVISION				

ments in your office or those you have received from other companies. You might also look at some of the catalogs of standard forms from office supply companies.

For small runs of forms—100 copies or so—it most likely makes sense to use a high-quality photocopier as your duplicator. For a larger number of copies, take your completed form to an offset printshop.

A few more examples of forms created under 1-2-3 and enhanced with Allways follow. We show you first the unadorned 1-2-3 worksheet and then the Allways output.

A Sales Slip

The goal here was to personalize a standard form. We took an example from a standard office supply company's form; you might want to work from a copy of a bill from a company that performs a service similar to yours or sells a similar product. This simple form uses seven equal-width columns.

A portion of the basic 1-2-3 file can be seen in Figure 11.8. (For purposes of the screen picture shown here, we took out some rows in the middle of the worksheet to get more of the form on the screen.) A portion of the unadorned Allways screen, also with some missing middle rows, can be seen in Figure 11.9.

Working within Allways, we can begin to enhance the worksheet. One portion or another of each of the columns is ruled. The row height for the middle of the form, where the clerk is to fill in items sold, has been adjusted to make enough room for handwritten entries.

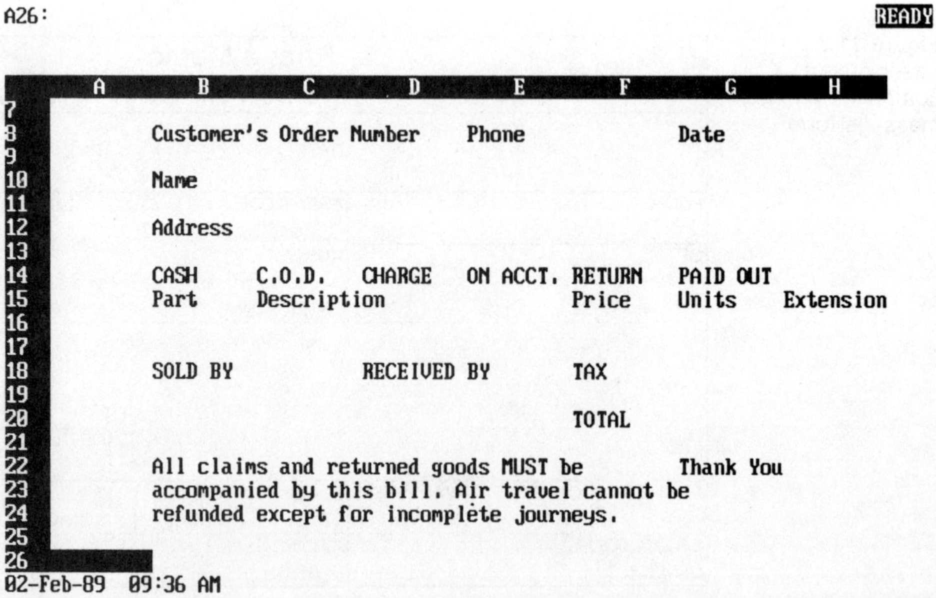

Figure 11.8
1-2-3 Worksheet for
Sales Slip

A26:   READY

```
        A        B        C        D        E        F        G        H
7
8       Customer's Order Number    Phone              Date
9
10      Name
11
12      Address
13
14      CASH     C.O.D.   CHARGE   ON ACCT. RETURN   PAID OUT
15      Part     Description                Price    Units    Extension
16
17
18      SOLD BY           RECEIVED BY       TAX
19
20                                          TOTAL
21
22      All claims and returned goods MUST be         Thank You
23      accompanied by this bill. Air travel cannot be
24      refunded except for incomplete journeys.
25
26
02-Feb-89  09:36 AM
```

Figure 11.9
Always display of
unenhanced Sales
Slip text

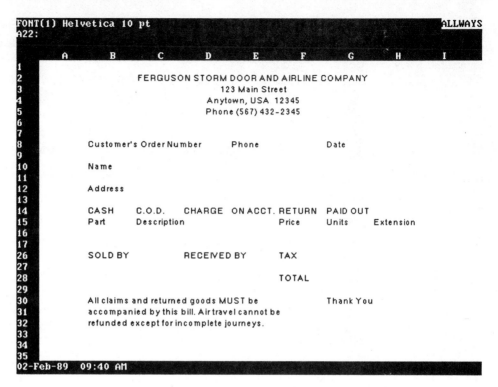

We add an empty row at top and empty columns along the left and right sides of the 1-2-3 worksheet to allow Always to draw a frame around the form.

We can make made use of one of the extra features of a PostScript printer, such as the QMS-PS 810 used for many of the examples in this book, to reverse print white type against a black background for the category line of the sales form. To reverse print type, use the **/Format Color** command and set the text color to **White** for the range you wish to reverse. The on-screen display of text in that range will disappear on a black-and-white screen, since both foreground and background are now set at white. Next, use the **/Format Shade** command and set the same range of cells to **Solid** shading. The type will be reversed on screen, and will print as such on some printers.

In addition to PostScript printers, this technique works on dot-matrix printers when the printer is instructed to use a downloaded soft font for the white text. As noted earlier, this technique also works on the original H-P LaserJet, as well as printers that emulate that particular device. However, the technique will *not* work on Hewlett-Packard LaserJet Plus or Series II machines, or printers that are set up to emulate these devices, because this type of printer can only print text in black.

The form, as enhanced using Allways, can be seen in a screen picture in Figure 11.10. A laser printer final copy is shown in Figure 11.11.

A Worksheet to Plan Forms

Earlier, we promised to show you how to draw your own sheet of graph paper for use in planning forms.

We started in 1-2-3 and created a pseudoworksheet within the worksheet, setting up columns A through J and rows 1 through 25. (Hint: To save having to enter the numbers 1 through 25, we used the 1-2-3 **/Data Fill** command and instructed the system to fill the range from 1 to 25 at a step of 1.) The labels for the columns are entered with the ^ symbol so that they are centered.

The 1-2-3 unadorned worksheet can be seen in the screen picture in Figure 11.12. We set the column width at 6 characters; as you will see in the next step under Allways, the cell width will be a function of the point size chosen for the font used as labels for the graph paper. You'll have to conduct some simple experiments if you want to use different size boxes and type from that in the example.

Moving into Allways, our first task is to create square boxes for graphing. Note that 1-2-3 has set up the columns using our specified width of 6 characters. We'll keep that and seek to space out the rows so that the boxes will be square. Using the **/Format Font** command, we select 20-point Helvetica and apply it to all of the row and column labels.

To draw the actual boxes for the graph paper, we can use either the **/Format Lines** or the **/Layout Options Grid** command.

Figure 11.11
Laser printout of
Sales Slip

FERGUSON STORM DOOR AND AIRLINE COMPANY
123 Main Street
Anytown, USA 12345
Phone (567) 432-2345

Customer's Order Number	Phone	Date			
Name					
Address					
CASH	C.O.D.	CHARGE	ON ACCT.	RETURN	PAID OUT

Part	Description			Price	Units	Extension
SOLD BY	RECEIVED BY			TAX		
				TOTAL		

All claims and returned goods MUST be accompanied
by this bill. Air travel cannot be refunded except for
incomplete journeys.

Thank You

To make the boxes with solid lines, we can use the **/Format Lines** command, selecting **All** for the placement of the lines and applying the command to the range enclosed within the rows and columns. We've also gone into the **/Layout Options LineWeight** command and selected **Light** as the line weight.

A portion of the resulting on-screen display within Allways can be seen in Figure 11.13. A laser printer output of the graphing paper is shown in Figure 11.14.

As we've noted, with Allways you can adjust the line weight (the thickness or heaviness) of lines drawn in the worksheet through the **/Layout Options**

Figure 11.12
The 1-2-3 screen
for planning forms

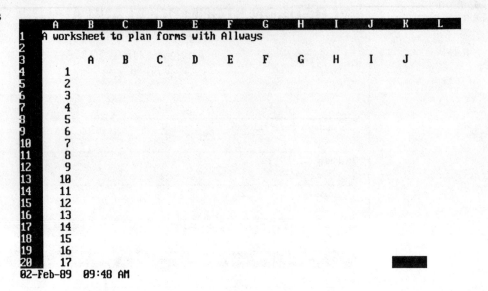

Figure 11.13
Allways display of
formatted planning
form

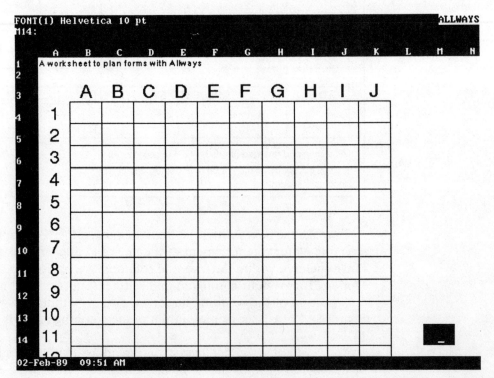

Figure 11.14 Laser printout of finished planning form

A worksheet to plan forms with Allways

	A	B	C	D	E	F	G	H	I	J
1										
2										
3										
4										
5										
6										
7										
8										
9										
10										
11										
12										
13										
14										
15										
16										
17										
18										
19										
20										
21										
22										
23										

LineWeight command. Available options are Normal, Light, or Heavy. Whatever option you select, though, is applied to all lines in a chart. There is no way to apply different weights to different lines.

However, you can achieve a similar effect by adding columns and rows to your worksheet, filling them with the **/Format Shade** command, and adjusting their widths or heights individually. You can also experiment with use of light, dark, or solid black shading.

An example of this procedure at work can be seen in Figure 11.15. We've identified six settings, including 1-, 2-, and 4-point horizontal rules and 1- and 2-character-wide vertical rules, and used light, dark, and solid line weights. Whether fine differences between light, dark, and solid shades or between 1- and 2-point-high rules can be discerned depends on the quality and resolution of your output device.

For comparison purposes, we've also included in the figure an example of a block of type enclosed within the normal line weight obtained using the **/Format Lines Outline** command. Note that it is the thinnest of the lines displayed here.

Varying the line weight will have a noticeable effect only on certain types and qualities of printers, principally high-resolution laser printers and high-density dot matrix devices. You'll have to experiment with your output device to see what options are available to you.

Figure 11.15   Shading variations within Allways

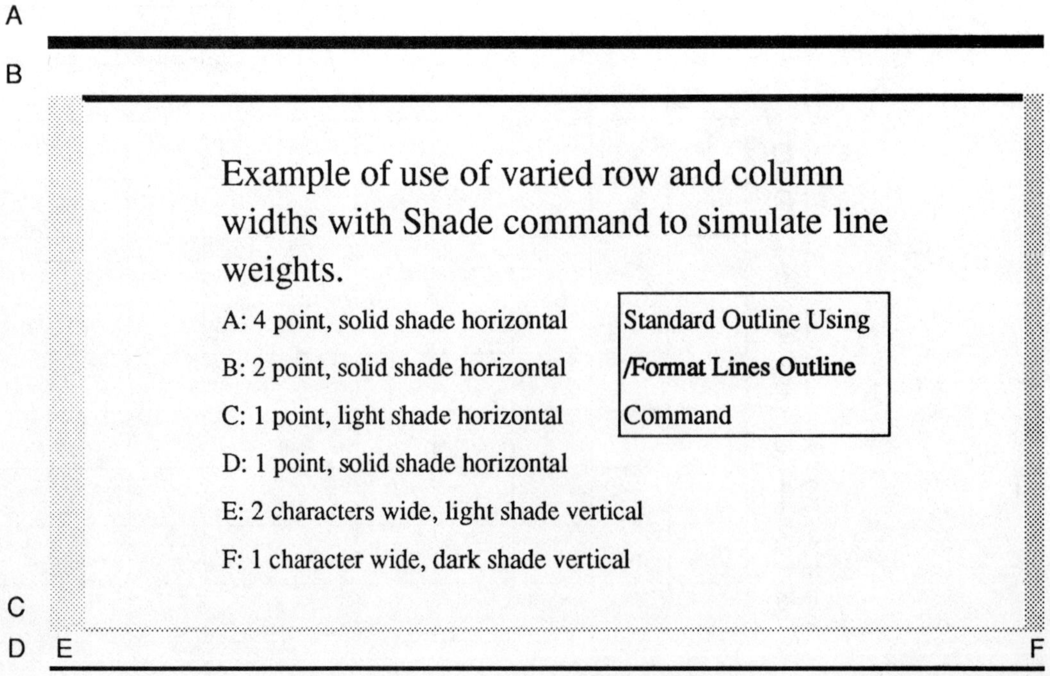

Example of use of varied row and column widths with Shade command to simulate line weights.

A: 4 point, solid shade horizontal

B: 2 point, solid shade horizontal

C: 1 point, light shade horizontal

D: 1 point, solid shade horizontal

E: 2 characters wide, light shade vertical

F: 1 character wide, dark shade vertical

Standard Outline Using

/Format Lines Outline

Command

An alternate means of drawing the boxes is to use the **/Layout Options Grid** command to turn on the lightweight dashed grid lines. The F8 function key serves as a toggle to perform the same instruction. The grid lines will cover the entire worksheet, including the titles, but for our purpose in producing a planning sheet, this is acceptable.

A laser printer output version of the graphing paper using the **Grid** command is shown in Figure 11.16.

Figure 11.16 Laser printer output of shaded form planner

A worksheet to plan forms with Allways

	A	B	C	D	E	F	G	H	I	J
1										
2										
3										
4										
5										
6										
7										
8										
9										
10										
11										
12										
13										
14										
15										
16										
17										
18										
19										
20										

Taking a Flyer

In Figure 11.17, you see a simple example of a flyer created using the 1-2-3/Allways combination.

This simple form uses a few special tricks: Two rows are reduced to 4 characters in height and filled with solid shading to create the bars at the top. The PostScript printer's capabilities are used to set white type inside a black box.

In a flyer of this sort, a less formal presentation, it is permissible to be a bit more adventurous in your choice of type faces. However, even here, we have been careful not to mix too many fonts. This flyer was made up using styles from just two type families: Avant Garde Gothic® in standard, heavy, and italic faces, and ITC Zapf Chancery® Italic for the emphasis font.

A Taxing Example

Our final, most complex form makes use of the text justification and variable column width and row height features of Allways to produce a questionnaire. In this case, we will reproduce a version of an IRS tax form.

We're not going to go step-by-step here—there are too many small steps involved. Instead, we'll check into the progress of the form at several key steps and point out some of the work that has been done.

Figure 11.17
A simple flyer

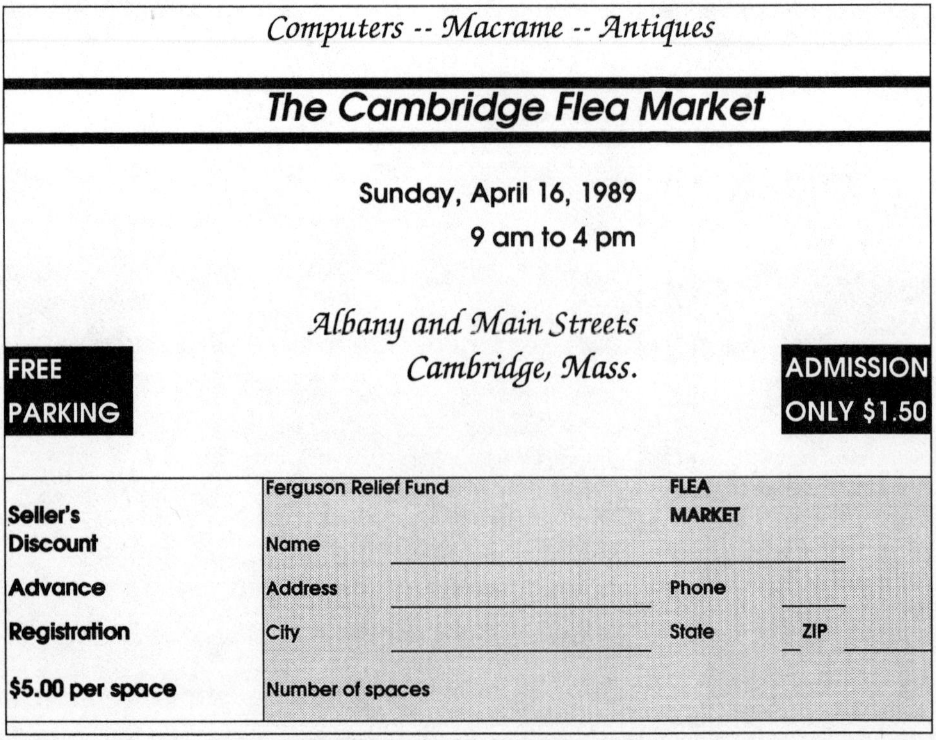

Computers -- Macrame -- Antiques

The Cambridge Flea Market

Sunday, April 16, 1989
9 am to 4 pm

Albany and Main Streets
Cambridge, Mass.

FREE
PARKING

ADMISSION
ONLY $1.50

Seller's Discount	Ferguson Relief Fund	FLEA MARKET
Advance	Name	Phone
Registration	Address	State ZIP
	City	
$5.00 per space	Number of spaces	

Figure 11.18 shows "Schedule A—Itemized Deductions" as printed and distributed by the IRS.

We enter 1-2-3 and produce a rough worksheet version. You'll quickly find that 1-2-3 columns, created using the standard video screen font, will not

Figure 11.18
An official IRS form

SCHEDULES A&B (Form 1040) Department of the Treasury Internal Revenue Service (3)	Schedule A—Itemized Deductions (Schedule B is on back) ▶ Attach to Form 1040. ▶ See Instructions for Schedules A and B (Form 1040).	OMB No. 1545-0074 1988 Attachment Sequence No. 07

Name(s) as shown on Form 1040 — Your social security number

Medical and Dental Expenses (Do not include expenses reimbursed or paid by others.) (See Instructions on page 23.)	**1a** Prescription medicines and drugs, insulin, doctors, dentists, nurses, hospitals, medical insurance premiums you paid, etc . .	**1a**
	b Other (list—include hearing aids, dentures, eyeglasses, transportation and lodging, etc.) ▶	
		1b
	2 Add lines 1a and 1b, and enter the total here . .	**2**
	3 Multiply the amount on Form 1040, line 32, by 7.5% (.075) . .	**3**
	4 Subtract line 3 from line 2. If zero or less, enter -0-. **Total** medical and dental . . ▶	**4**
Taxes You Paid (See Instructions on page 23.)	**5** State and local income taxes	**5**
	6 Real estate taxes	**6**
	7 Other taxes (list—include personal property taxes) ▶	
		7
	8 Add the amounts on lines 5 through 7. Enter the total here. **Total** taxes . . ▶	**8**
Interest You Paid (See Instructions on page 24.)	**Note:** *New rules apply to the home mortgage interest deduction. See Instructions.*	
	9a Deductible home mortgage interest you paid to financial institutions (report deductible points on line 10)	**9a**
	b Deductible home mortgage interest you paid to individuals (show that person's name and address) ▶	
		9b
	10 Deductible points. (See Instructions for special rules.) . . .	**10**
	11 Deductible investment interest (see page 24)	**11**
	12a Personal interest you paid (see page 24) . |**12a**|	
	b Multiply the amount on line 12a by 40% (.40). Enter the result .	**12b**
	13 Add the amounts on lines 9a through 11, and 12b. Enter the total here. **Total** interest ▶	**13**
Gifts to Charity (See Instructions on page 25.)	**14** Contributions by cash or check. (If you gave $3,000 or more to any one organization, show to whom you gave and how much you gave.) ▶	**14**
	15 Other than cash or check. (You must attach Form 8283 if over $500.)	**15**
	16 Carryover from prior year	**16**
	17 Add the amounts on lines 14 through 16. Enter the total here. **Total** contributions . ▶	**17**
Casualty and Theft Losses	**18** Casualty or theft loss(es) (attach Form 4684). (See page 25 of the Instructions.) . ▶	**18**
Moving Expenses	**19** Moving expenses (attach Form 3903 or 3903F). (See page 26 of the Instructions.) ▶	**19**
Job Expenses and Most Other Miscellaneous Deductions (See page 26 for expenses to deduct here.)	**20** Unreimbursed employee expenses—job travel, union dues, job education, etc. (You MUST attach Form 2106 in some cases. See Instructions.) ▶	**20**
	21 Other expenses (investment, tax preparation, safe deposit box, etc.). List type and amount ▶	
		21
	22 Add the amounts on lines 20 and 21. Enter the total.	**22**
	23 Multiply the amount on Form 1040, line 32, by 2% (.02). Enter the result here	**23**
	24 Subtract line 23 from line 22. Enter the result (if zero or less, enter zero) . . . ▶	**24**
Other Miscellaneous Deductions	**25** Other (from list on page 26 of Instructions). Enter type and amount ▶	
		25
Total Itemized Deductions	**26** Add the amounts on lines 4, 8, 13, 17, 18, 19, 24, and 25. Enter the total here. Then enter on Form 1040, line 34, the LARGER of this total or your standard deduction from page 17 of the Instructions . . . . ▶	**26**

For Paperwork Reduction Act Notice, see Form 1040 Instructions.   Schedule A (Form 1040) 1988 accommodate as much text as the smaller, proportionally spaced typefaces we will use under Allways. It is also evident that it would be a nearly impossible task to attempt to justify type to fit a particular space as we enter the type. Instead, on the basis of the form you're working from or the sketch you've worked out on paper, enter the copy to fill a range of cells roughly. In Figure 11.19, you see a screen picture of a portion of the unadorned and confusing 1-2-3 worksheet. Many of the columns have overprinted text that spills beyond cell widths.

When we switch over to Allways, before we do anything else, we'll reset the entire form in a default type size of 8 point, typical for this sort of form. You can see the still-unusable first-pass result in Figure 11.20.

Now we can get down to work. We reset the line spacing between each row to 10 points, tightening up the text's appearance. Then, we set the system to display an on-screen grid to help in positioning text (/**Display Options Grid**).

Next, we adjust the column widths. We widen column A to include all of the category listings, tighten column B to just 4 characters wide to hold option numbers, and widen column C to carry all of the text. We narrow column D to a single character (just wide enough to serve as a position holder for centering the title at the top of the worksheet) and then eliminate columns E and F by setting their widths at 0. These adjustments made, we use the /**Special Justify** command to readjust the appearance of the text blocks. The Allways worksheet, as it exists now, can be seen in Figure 11.21.

Many steps later, after we finished adjusting column widths, we're ready to apply fonts, lines, and shading. We've remained within the Helvetica family

Figure 11.19
Screen picture of
1-2-3 text for tax
form

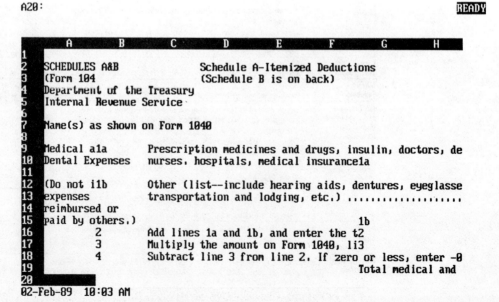

A20:   READY

```
         A         B         C         D         E         F         G         H
1
2  SCHEDULES A&B                    Schedule A-Itemized Deductions
3  (Form 104                        (Schedule B is on back)
4  Department of the Treasury
5  Internal Revenue Service
6
7  Name(s) as shown on Form 1040
8
9  Medical a1a          Prescription medicines and drugs, insulin, doctors, de
10 Dental Expenses      nurses, hospitals, medical insurance1a
11
12 (Do not i1b          Other (list--include hearing aids, dentures, eyeglasse
13 expenses             transportation and lodging, etc.) ...................
14 reimbursed or
15 paid by others.)                                              1b
16         2           Add lines 1a and 1b, and enter the t2
17         3           Multiply the amount on Form 1040, li3
18         4           Subtract line 3 from line 2. If zero or less, enter -0
19                                                      Total medical and
20
02-Feb-89  10:03 AM
```

Figure 11.20
Screen picture of
unenhanced
Allways version of
tax text

Figure 11.21
Allways enhance-
ment of tax form in
progress

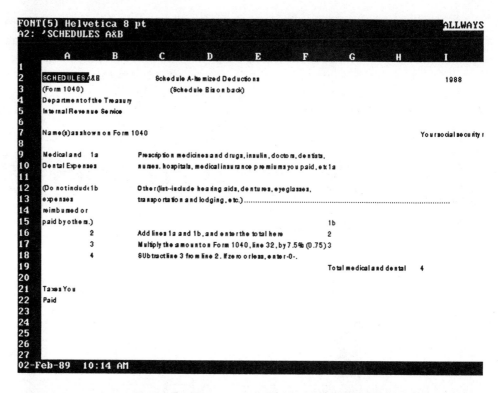

throughout, altering the point size and faces where appropriate: the overall title is in Helvetica Narrow Heavy, 17 point. Body copy is in Helvetica 8 point medium and bold; the fine print credits are in 6-point type.

In preparing the chart, we left the grid marks on the screen to help identify ranges to be outlined. Figure 11.22 shows the on-screen display with grid lines, just prior to completion of the chart. Figure 11.23 shows the final form, printed using the QMS-PS 810 laser printer.

Figure 11.22
Near-complete
Allways version of
tax form

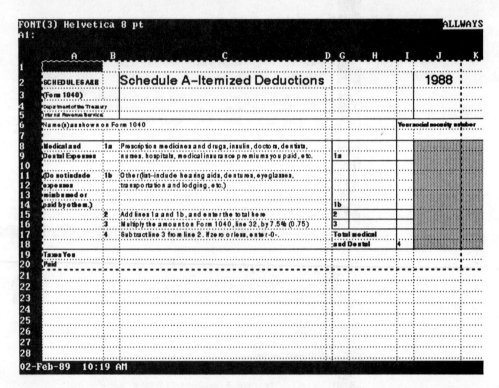

Figure 11.23
Laser printer output
of tax form

12 Printing with Allways

All of the advanced design and layout features of Allways are of little value if the user cannot obtain a printed version of the improved 1-2-3 spreadsheet.

Toward that end, Allways is intended to work with a range of state-of-the-art printers, including lasers, dot matrix, and other graphics-capable devices. The software, as well, offers a range of facilities that afford a great deal of control over the printing process.

Some of the options available to the Allways user at printing time are

≡ Sending a formatted worksheet to the selected printer.
≡ Creating a formatted worksheet file and storing it on disk for later printing or electronic distribution.
≡ Selecting an alternate printer from among the drivers available.
≡ Changing the output port (interface).
≡ Selecting the range of cells or pages to be printed.
≡ Setting page breaks.
≡ On laser printers, selecting portrait or landscape orientation.
≡ On certain laser printers, choosing the printing resolution.
≡ Selecting font cartridges on printers with this feature.
≡ Specifying pagination options for headers and footers, including page numbers.
≡ Choosing options specific to the printer being used, including selection of paper tray or manual feed.
≡ Specifying the number of copies to be printed.

Before You Begin

Printing (to an output device or file) a worksheet formatted under Allways must be done from within the Allways program because the underlying 1-2-3 worksheet is not altered by Allways. Instead, a second file, with formatting instructions, is prepared by Allways, and the program uses the two files to create the instructions for your printer.

NOTE: The file that Allways creates carries the same file name as the 1-2-3 worksheet with which it is associated. The 1-2-3 file has a file name extension of .WK1, and the Allways file uses an extension of .ALL. Because the Allways file is saved at the same time as the 1-2-3 worksheet is saved, both will display the same date and time (within a few seconds) in the MS-DOS or PC-DOS directory.

We will assume that you have already loaded 1-2-3 with Allways added, and have entered into Allways to format a worksheet for printing. The worksheet should appear on the screen.

If there are no special settings for the worksheet, printing is as easy as this:

1. Set the range for printing.
2. Select **Go**.

As simple as that procedure is, it is still important to know about all of the various settings to which the Allways user has access. Following is a more detailed path to printing. We'll go into detail on each of them soon:

1. Set the range for printing.
2. Select Print Settings.
   a. Page to begin printing
   b. Page to end printing
   c. Page number given to first page
   d. Number of copies to be printed
   e. Instructions to the program whether to wait after each page is printed to allow manual feeding of paper stock
3. Select the Printer Configuration.
   a. Choose the printer from available printer drivers
   b. Select the appropriate interface from available parallel and serial choices
   c. Choose a paper orientation between portrait and landscape (on laser printers only)
   d. Select from available paper bins for the printer in use
   e. On selected printers, choose from available printing resolutions
   f. On selected printers, choose from available font and personality cartridges
4. a. Choose **Go** to print to the printer, *or*
   b. Choose **File** to create a printer-ready file on disk.

Printing to a File

Printing to a file is a valuable facility available under Allways. In this option, the program outputs a complete file, bringing together the underlying 1-2-3 worksheet and the Allways formatting codes in one place.

Later, you can send a group of these files to a printer in a batch mode, or you can bring the disk to another printer or another computer/printer setup. The file can also be electronically transmitted over a network or a telecommunications hookup.

In effect, printing to file is creating a "run-time" version of a 1-2-3 file formatted under Allways. As the user of the file itself you need neither 1-2-3 nor Allways to output a printed copy.

To create a print file

Press / and select **Print File**.

Enter the file name for the print file to be created. Allways will supply a file name extension of .PRN if you do not specify one.

To later send the print file to a printer, use the **COPY** command of DOS, directing the file to the proper interface. For example, to send the file to a printer attached to the standard LPT1 parallel interface, type

COPY filename.ext/B LPT1:

and press **ENTER**.

The **/B** switch is a parameter of the **COPY** command that helps prevent the printer from misinterpreting certain printer codes as an end-of-file mark, which would prematurely end printing. Use of the **/B** switch is recommended.

We've mentioned that the resulting file is the equivalent of a run-time version of Allways. Included in the .PRN file are all of the instructions needed to make your printer produce a full copy. Depending on the type of printer in use, this could result in quite a large file. For example, we took a simple bar graph created from a 1-2-3 worksheet, and gave a small amount of enhancement under Allways. We printed that Allways image as a .PRN file that could be sent to a PostScript printer for output. Here are the files and their sizes.

123WSHET.WK1	2204 bytes	(1-2-3 worksheet)
123GRAPH.PIC	1057 bytes	(1-2-3 graph)
ALLWSHET.ALL	1248 bytes	(Allways enhancements)
ALLPRINT.PRN	49462 bytes	(Allways .PRN file)

As you can see, the .PRN file for a PostScript printer ballooned to a size more than ten times as large as the total of the two 1-2-3 files plus the Allways enhancement.

The same worksheet printed to a file for output on an HP LaserJet is 158,667 bytes. Printed to a file for output on the Toshiba P351 printer, the file is 169,378 bytes.

NOTE: If you do print Allways output to a .PRN file for later printing, keep an eye on the amount of storage space you are devoting to such files. Five or six files can easily total a megabyte of storage.

Choosing a Range for Printing

Before printing can begin, it is necessary to specify the range of cells to be printed.

Press / and select **Print Range**.

You will be offered a choice to **Set** or **Clear** the range. Setting the range to a new parameter automatically clears the previous range description. Highlight the range to be printed by

≡ Entering the cell coordinates for beginning and end of the range or
≡ Putting a period at one corner or the other of the range and thereby anchoring it, then moving the cursor to the diagonally opposite corner.

The selected range will be indicated in reverse video until you press the ENTER key to accept the range.

After Allways receives its instructions for a print range, it returns the screen display to the default set of colors. The selected print range now is indicated on screen by a dashed-line box around the cells to be printed. In Figure 12.1, we can see the top left corner of a print range in a screen picture of an Allways

Figure 12.1
Allways print range

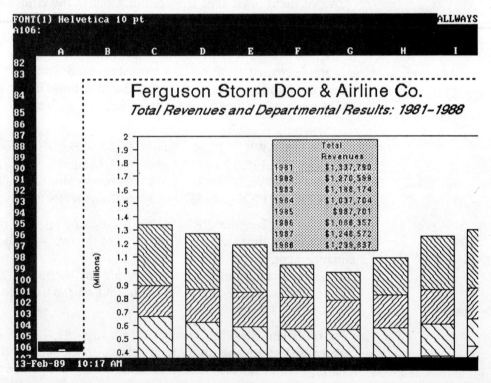

display. In this case, the print range begins in Cell B83 and extends to the right and down, beyond the screen display.

Unfortunately, Allways uses the same dashed line to indicate page breaks for printing. If your worksheet is too wide or too long to be printed on a single piece of paper using the print range you have specified, you will find at least two sets of dashed lines on the horizontal edge, the vertical edge, or both edges of the worksheet. We created an extreme example for Figure 12.2, with a screen that includes the bottom left corner of the user-specified print range as well as two Allways-imposed page breaks, one a vertical page break between columns G and H, the other a horizontal page break between rows 104 and 105.

This is, of course, a relatively minor problem. You will only see the doubled set of dashed lines if you have specified a print range wider than can be accommodated on a single piece of paper. Remember, the outer set of dashed lines represents the print range; the inner set represents the page break(s).

NOTE: One makeshift solution to the problem of confusion between user-specified print ranges and system-specified page breaks can be seen in the same figure. If you insert a blank column, A, the system's horizontal page breaks will extend across the entire screen, crossing the line of the

Figure 12.2
A confusion of
dashed lines

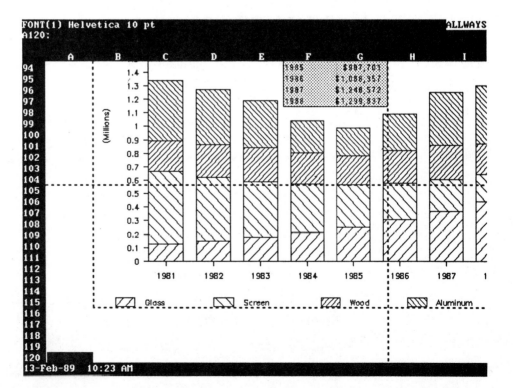

print range, and they'll be easier to see. Similarly, the system's vertical page break descends to the bottom of the screen, crossing the lower extent of the print range. In any case, you'll have to consider carefully the purpose of any dashed lines you see on your Allways screen.

One special feature of **Print Range** is convenient if you have created a worksheet that has a column of confidential numbers you do not want to print at this time. Place the nonprinting row or column at the top, bottom, left edge, or right edge of the worksheet, and exclude the row or column from the print range. One possible example of such a worksheet is a price list that includes both retail and wholesale prices. The worksheet handed to the retail customer would not have wholesale prices.

An alternate way to accomplish the same thing is to place the wholesale figures in a column or row at one of the edges of the worksheet, then issue a manual page break to exclude these numbers from printing. You see a screen picture of such a form in progress under Allways in Figure 12.3. Here, we have manually added a vertical page break between columns E and F for the version of the price sheet that will be printed out for retail customers. For wholesale customers, the vertical page break must be removed before printing.

Specifying Page Breaks Manually

As noted, Allways automatically inserts horizontal page breaks when a worksheet is too long or vertical page breaks if the worksheet is too wide to be printed on a single piece of paper.

NOTE: If the worksheet is too wide, Allways starts printing in the top left corner of the first page of the print range and goes as wide as it can before printing the page *below*. Once it has completed going down the worksheet, it will return to the top left corner of the next column break and work its way down any pages it finds there.

You can insert page breaks manually as well, to avoid page or column breaks that interfere with communication of information.

To add a row (horizontal) page break:

Press / and select **Worksheet Page Row**.

Move the cell pointer to the horizontal row where the new page should begin and press **ENTER**.

To add a column (vertical) page break:

Press / and select **Worksheet Page Column**.

Figure 12.3
A manually inserted
vertical page break

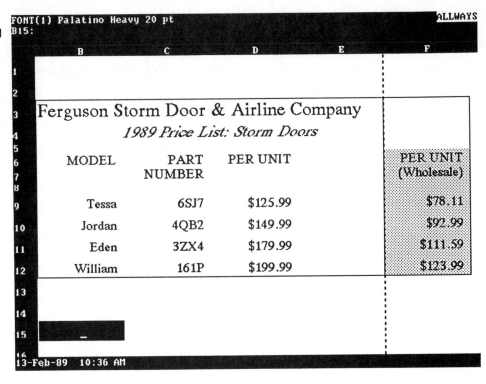

Move the cell pointer to the vertical column where the new page should begin and press **ENTER**.

NOTE: If you merely need to print out a portion of a worksheet, set a print range that is smaller than the entire Allways worksheet and send just that range to the printer.

Selecting the Configuration

The configuration window in Allways shows a range of printer options, including choice of printer and interface. Depending on the printer drivers you select, from among those loaded into the Allways program at first installation or installation update time, you may also have access to the following options:

≡ Font cartridge or cartridges
≡ Portrait or landscape orientation (available on nonimpact printers such as laser devices)
≡ Graphics resolution
≡ Paper bin or tray

You only have to enter the **Print Configuration** menu if you want to change the default device or adjust one of its settings.

As part of the installation process, you will be asked to specify one or more printer drivers. The first driver chosen is considered by Allways to be the default device; at the time of printing, you can instruct the system to use the driver for one of the other available printers. If you have added a printer since the Allways program was last installed and want to use that printer for output under Allways, you will need to exit from the program and load the AWSETUP program. Select **Add a Printer** and follow the on-screen instructions. Once you have added the printer drivers for the various printers you will be using with Allways, you can select among them by issuing the **/Print Configuration Printer** command.

After you have entered the **Print Configuration** menu but before you select **Printer**, Allways will display the default settings for a printer. An example is seen in Figure 12.4. In this case, we have instructed Allways to use the driver for the **Apple LaserWriter Plus** or **II** model (which also functions as a generic driver for most PostScript printers, such as the QMS-PS 810 actually used in this setup). The selected interface is **Parallel 1**, which in most systems is equivalent to MS-DOS device LPT1.

The orientation in this instance is **Landscape**, which rotates the image 90 degrees to print the image across the length of the paper, like an ordinary

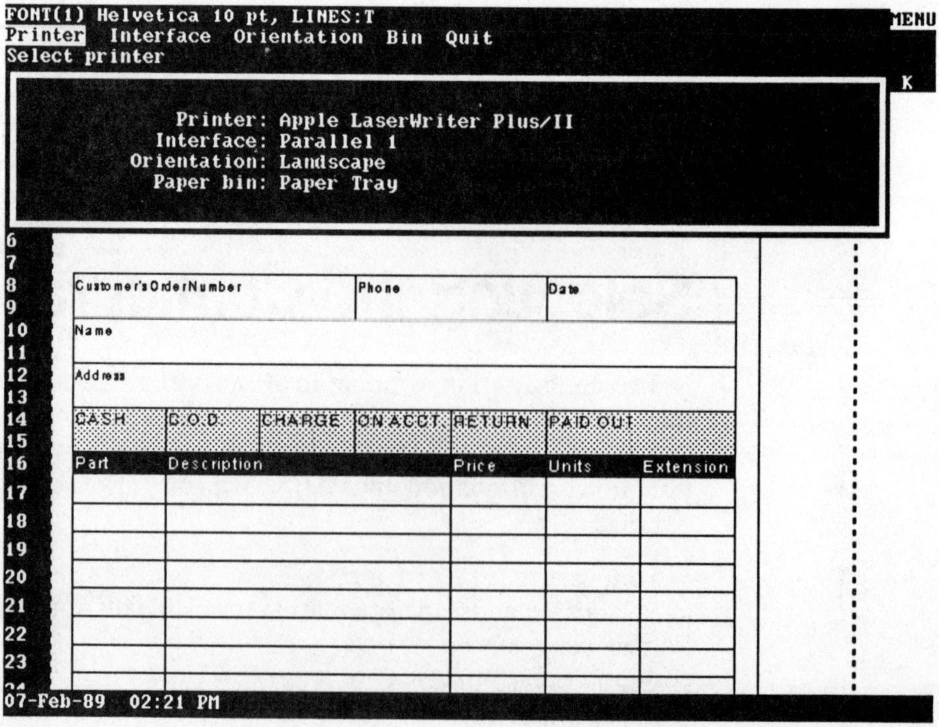

Figure 12.4
Allways Printer
Options menu

postcard. The standard orientation for laser printing is **Portrait**, which produces an image across the width of the paper, like a playing card. The paper bin selected is the standard paper tray; some printers will have more than one available tray.

If we were to select **Printer** at this point, we would next see a window listing those printer drivers we have installed to work with our copy of Allways. Figure 12.5 shows the three available choices on one of our test computers. The **Apple LaserWriter** is highlighted in this example. Figure 12.6 shows the choices of available printer ports. As noted, on most systems **Parallel 1** is the same as the device LPT1; if, for some reason, your system has reassigned those devices, you have other options.

If you plan to print graphs as part of an Allways worksheet, it is necessary to have the 1-2-3 graph fonts installed in the system. These fonts, with file name extensions of .FNT, should have been copied to your system as part of the Lotus 1-2-3 installation process. If, for some reason, they were not installed, place the PRINTGRAPH disk in drive A, set the default subdirectory of your hard disk to the location of the 1-2-3 files, then copy the files. If, for example, your 1-2-3 files reside in a subdirectory called \123 on the C> hard disk, use the command

   A>COPY *.FNT C:\123

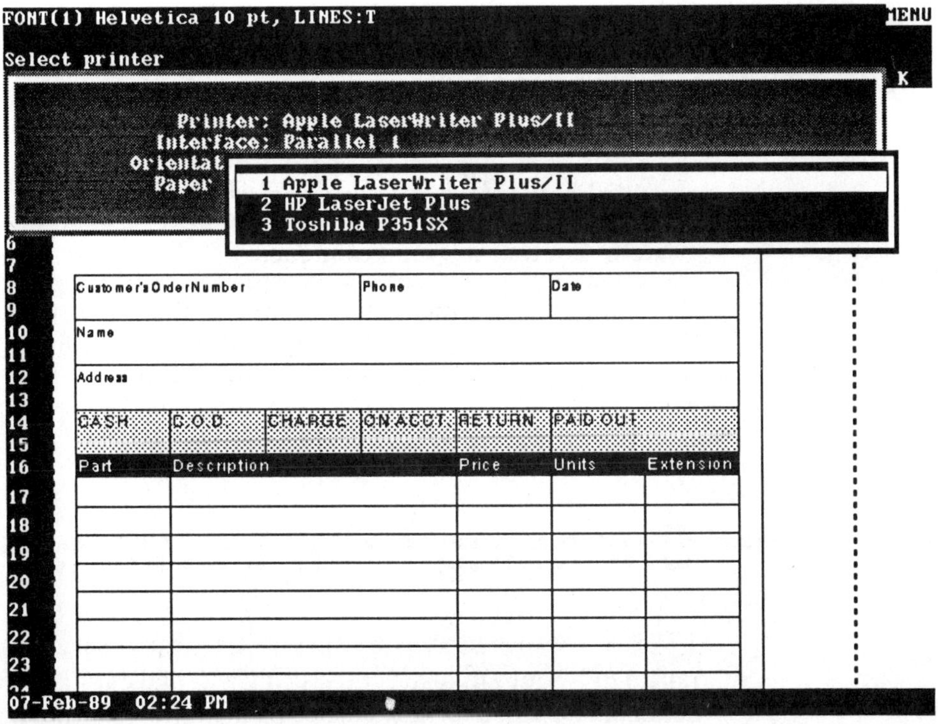

Figure 12.5
Allways Printer
Selection menu

Figure 12.6
Allways Printer Port
menu

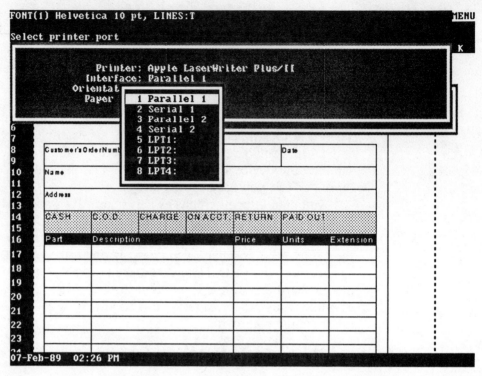

On certain printers, Allways enables you to choose the output resolution for graphics. The HP LaserJet, for example, can be directed to use one value from a range of resolutions between 75 and 300 dots per inch.

NOTE: On the HP LaserJet, changing the graphics resolution only affects the printing of graphs. Soft fonts are printed by downloading them and are not output in graphics mode.

For graphics, the higher the resolution, the better the quality of the output. You may, though, want to pick up a bit of speed while working on drafts of worksheets by selecting a low resolution level. You may also be forced into using a lower resolution if your laser printer does not have sufficient memory to handle the file sent it.

Choosing Print Settings

As an Allways user, you can select a certain set of pages (within a print range) to be output, instruct the printer to make multiple copies of the pages, and assign a value for the start of page numbering (if that has been included as part of the worksheet). A screen picture of the **Print Settings** menu within Allways is shown in Figure 12.7.

Beginning or Ending Pages for Printing

To control which pages within a print range are output, press / and select **Print Settings**. Then select **Begin** or **End**. Enter the beginning or ending page numbers.

If you assign only a beginning page number, Allways will print from that page to the end of the pages within the print range. Similarly, if you select only an ending page number, Allways will print from the first page of the print range to the page with the ending page number. You also can select both a beginning and an ending page number to select a set of pages from within the range.

NOTE: The beginning and ending page numbers are *relative* to the pagination numbering specified using the **First** command. If the first page has been numbered as 15, the beginning range under the **Print Setting Begin** command is 15. Selecting a beginning page number for printing of 20, for example, will start printing five pages into the range of pages here, on the page numbered as 20, *not* on the twentieth page of the range.

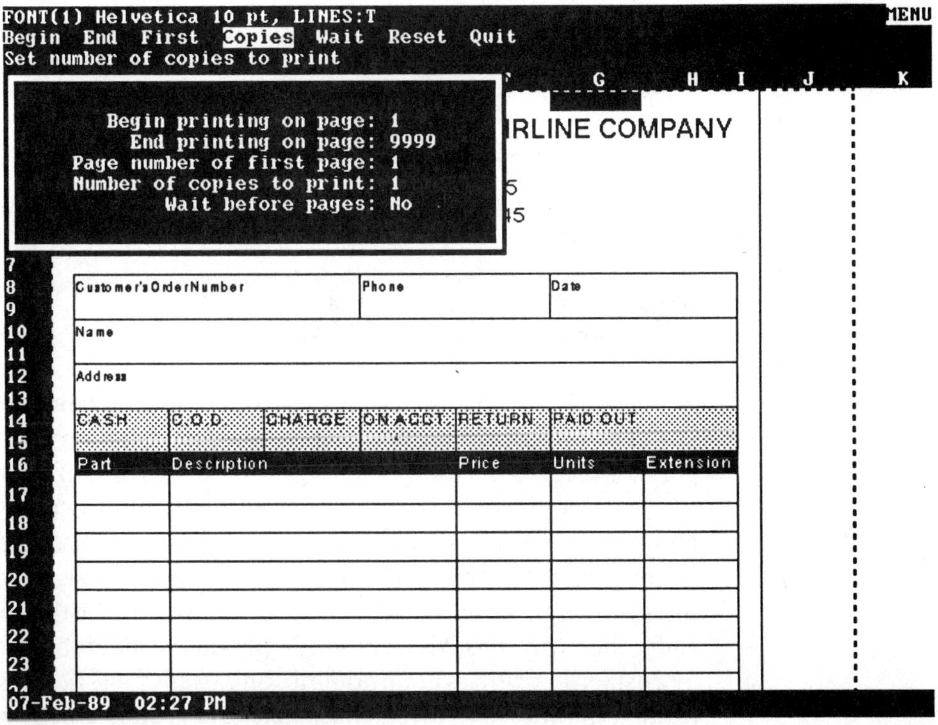

Figure 12.7
Allways Print
Settings menu

Page Numbering

To specify the value for the first page number in a header or footer, press / and select **Print Settings First**. Then enter the number for the first page.

NOTE: Page numbering will only result when the # symbol has been included in a header or footer. The default value for the first number is 1.

To add a header or footer, select **/Layout Titles**, select **Header** or **Footer**, and enter the text (up to 240 characters). To include the date in a header or footer, put an at sign (**@**) in the text. To include the current page number, put a pound sign (**#**) in the text.

To create justified sections, use a vertical bar (|) to separate the sections. For example, @|**Second Quarter**|**Page** # results in a left-justified date, **Second Quarter** centered, and the page number right-justified.

To remove a header and/or footer, use the **/Layout Titles Clear** command.

Printing Multiple Copies

To output multiple copies of the specified print range, press / and select **Print Settings Copies**. Enter the number of copies to be produced.

Wait Before Printing

The default setting for printing is **Continuous**, which assumes the use of fanfold computer paper or an automatic single sheet feeder. If, however, you want the printer to pause after printing each page to allow use of a manual feeder, press / and select **Print Settings Wait Yes**.

Restoring Print Settings

To return all print settings to their default values, press / and select **Print Settings Reset**.

PostScript Files

PostScript is a page description programming language that transmits instructions to a printer or other output device about the appearance of text, graphic shapes, and images. It requires the presence of a PostScript interpreter. In most instances this interpreter is physically located inside the printer, although it is also possible to have the interpreter installed in an adapter card in the computer or inside the computer itself. Now, there are also software interpreters that will convert graphic images to PostScript or PostScript-like code; they will, though, generally operate considerably slower.

PostScript printers are by definition raster image devices, that is, they create printed output by drawing characters and graphics with very fine, individual dots translated to the page in a television-like scan from side to side or top to bottom. Most are nonimpact printers, such as laser or ink jet printers, although it is possible to draw PostScript pages with any dot matrix printer, including impact printers. As the interpreter executes commands to create characters, graphics, or images, it converts from the PostScript description to the low-level and machine-specific raster data format of the output device.

PostScript is a very powerful language in and of itself, but it does require brute-force instructions from the computer to the printer to accomplish its output. If you have selected a PostScript printer as the current output device and want to take a look at what the instructions are like, print an Allways image as a file, rather than outputting it to the printer. Allways will save the file with a .PRN extension. Exit from Allways and 1-2-3, then type the file to your screen or examine this straight ASCII file by uploading it to a word processor.

We've created a simple printed output of a promotional card for Ferguson Storm Door & Airline. The finished product can be seen in Figure 12.8. We also saved that image as a .PRN file. The file itself was more than 10 KBytes in size for the QMS-PS 810 printer, including 293 lines of code and comments! We've reproduced just a sample of the code, as follows:

```
%!PS-Adobe-1.0
%%Creator: Allways by Funk Software, Inc.
%%Pages: (atend)
%%EndComments

/bdf { bind def } bind def
/pt2dot { 300 mul 72 div } bdf
/dot2pt { 72 mul 300 div } bdf
/_aws7 0.00 def
/_aws6 0.12 def
/_aws5 0.44 def
/_aws4 0.54 def
/_aws3 0.78 def
/_aws2 0.88 def
/_aws1 0.97 def
/_aws0 0.99 def
```

Figure 12.8
Simple example of
PostScript output

Ferguson Storm Door & Airline

Our Doors Are Always Closed For You!

```
/_port    true      def
/_yoff    792       def
/an { /AvantGarde-Book-ExtAscii /AvantGarde-Book } bdf
/ani { /AvantGarde-BookOblique-ExtAscii /AvantGarde-BookOblique } bdf
          . . .
/FontName get exch definefont pop
} bdf
/awb {
gsave setgray
newpath neg moveto
exch dup 0 exch neg rlineto
exch 0 rlineto
0 exch rlineto
closepath fill
          grestore
            } bdf
/awg {
      1 true [ 1 0 0 1 currentpoint neg exch neg exch]
        } bdf
/awi { imagemask } bdf

/awl { gsave setgray 2 setlinewidth newpath neg moveto neg lineto
stroke grestore } bdf
          . . .
2 1049 300 300 _aws7 awb
99 2 300 300 _aws7 awb
99 2 1347 300 _aws7 awb
7 ph awf
372 awv
308 awh
(Ferguson Storm Door & Airline ) awt
99 2 300 397 _aws7 awb
99 2 1347 397 _aws7 awb
99 325 300 494 _aws1 awb
          . . .
```

As you can see, it is better to have Allways do the work than to attempt
to do it yourself.

Idiosyncratic Printers

As any experienced user knows—and as any new user quickly learns—computers are still not all science. Despite lofty claims of "compatibility" and
"emulation" across heterogeneous operating systems and architectures, not

every device will work as advertised with every other device it finds. Therefore, in the absence of science, the user must apply some art. Here are a few observations we have made in the course of researching this book about a few idiosyncratic printers in use with the 1-2-3/Allways combination.

The popular Toshiba P1300 and P300 series of printers, including the P1351 and P351, are very high-quality, speedy impact dot matrix printers. They include a number of resident typefaces, a cartridge slot, and the ability to accept downloaded fonts. They are quite good at handling word processing assignments and the printout of 1-2-3 worksheets as ordinary text documents.

The Toshiba printers are also "graphics capable," but they employ an unusual protocol that gives some programs, including Allways, a great deal of difficulty when output is sent as graphics files. In the initial releases of Allways, versions 1.0 and 1.01, the Toshiba printers could not handle both graphics and text in the same file.

Another problem involves the ubiquitous Hewlett-Packard LaserJet. Nearly every software maker, including Lotus and Funk, has added drivers to support the HP products. At the same time, nearly every laser printer manufacturer, no matter how capable its own machine is, has been forced by market pressures to include a LaserJet emulation mode. Unfortunately, it appears that there are HP emulators and HP emulators—some are better than others. If you are using a non-HP laser printer operating in an HP emulation mode and are getting unplanned form feeds, garbled characters, or other unacceptable output, check with Funk Software support to see if a software fix has been created for your printer.

The earliest versions of Allways included only one PostScript driver, for the Apple LaserWriter II. In fact, almost all PostScript laser printers will operate without any problem when identified to the program as an Apple LaserWriter, and this option should be chosen. The QMS-PS 810 laser printer used for part of the preparation of this book used that driver. Future versions of Allways and other software programs will likely include some specialized PostScript drivers.

When Is What You See *Not* What You Get?

In most instances, Allways delivers on its promise as an example of that much-sought-after creature, "What You See Is What You Get" software. WYSIWYG software shows on-screen a representation of all characters and symbols to appear on a printed page, including those that appear beyond the standard 80-character width of the screen or the 24- or 25-line depth. The viewer of a WYSIWYG screen can see exactly where sentences break or are hyphenated and where page breaks occur.

A graphics-based program such as Allways also displays—on a graphics-capable monitor—representations of shadings, lines, and type font styles and sizes.

Here, then, is what Allways *will* display:

≡ Serif or sans-serif type, as directed by the user for a particular range of cells.

≡ Relative type size scales, with 36-point characters roughly twice the size of 18-point characters, and so on.

≡ Differences in column widths and row heights.

≡ Shadings, in light, dark, and solid weights.

≡ Rules and boxes.

≡ Imported graphics files, brought in as .PIC files from 1-2-3.

So, when is What You See *not* What You Get? The problem arises when you use a proportional typeface, such as many of those available in PostScript and other type families. These typefaces achieve a more finished appearance by allowing narrower letters to occupy a smaller space than wider ones. (In printing, the narrow lowercase letters are usually l, i, f, t, and j; wide characters include m and w.) You are most likely to run into this problem if you set a tight box or shade around a block of type, or if you extend type to the edges of a print range.

Figure 12.9 shows a screen picture of an Allways display. In the upper box, we can see a block of type that—on the VGA monitor—extends beyond the right side of the outline box. In the bottom box, the figure shows a block of type that appears, on screen, to fit more tightly within the box; only the hyphen breaks through the box.

Figure 12.10 shows a printout of the same file, using the QMS-PS 810 laser printer, in which the same text fits tightly within the upper box. In this case, the typeface and the particular letters used in the example are narrower than their on-screen equivalents under Allways. In the printout of the bottom box, the same block of type bursts out of its box. In this case, the typeface and letters used in the example are wider in printed form than they are in their on-screen electronic representations.

What is the solution for the Allways user? If you are using a proportional typeface and are tightly enclosing type within boxes or shading, or if your type extends close to the print range boundary you have set, you may have to experiment with your hard copy output and adjust column widths, row heights, or justify blocks of text to take account of the realities of the typefaces you are employing.

Figure 12.9
WYSIWYG screen
picture within
Allways

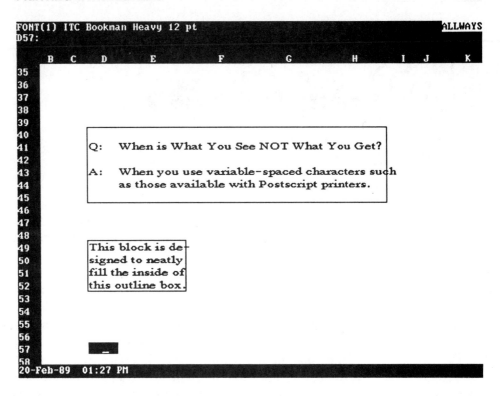

Figure 12.10
WYSIWYDG
PostScript printout
of same file

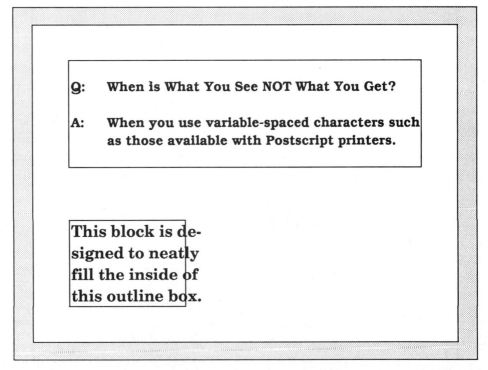

13 Macros for 1-2-3 and Allways

Although Allways does not have a separate macro command facility, you can construct macros inside a 1-2-3 spreadsheet that will execute commands within Allways.

Macros are useful keystroke programs that can help you toward more efficient and easier use of 1-2-3 and Allways. They are excellent additions to such programs, because even experienced users can find the range of 1-2-3 and Allways commands and functions intimidating and difficult to remember.

Although many software developers have copied the popular 1-2-3 menu design, making it a common user interface, with products as rich as 1-2-3, it is difficult to find just the right menu sequence for a specific job. As a 1-2-3 add-in product, Allways has copied the 1-2-3 menu structure and, basically, is easy to use. However, like 1-2-3, Allways commands—especially the ones you do not use frequently—can be difficult to remember. This is particularly frustrating when you have done the same task before but can't remember how to do it again. One way to reduce this frustration and save keystrokes with repetitive tasks is to preprogram common procedures with 1-2-3 macros.

In this chapter you learn the basics of designing and writing macros in 1-2-3 so you can tap this programming power in your use of Allways. In addition, we give you some hints on using mathematical formulas and procedures in 1-2-3 and discuss how to handle 1-2-3's powerful and useful range-naming capabilities. All of these areas are important to Allways users.

What Is a Macro?

A *macro* basically is a simple computer program that enters a series of keystrokes, menu selections, or commands for you. Lotus Development at one time called worksheet macros "The Typing Alternative." A macro can turn dozens or even hundreds of keystrokes into a simple two-key combination. You can use macros to automate lengthy, complicated procedures or simply to make repetitive tasks quicker and easier to execute.

Macro commands are entered as cell labels in a separate portion of the worksheet and are given special range names that identify them as macros. You can do anything with macros that you can do directly from the keyboard. There are even some macro commands that cannot be entered from the keyboard.

Although you still must understand the commands and functions you use in macros, these simple worksheet programs can help you be more consistent in worksheet operations. They can apply potentially difficult command sequences easily by reducing them to a few keystrokes.

When to Use Macros

Use worksheet macros any time you have to enter a series of repetitive keystrokes or to simplify difficult procedures. Don't save macros for special applications; get in the habit of using them for many of your day-to-day worksheet operations. For example, a simple macro can make it easy to save worksheets regularly, a process that requires at least five keystrokes. With the **save** macro shown later, you can do it in two keystrokes. You can reduce a 50- or 100-key command to the same two keystrokes.

Although Allways does not have its own macro capability, you can write macros inside a 1-2-3 worksheet that call up Allways, perform Allways functions, then return to 1-2-3. You can use this feature, for example, to enter Allways, merge a formatting worksheet with the current one, print the formatted results, and return to 1-2-3. If you use the LEARN program (see the discussion under "Lotus LEARN") you can record the necessary Allways keystrokes in the worksheet automatically.

Writing Macros

To write a macro, select an out-of-the-way area of the 1-2-3 worksheet and enter the label: **MACROS**. Move down two rows under the **MACROS** label and type:

'/fs~r

This command translates to **/file save RETURN Replace**. Notice the apostrophe in front of the macro sequence. This tells 1-2-3 to enter the keystrokes as a cell label. Without the apostrophe the slash bar key will invoke the 1-2-3 menu and instead of writing a macro you will execute the **Save** command sequence.

The tilde (˜) is the 1-2-3 shorthand for the RETURN key. Use the tilde in your macros when you would press RETURN if you were entering the same sequence of commands from the keyboard.

Before using this macro you must give it a macro name. Move the cursor to the cell that contains the macro and issue the **/Range Name Create** command. Enter \S (backslash S) and press **RETURN** when 1-2-3 asks for the range name. Finally, press **RETURN** to define the single-cell range under the cursor as the macro range.

Document macros with the macro name and a short description of the function. We usually put the macro name in a cell to the left of the first cell in the macro and enter a short description in a cell to the right of the macro area:

\S   '/fs~r   <<<<<**Save the Current Worksheet**

With the macro designed, written, and documented, you now can save the current file by typing **ALT-S** instead of the usual 1-2-3 menu sequence.

NOTES: You only have to name the initial macro cell, even if the macro occupies many cells.

Make certain you want to save the file by the same name as it was retrieved. If not, use the 1-2-3 menu sequence to save the file manually under the name you want to use. Thereafter the ALT-S sequence will use the new name to save the file.

HINT: Create a macro worksheet that holds the macros you will use for all or most of your worksheets. To create a new worksheet, first load the macro worksheet to make the set of common macros available. Next, save the worksheet, using keyboard commands, under the new name. Thereafter, you can use the **ALT-S** macro to save the file. If you use **ALT-S** without specifying a new name for the file, the new worksheet will be saved into your macro file.

As you learn to apply macros regularly, you will use temporary macros to type such repetitive information as column labels or worksheet format commands. We frequently use \Z for temporary keyboard macros because the ALT key and the Z key are next to each other at the lower left of the keyboard, making one-hand execution easy. (On non-IBM computers the MACRO key may be something other than the ALT key.)

Lotus LEARN

Lotus Development Corporation now provides an add-in program called LEARN that simplifies macro writing. LEARN attaches to 1-2-3 with the Add-In Manager in the same way as Allways and is invoked either through the **Add-In Manager** menu or with one of the hot keys you specify during installation.

With LEARN you do not have to write each macro step by hand. All you have to do is invoke LEARN, then step through the sequence of commands you want in the macro, and LEARN remembers the commands and writes the macro into the worksheet. LEARN will record any keystroke sequence you can enter from the keyboard, but you cannot use 1-2-3's advanced macro commands. (See the discussion of "Advanced Macro Commands" later in this chapter.)

At one time LEARN was sold as a separate program. Then Lotus offered it free through 1-2-3 dealers as part of a "Value Pack" diskette and documentation package when the decision was made to remove copy protection from 1-2-3 releases 2.0 and 2.01. LEARN is now part of the standard 1-2-3 package. If you are using an older release of 1-2-3 release 2.0 or later and you do not have the LEARN program, contact your dealer or Lotus Development Corporation directly. Although LEARN does not produce flawless macros (you probably will have to edit them to produce the final working version), it is invaluable to anyone who writes even simple macro code.

When you invoke LEARN, the following menu is displayed:

Range Erase Cancel No Yes Quit

As you highlight each menu item, the following prompts are displayed:

Range	Specify range to store keystrokes
Erase	Erase all cells in the LEARN range
Cancel	Cancel the LEARN range
No	Turn LEARN mode off
Yes	Turn LEARN mode on
Quit	Leave the LEARN add-in

The first step in writing a macro with LEARN is to specify the worksheet range to hold the program. This is one of LEARN's both strongest and weakest points. On the one hand, LEARN will not write into areas of the worksheet you have not previously set aside for the current macro, which avoids the possibility of destroying existing cell entries. On the other hand, you have to know in advance how many commands your macro will include so you can set aside the proper amount of space in the worksheet for it.

One way around this problem is to reserve several columns, top to bottom, as macro space. Then, when you write a macro with LEARN, specify one entire remaining column, or what is left of it below existing macros, as the new macro range. This way you will be assured of having enough space reserved for the new macro. If the range you specify is too small to hold the entire macro, LEARN reports an out-of-macro-space error and stops recording keystrokes.

After you have entered the last keystroke of the current macro you are recording with LEARN, invoke the LEARN menu again and select **No**, which means to stop saving keystrokes in the macro range. The last entry in your macro will show these keystrokes:

```
/fs~r
{APP2}n
```

This sample macro, the file-save macro discussed earlier in this chapter, written with LEARN shows that LEARN is installed as the second Add-In Manager program ({APP2}). After you have turned off keystroke recording, use **/Range Erase** to delete the final series of keystrokes in the macro. Although turning off LEARN as the final step of a macro as it plays back would not affect the results of the macro, it is an extra step that is not required; the command sequence uses up unnecessary worksheet space.

A slight problem surfaces when you use LEARN with Allways. Although keystrokes entered while you use Allways will be recorded into the specified worksheet macro range, each keystroke or command is entered into a separate cell. A LEARN-produced macro to invoke Allways, select the **Format** menu, and select font number 7 for the current cell, for example, records like this:

```
{APP3}
/
f
~
7
~
{ESC}
{APP2}n
```

Although it is desirable to separate commands into logical groups for ease of editing and documentation, you usually will want to put more than one keystroke into each cell. This simple macro could be rewritten like this:

```
{APP3}
/f~7~
{ESC}
```

Note that you must exit Allways before you can invoke LEARN to turn off keystroke recording. The {ESC} command in this macro returns you to the 1-2-3 worksheet. You also could use the main Allways menu to return to 1-2-3:

```
{APP3}
/f~7~
/1
```

Note that although LEARN greatly simplifies macro writing, it does not obviate the need for careful macro planning and design. The following section provides some hints on macro design that can be valuable, whether you are writing macros with LEARN or by hand.

Macro Design

Careful worksheet and macro design can reduce end user problems and enhance the usefulness of your applications. Software development—whether it is a complex application with many lengthy programs or a simple worksheet macro—consists of at least four stages.

≡ Specify what the program will do.
≡ Design the program.
≡ Write the program.
≡ Test and debug the program.

The final step, testing and debugging, can take up to half of the total program development time. Development time can be shortened by careful specification and design work. Writing a computer program or macro is a little like building a house. The end result must have a well-designed structure built on a solid foundation. Building contractors start with a detailed blueprint. Successful programmers start with detailed specifications.

Every programmer or application user probably has a different approach to program specification and design. When designing macros for 1-2-3 and Allways, you probably have gone through the specification and design stages by doing the tasks you want to program by hand. You already have a good idea of what the program must do, and you may have performed the program steps many times. That makes writing the macro relatively easy; however, you still should perform a few structured procedures to make sure the results are what you want.

≡ Define the output first.
≡ Write a description of the program.
≡ Write specifications.
≡ Design and write macro modules.
≡ Test the program.
≡ Document the program.

Define the Output First

With simple macros this phase is easy. With the **Save** macro described above, for example, the only output is to get the file saved to disk. If you are designing a macro to load Allways, format the worksheet, print it, and return to 1-2-3, the output specification has several parts, and the complete program has several identifiable components. No matter how simple or how complicated the procedure, you still must understand what results you hope to achieve before you can write a successful macro.

Write a Description of the Program

Part of the program design should include writing a description of the program steps as well as an output definition. With 1-2-3 and Allways this phase can be as simple as jotting down the menu sequence if the macro involves only menu selections. When the final program will include separate identifiable modules, this is a good time to separate the modules in your design. If you don't, you may find that the more macros you write, the more you are doing some of the same things over and over again.

By understanding fully the discrete components of your program, you can build a macro module library with routines you can use later like bricks to stack finished programs together. Obviously, the write-it-down stage will be very simple for short and simple modules. It will be more involved as the macros you design get more complicated.

Even if you are using the Lotus LEARN program to build macros, you want to understand the program sequence to minimize wrong keystrokes. It is true that with LEARN your precise keystrokes are remembered, so that even if you push the wrong key, then correct it, the end result will be correct. However, such programmed mistakes take up room on the worksheet, and they make your programs run slower. You can reduce the time you spend editing the programs that LEARN writes for you by paying attention to the program design steps, including writing down the steps.

Design and Write Macro Modules

Using LEARN or by writing a series of cell labels yourself, write the individual modules. Simple programs consist of only one module. They do one task or a series of closely related jobs to produce simple output. More involved programs may have dozens of modules.

In either case, think of your evolving macro as a series of modules or tasks. Group the tasks logically, and write the instructions to carry them out in a sequence that makes sense to you.

After the commands are entered, use **/Range Name Create** to name the first cell of the macro with an appropriate macro name. You can use any alphabetic key preceded by a \ as the macro name. If other range names exist when you invoke the create range command, 1-2-3 will show you existing names. Remember, if you specify a name that already exists, the pointer to the existing range associated with the existing name will be changed to point to the new range. If this is what you want to do, fine. Make sure, however, that you want to replace an existing range before selecting an existing name.

Test the program

Simple macros can be tested easily. You simply hold down the ALT key, press the proper macro key, and observe the results. For more complicated programs, the test procedure should be more involved. One of the dangers of automated procedures is that incorrect data can be entered or generated and go unnoticed.

During testing, use data that can be traced or checked by hand. You can separate macros into individual modules and run the modules separately. Once you are satisfied that each module is running properly, recombine the individual elements into the complete macro.

NOTE: Macro commands must be entered in contiguous cells. You can separate a macro into modules by inserting a blank row between macro elements. Use **/Range Name Create** to temporarily name the separate segments so they can be executed individually.

Document the Program

Even simple macro routines should be fully documented. As you first begin using macros, the few uncomplicated programs you write will be easy to understand. You can easily find out which routine does what if you need to modify a macro later.

As you gain more experience, however, the number of macros you use on a regular basis will grow, and each macro will become more involved. Moreover, as you learn to build macro libraries of useful subroutines (modules), you want to be able to pull these program pieces out of a master list for easy inclusion in other macros.

Therefore, get in the habit of properly documenting each macro or macro module from the very beginning. As we mentioned earlier in this chapter, one method of macro documentation is to place the actual macro name in the cell immediately to the left of the first cell in the macro, then put a brief description of the macro in a cell to the right.

\S   '/fs~r   <<<<<Save the Current Worksheet

Macros that include more than one functional module should carry separate documentation for the beginning of each module. In some cases when the macro function is not immediately clear, you may want to include documentation on each line.

If you are writing macros for use by others, people who may have to make their own changes later, then go one step further. Select a section of the worksheet as the macro documentation section and write a brief description of what each macro does, including how to use it and when to use it.

If you are using release 2 or later of 1-2-3, you have access to a convenient tool to aid with this additional documentation, the **/Range Name Table**. This command sequence generates an alphabetical range name table list in the worksheet.

Such a list shows macro locations, as well as other range names you may have created in the worksheet. Create the list in the documentation area of your worksheet, and add to it notes about the function of each range. Remember, however, that if you create a number of new range names after the documentation is written you must use the **/Range Name Table** command again or your notes won't match the range names in the table.

NOTES: Use a formula instead of a hard cell reference when creating macro range names. Precede the range name with a plus (+) sign, and format these range definition cells as text cells. This will cause the range name table to adjust itself when you rearrange the worksheet, if you reissue the **/Range Format Text** command for the formula cell.

Consider creating a separate worksheet to hold macros and documentation. Use the separate documentation file as a computer-based reference or print it for a written reference.

Make sure you update the macro documentation any time changes are made to the programs. Incorrect documentation can be worse than no documentation at all.

This attention to documentation may seem troublesome, but the effort will pay for itself later when you or someone else has to make changes or additions to your macro programs.

Physical Presentation

Carefully design the presentation of each macro on the worksheet data. 1-2-3 places some constraints on creative program design because there can be no spaces between macro commands, and the cell-oriented layout of the worksheet prevents you from conveniently indenting macro commands. There are a few things to remember about macro command presentation that can make the code more useful and easier to follow.

≡ Place macro modules so each module is called logically.
≡ Use mnemonic macro names to make using them convenient.
≡ Prominently label all macro range names.
≡ Describe each macro module's function right on the worksheet.
≡ Try to place macros in the same worksheet area each time.
≡ Use the same range names and macro names from worksheet to worksheet.
≡ Write modular code so you can reuse tested modules.

Formulas in 1-2-3

Although 1-2-3 is used for a wide range of applications, one of the most common ways that users apply this versatile program is for analysis and processing of mathematical formulas. The program is supplied with more than 100 built-in mathematical formulas in the form of @ functions, and these procedures, really formulas and programs that are part of the main 1-2-3 program, can be used directly in your spreadsheets.

There are other applications, however, where you will need to construct your own formulas and procedures. This section gives you some guidance in using 1-2-3 to process custom formulas and mathematical procedures.

Mathematical Symbols in 1-2-3

First, some basic review on mathematical processing in 1-2-3. For the most part you can use familiar mathematical symbols and procedures in 1-2-3, but there are some differences to remember. 1-2-3 uses the plus (+) and minus (–) symbols in the normal fashion. To divide one number by another, separate the two numbers with the forward slash (/) with the dividend first. To multiply two numbers together, separate them with an asterisk (*). The table in Figure 13.1 summarizes how these symbols are used.

NOTE: Cell references can be used in 1-2-3 formulas and other mathematical functions as if they were literal numbers. This capability is similar to the concept of variables in algebra.

The Order of Mathematical Operations

The examples in Figure 13.1 are simple and produce predictable results. Actual applications in your formulas probably will be more complicated, and it may be more difficult to predict the results because of the way 1-2-3 conducts mathematical operations. The table in Figure 13.2 shows the order in which mathematical operations are conducted.

Converting Formulas to 1-2-3 Format

Here is a simple formula of the type you might want to use in 1-2-3, showing the use of multiplication, division, and subtraction:

Figure 13.1
Formula symbols

Lotus 1–2–3 Math Operations

Math Operation	Lotus 1–2–3 Symbol	Examples
Multiplication	*	36 * 6; B12*C5
Division	/	536/6; C5/B12
Addition	+	52 + 3; C5+B12
Subtraction	–	75 – 15; B12–C5
Raising to a Power	^	4*2; B12^C5

Figure 13.2
Order of operations

Math Order of Operations

1 Raising a number to a power (^)
2 Multiplication and Division   (*, /)
3 Addition and Subtraction   (+, −)

NOTE: Mathematical operations are conducted left-to-right.
Operations inside parentheses are conducted first.

((C10/D10)*100)-100

If this formula were entered in a 1-2-3 cell, the value in cell C10 would be divided by the value in D10, the result of that operation would be multiplied by 100, and the literal value 100 would be subtracted from the result. This formula computes the percent increase of one value over another.

Here's a practical application for the formula: A computer vendor announces that it will market the personal computers manufactured by another vendor. The vendor announces that the price for a basic configuration of the high-end PC product, which contains some custom modifications to the original design, will be $4200. The original manufacturer sells its version of the machine for $3999. How much more, as a percent, does vendor two charge for its PC?

Enter the larger number, $4200, in cell C10 and $3999 in Cell D10. Next, enter the formula in cell A1. As soon as you press **RETURN** after entering the formula, 1-2-3 should display the value 5.026256, which is the percent increase of the larger number over the smaller one.

NOTE: 1-2-3 displays the results of formulas in the cell where the formula is entered. The formula itself appears on the prompt line above the worksheet grid.

In this example we used parentheses to document the formula. Remember that 1-2-3 conducts operations inside parentheses first. If there are parentheses within parentheses operations inside the *innermost* set of parentheses are done first. However, because mathematical processing also progresses left to right, multiplication and division first, this formula would produce the same results without the parentheses.

We used parentheses here—and you will want to use them in many of your formulas—to self-document the formula. Once you understand how 1-2-3 computes formula results, such groupings can help you understand how to construct the formula in the first place and how to modify it later if necessary.

NOTE: If you enter this formula without the parentheses you must precede the formula by a + to tell 1-2-3 that the cell entry is a formula and not a literal value.

As you work with more complex formulas, the secret to successful conversion is to work in modules, converting pieces of the formula, step by step, until the entire formula is in 1-2-3 format and is working properly.

Just as writing macros in modules can reduce errors and make the macros easier to edit, writing formulas in modules has the same benefit. You can place individual formula components into separate cells, then write a master formula that uses these cell results. If you use descriptive range names for the individual formula components, the master formula is self-documenting and becomes quite easy to debug or modify.

Range Naming Tips

An excellent 1-2-3 feature that also saves time and effort in Allways is the ability to name worksheet ranges. Carefully designed naming conventions will save you macro programming time and will help make formatting a worksheet with Allways easier. You must name at least the beginning cell of any macro range to use it. Get in the habit of using range names for other areas of the worksheet as well. Macros can call these range names instead of numeric cell references. That way, if you rearrange the worksheet, you won't have to rewrite any macros that refer to the moved range. In addition, by getting in the habit of using the same range names for similar functions in all worksheets, moving a macro from one worksheet to another will be easier.

Specifying Ranges

Use the /**Range Name Create** sequence to name a section of a worksheet. As part of this process, you must tell 1-2-3 what name you want to use and the range of cells to include with the name. You can specify the range by entering the range of cell references—**A1..B6**, for example—or by using 1-2-3's point feature to paint the appropriate cells.

HINTS: Use the /**Range Name Labels** command to assign cell labels as range names to adjacent cells. You can assign existing labels as range names for cells to the right, left, above, or below the label. This procedure simplifies naming multiple ranges.

Use the <F3> (name) key to recall existing range names. The F3 key also works during the /**Range Name Create**, /**Range Name Delete**, and /**Range Name Table** commands. When using the /**Range Name** command sequence, if you press F3 a second time you will get a full-screen listing instead of the horizontal list resembling the 1-2-3 menu at the top of the screen.

NOTE: You can assign more than one name to the same range. This can help with worksheet documentation. For example, macro names consist of only two characters, a backslash and a character. You can assign the same range a more descriptive name to aid in documentation and to make macro branch operations more clear.

Naming Ranges

1-2-3 allows range names of up to 15 characters for any single cell or range of cells. You can choose just about any name you like, but consider these practical restrictions:

≡ Use descriptive names. You should be able to tell at a glance what type of data is contained in a given range.
≡ Do not use names that can be confused with cell addresses. AS89 for annual sales in 1989, for example, or ST12 for sales totals in December, are valid range names, but they also can be cell addresses. Such confusing names can cause formulas that refer to these cells to perform incorrectly, and macros that use {goto} could end up in the wrong place.
≡ Avoid characters that could be mistaken for logical or arithmetic operators. Such names as Sales-1989, for example, could be interpreted as a subtract operation: The location Sales *minus* 1989. Names that use NOT, AND, @, +, *, or # also are poor choices.
≡ Use an underscore between words in a range name. The name TOTAL_DUE is easier to interpret than TOTALDUE, for example. You can use spaces in 1-2-3 range names, but these separate words could be misinterpreted.
≡ Use alphabetic instead of numeric characters to begin a range name. Range names with numbers at the end instead of the beginning are less confusing.

Macro Notation

1-2-3 macros actually take two forms. Just as the release 1A user's manual indicated by calling macros "The Typing Alternative," macros can be used to store a series of keystrokes so you can recall them in sequence when you need them. In this case, you simply place the keystrokes in a series of 1-2-3 cells as labels.

Early releases of 1-2-3 also included a few "bracket commands" to support the keystrokes that could not be typed directly from the keyboard as labels: function keys, for example, and the cursor movement keys. Since release 2.0, 1-2-3 users have had access to a much larger collection of Advanced Macro

Commands, which function like earlier bracket commands but offer expanded functionality.

Special Keys

Using 1-2-3 menu commands and functions in macros is as simple as typing these commands into a cell as a label instead of directly from the keyboard. The difference is that you have to precede these commands with the ' label prefix, and you have to use a few special commands to substitute for keys you can't enter directly as a label.

The RETURN key, for example, signals the end of a cell entry. If you need to use the RETURN key as part of a macro command, you type the tilde (~) where the RETURN should go.

To move the cursor from cell to cell within a 1-2-3 macro, use the commands in braces shown in Figure 13.3. Other standard curly bracket commands also are shown in this illustration.

Advanced Macro Commands

Release 2 of 1-2-3 added several significant enhancements to the software's macro language. Enhanced support for existing special keys is provided, for one thing. With the new release you can use more English-like commands to build macros, there are more true programming functions, and external file access is supported.

These advanced commands are also enclosed in braces ({}). Some of the commands require arguments in much the same way that some @ functions take arguments. There are some differences, however. For one thing, whereas the arguments with @ functions are set off in their own parentheses, the macro commands and their associated arguments are enclosed in the braces:

{MACRO Argument1, Argument2, Argument3,...ArgumentX}

Although this macro syntax is precise and must be followed every time, you can use all uppercase characters, all lowercase characters, or a combination of the two to construct your macros. Remember, the goal is to build easy-to-use and self-documented code. Use whatever combination of characters fits your application. Also be aware of an important difference in the way macros function. Most formulas and functions inside a worksheet are dynamic. As you move ranges or delete cells, the references to these locations in formulas and functions are updated automatically. This doesn't happen with macros because macros are entered as labels.

That's one reason you should establish the worksheet and get it functioning properly before building complicated macros to support it. That's also another reason to use carefully planned range names in your worksheets as much as

Figure 13.3
Basic 1-2-3 macro
commands

Standard Macro Commands

Cursor Movement Keys

{down}	Move cursor down one row
{PgDn}	Move cursor down one page
{right}	Move cursor right one column
{home}	Move cursor to first worksheet cell (A1)
{up}	Move cursor up one row
{pgUp}	Move cursor up one page
{left}	Move cursor left one column
{end}	Move cursor to first empty cell (if current cell contains data) or to first full cell (if current cell is empty). Used before {up}, {down}, {left}, {right} to determine direction of move.

Function Keys

{edit}	F2
{name}	F3
{abs}	F4
{goto}	F5
{window}	F6
{Query}	F7
{table}	F8
{calc}	F9
{graph}	F10

Other Special Keys

{del}	DEL
{bs}	Backspace
{esc}	ESCAPE
{?}	Pause for input from the keyboard. Macro resumes when the user presses return.
~	Return. Use without curly brackets.
{bs}	Backspace
{esc}	ESCAPE

possible. If macros call ranges instead of discrete cells, as you move things around on the worksheet, the macro will still work, as long as the same range name is associated with the desired operation.

In addition to the standard macro commands, you can use the commands shown in Figure 13.4. Note that some of the advanced commands (such as {**WINDOWSOFF**}) stand alone, while others require arguments. A third type of command can be used with an optional argument. Where arguments are used, they appear inside the braces to the right of the command. In the command list below, we have shown generic arguments with the commands that use them. Arguments that are enclosed in angle brackets (< >) are optional.

The advanced commands generally should be terminated with a carriage return (~).

The list below is selected from 1-2-3 advanced macro commands that may have direct application to Allways macro programmers. You probably can use many other 1-2-3 macro commands and functions to your advantage. Study the 1-2-3 manual or one of the excellent texts available on 1-2-3 macro programming.

Control and User Interface

{**BEEP** <number>}

Causes the computer speaker to issue a short beeping sound. **number** changes the frequency (sound) of the beep.

{**BREAKOFF**}

Prevents macro interruption by disabling the BREAK key. Normally you can halt a running macro by pushing CTRL/BREAK. {**BREAKOFF**} disables CTRL/BREAK.

{**BREAKON**}

Restores the normal function of the CTRL/BREAK key combination, canceling a {**BREAKOFF**} command.

Figure 13.4
Advanced macro commands are enclosed in braces

Advanced Macro Commands	
{bigleft}	Moves cursor left one screen (SHIFT/TAB)
{bigright}	Moves cursor right one screen (TAB)
{right x}	Moves cursor right by x columns
{backspace x}	Issues x backspace commands
{delete x}	Issues x DEL commands
{escape}	Equivalent to {esc} in Release 1A
{backspace}	Equivalent to {bs} in Release 1A
{delete}	Equivalent to {del} in Release 1A
{~}	Displays the tilde character (~)
{{}	Displays the left bracket character ({)
{}}	Displays the right bracket character (})

{WAIT time}

Causes a macro to halt execution until the specified time of day occurs. In 1-2-3 the current time and date is tracked with a serial number that specifies time from .00000 for midnight to .99999 for one second before midnight (11:59:59).

Data Management

{BLANK location}

Erases specified location; equivalent to the /Range Erase command.

{CONTENTS destination,source,<width>,<format>}

Assigns a string value to a specific cell. Resulting string represents the numeric contents of another cell. **Destination** specifies the *to* cell; source is the *from* cell. You can optionally specify a width for the destination cell, and a format for the resulting display. **Destination** contains a string value, not a numeric value. **format** requires a numeric format for the **source** cell.

{LET location,contents <:type>}

Assigns values to a worksheet cell without moving the cell pointer. String and numeric values supported; **location** can be a cell address or a named range. If a range contains more than one cell, {LET} assigns the specified value to the upper left cell in the range.

{PUT range,column,row,contents}

References cells only within **range** by column and row. A variation of the {LET} command, which references location within the whole worksheet.

File Management

{CLOSE}

Writes to disk any open file buffers and closes a file previously opened with the {OPEN} command; ignored if no files open.

{FILESIZE location}

Stores in **location** the size in characters of opened file.

{GETPOS location}

Stores in **location** the position of the file pointer in an open file; ignored if no file is open.

{OPEN <path>filename,mode}

Opens an external file and prepares it for use. **<path>** required only if **filename** is not in current directory.

{READLN location}

Reads information from the current file pointer location up to but not including the next carriage return/line feed. Data stored at **location**.

{READ No_Characters,location}
Copies a specified number of characters from the current file pointer position to **location**. The file pointer is updated to show where the read operation terminated.

{SETPOS position}
Sets the file pointer within an open file to **position**. Remember that the first character in a file is at position 0.

{WRITELN string}
Writes **string** to the currently open file at the file pointer position. The string is terminated with a carriage return/line feed. The **string** argument can be a literal, or a valid 1-2-3 cell reference.

{WRITE string}
Writes **string** to the currently opened file at the present file pointer position. Does not automatically terminate the written data with a carriage return-/line feed.

Keyboard Input

{GETLABEL prompt,location}
Accepts alphanumeric data from the keyboard and stores it at **location**. The **prompt** displays in the control panel to tell operator what information to enter. A RETURN terminates input.

{GETNUMBER prompt,location}
Accepts numeric data from the keyboard and stores it at **location**. The **prompt** displays in control panel to tell operator what information to enter. A RETURN terminates input.

{GET location}
Pauses macro and accepts a single character input from the keyboard and stores it at **location**. Accepts function keys (<F1> through <F12>). RETURN terminator not required.

{LOOK location}
Scans keyboard input location to see if a character has been entered since the macro started. First character in the keyboard buffer is stored at **location**. If the keyboard buffer is empty, 1-2-3 erases **location**.

Program Control

{BRANCH location}
Transfers macro execution to the **location**. Equivalent to GOTO in BASIC.

{DEFINE location1: type1, <...locationx:typex>}
Specifies storage locations for variables passed to a subroutine; sets variable type for each location.

{DISPATCH location}

Indirect branch. Program execution moves to **location**, which contains a second address that is the final destination of the branch.

{FORBREAK}

Ends a {**FOR**} loop immediately; exits loop before the specified count is reached. Use {**FORBREAK**} after a condition check to stop the loop if desired.

{FOR counter,start,stop,step,location}

Initiates **FOR-NEXT** loop. A loop is a series of program statements that executes repeatedly until some condition is met.

{IF condition}

Initiates IF-THEN-ELSE conditional compare. When **condition** is true, the THEN clause is executed; when **condition** is false, the ELSE clause is executed. {**IF**} continues with the next macro command if **condition** is false or executes macro commands that follow {**IF**} in the same cell if **condition** is true.

{MENUBRANCH location}

Branches to **location** where custom menu resides. Macro halted; execution continues at location determined by the selected menu choice.

{MENUCALL location}

Branches to **location** where custom menu resides. Macro halted; after selected menu code is executed, control is returned to the calling routine. Compare with {**MENUBRANCH**}.

{QUIT}

Halts macro execution and returns control to the console.

{RESTART}

Cancels subroutine association with a calling routine. After {**RESTART**}, macro execution ceases when a {**RETURN**} instruction is processed or when a blank cell is encountered.

{RETURN}

Terminates a subroutine and returns control to the calling routine.

{subroutine <variable1,...variablex>}

Executes **subroutine**, which is another named macro. Optionally passes variables from the calling routine to the subroutine. Variable passing requires the {**DEFINE**} command.

Screen Control

{INDICATE <string>}

Changes the mode indicator in the upper right corner of the control panel.

The **string** replaces default mode indicator. {**INDICATE**} without **string** restores default panel indicator.

{**PANELOFF**}

Turns off the control panel while a macro is executing.

{**PANELON**}

Reactivates the control panel during macro execution.

{**WINDOWSOFF**}

Freezes the worksheet window during macro execution to speed up macro execution.

{**WINDOWSON**}

Restores screen updating after it has been disabled with {**WINDOWSOFF**}.

Summary

This chapter serves as an introduction to the power of 1-2-3 macros. Among the strong features of Allways is its ability to interpret macro commands entered and executed within 1-2-3. This provides a level of macro capability with Allways, permitting autoexecution of potentially complex or time-consuming command sequences.

Chapter 14 shows you how to construct a number of useful macros within 1-2-3 that will make your use of Allways more convenient.

14 Practical 1-2-3 and Allways Macros

Chapter 13 introduced the concept of macros in 1-2-3, provided some general guidelines for macro writing, and showed you how macros based in 1-2-3 can be used in Allways.

This chapter shows you how to use macros specifically for Allways applications and provides some sample macros you can either use as is or modify for your own needs.

Macros in Allways

Unfortunately, Allways does not have a macro language of its own. There are many functions within Allways that would be easier if they could be executed from within macros that originate inside the Allways program.

Fortunately, you can construct macros inside 1-2-3 that will conduct operations in Allways, then either return to 1-2-3 or leave you in Allways to complete other tasks manually. You can either write Allways macros as text labels in a 1-2-3 range or use the 1-2-3 LEARN add-in utility to generate macros in a specified spreadsheet range.

Although both methods will result in macros you can use, if you create Allways macro procedures in LEARN they may require some editing to conform to the physical arrangement and presentation we recommend in this book.

We advocate grouping macro procedures in logical modules with appropriate labels. This is easy to accomplish when you write macros as cell labels. When you generate macros for Allways from within LEARN, however, the commands are entered one command to a cell, stretching out the macro over several more rows than would be required to write the same macro procedure by hand.

If space is not a problem, and you don't mind the difficulty of documenting such macros, you can leave them as they are. We suggest, however, that you edit LEARN-produced macros to conform to the style presented here.

Even though you write Allways macros in 1-2-3, you can access almost all of the Allways commands and functions, using either standard Allways sequences or 1-2-3 names that function a little differently in Allways. For example, the function keys in both programs can be accessed through 1-2-3 macros. Each function key in 1-2-3 has a name that can be used in macro programs. The function keys in Allways are not named for macro execution, but you can use the 1-2-3 names to access their features.

The {WINDOW} function key from 1-2-3, for example, toggles between the graphics and text mode in Allways because {WINDOW} is F6 in 1-2-3 and F6 is the Text/Graphics key in Allways. You can use the 1-2-3 {ABS} function in Allways to carry out the F4 (zoom in) function, but there apparently is no way to issue the SHIFT-F4 (zoom out) function in a macro.

You can access the Allways small column width movements that are available during column width and row height adjustments from a 1-2-3 macro with the {Bigright} and {Bigleft} commands. Notice that these 1-2-3 commands have the opposite effect in Allways when you are setting row heights and column widths. Instead of moving the cursor a page at a time, as in 1-2-3, these commands move the cursor 1/10 of a character width. When doing normal cursor movement around the worksheet, however, these commands function as they do in 1-2-3.

Designing the Macro Master Spreadsheet

As mentioned in Chapter 13, many 1-2-3 users maintain a master macro spreadsheet that holds all of the common macros they use in spreadsheet design. When they build a new spreadsheet, they first load the master, then save it under the new spreadsheet name. That way such common macros as save a worksheet, enter Allways, change Allways defaults, and other utilities are available for all spreadsheets.

Even if you elect not to build a master spreadsheet at this time, the layout and design tips in this section will help you create better macros for the spreadsheets that need them.

As you enter these first utility macros, you can either turn on LEARN and let 1-2-3 record the keystrokes for you as you step through the process or refer to the menu diagrams in Chapter 2 to help you follow the process.

Move the spreadsheet cursor to the macro area. If you haven't already labeled this section, type MACRO at the top of a column, then move down two rows to start entering the macros.

Select an area for your macros that probably will be available in most of the spreadsheets you design. Later versions of 1-2-3 handle memory fairly efficiently, so you could place macros at the far right of the spreadsheet, beginning in column IM, for example.

The wide separation between spreadsheet data and the macro area will increase storage requirements slightly, but only slightly. As long as the majority of the spreadsheets you design aren't any wider than this, your macro area will be safely out of the way. Because you are not formatting the macro area of the spreadsheet with Allways, placing the macros in that far-flung region will not increase the size of your *.ALL format file, unless you try to format the entire spreadsheet with a nondefault font.

> **NOTE:** If you set the entire spreadsheet range to a nondefault Allways font, the storage requirements for the *.ALL file will grow dramatically. In one test we formatted a spreadsheet that required 17,566 bytes with two attributes at the head of the file, and the *.ALL file required 815 bytes. Next, we formatted the entire spreadsheet range, A1..IV8192, with the font in the number-2 position of the resident font list. The resulting *.ALL file required 66,317 bytes of storage.

Depending on the type of spreadsheets you regularly design, you could put all common macros into a single file or design separate macro master files for each type of spreadsheet you design. If you put everything together in one spreadsheet, then maintenance and application will be easier. But if you find that certain classes of spreadsheet never use large portions of your macro code, then consider redesigning your system to support separate spreadsheets.

For this discussion we'll assume that everything will go together in a single file. Adjust this scheme to fit your own requirements.

Allways Macros Described

To help you understand how macros work with Allways, we'll construct some practical macros in a 1-2-3 spreadsheet. Later in this chapter we'll summarize a number of macros with relatively little explanation. If you understand the initial macros—how they are entered in the 1-2-3 spreadsheet and what they do in Allways—then you'll be able to use or modify the provided samples for your own applications.

Remember to build macros in modules, that is, small groups of commands and functions that can stand alone or be incorporated into longer command sequences. This section suggests some basic utility macros, with each one building on the previous ones. This dependent module approach to macro programming is a sound one that makes later modifications to lengthy, involved macros much easier. By using the same modules over and over for as many tasks as possible, you can modify many complicated macros by changing just one or two modules. The alternative is to write discrete code for each program you design; but if you do this, you have to modify every program that contains certain procedures any time you want to change those procedures.

Save Current Spreadsheet

A macro you probably will want in every spreadsheet is one to save your work. Make **save** your first master macro by entering the following sequence in adjacent cells:

> **Save(\S) '/fs~r{Return} <----Save current spreadsheet**

Name the cell that contains the actual commands with the **/Range Name Create** sequence. Use backslash S (**\S**) as the range name. Now, when you press ALT-S, 1-2-3 will save the current spreadsheet to the predefined file name. Name the same cell again and call it **Save**, to make it easier to use this sequence as a subroutine within another macro.

Notice that a {**Return**} command has been added to this macro. This works like a RETURN from a GOSUB statement in BASIC to return program execution to the line or command following the subroutine call. When you execute the save command with the keyboard ALT-S combination, the {**Return**} command returns control to the keyboard. When you call the **save** macro from within another routine, control returns to the next macro command.

> **NOTE:** When using this macro, always save the spreadsheet the first time with the manual menu sequence. Otherwise you will either get an error or write over the master file you loaded to start building the current spreadsheet.

Invoke Allways

A macro module you certainly will use with many larger macro programs is a routine to call up Allways. Outside the macro environment, you enter Allways with an Add-In Manager hot-key sequence. If you have assigned Allways to ALT-F9, for example, you switch to Allways by holding down the ALT key and pressing F9.

To enter Allways from a macro, we suggest that you use the **Add-In Manager** menu. That way your macros will be more transportable, because they do not depend on Allways being assigned to the same hot key every time. The sequence for entering Allways from the Add-In Manager is: Press **ALT-F10** to display the **Add-In Manager** menu, select **Invoke** from the menu, then specify Allways as the application to invoke.

A macro to invoke Allways through the Add-In Manager after checking to make sure Allways is attached is shown in Figure 14.1. Be sure to leave at least one blank line between this macro and the **Save** macro previously discussed. Add as much documentation to the macro modules as you think necessary for easy update and modifications later.

This macro also has been given two names, one for keyboard execution and one for inclusion as part of a larger macro program. Although you can call a macro with its keyboard name (\A in this example), it usually is easier to use a more descriptive name for program execution. So, in addition to the keyboard macro name, the first cell in this macro is also called **Allways**. This makes it easier to follow the program logic and to make changes or fix bugs.

The first line of the macro uses 1-2-3's @ISAPP function to determine whether Allways is currently attached. This function returns a logical **1** if the

Figure 14.1
Makes sure Allways
is attached, then
invokes it through
the Add-In Manager

```
                          ┌──────────────────────────┐
                          │      M A C R O S          │
                          └──────────────────────────┘

Start Allways (\A)        {IF @isapp("Allways")=0}{Branch Err_No_Allways}
                          {Save}
                          {APP4}
                          I
                          Allways~
                          {Return}


Err_No_Allways            {Indicate Error}
                          {BEEP}
(Key_In = Cell IM2)       {Getlabel Allways not Attached!,Key_in}
                          {Indicate}
```

specified add-in is attached or a **0** if the application is not available. The {**IF**} command checks for a 0, which would mean that Allways is not available.

If Allways were not attached, then macro execution would jump to the error routine at **Err_No_Allways**, which writes the word **ERROR** in the upper right status display box, halts macro execution, and displays an error message in the display panel. By using the **Getlabel** command you can emulate the 1-2-3 error condition handler. The program waits for you to press a keyboard key, then returns to the Ready mode.

If Allways is attached, then execution of the macro continues on line two with the {**Save**} command. This shows how you can incorporate subroutines into the main program logic. {**Save**} uses the earlier **Save** macro to store the current file before entering Allways. This is just a safety measure to ensure that you have a safe copy of the file before you leave 1-2-3 and enter Allways.

Line three calls Add-In Manager with the {**APP4**} command. **Invoke** is selected from the **Add-In Manager** menu, and the Allways application is specified. A **Return** command also has been included in this macro so it can be used in conjunction with more involved routines.

Change Allways Defaults

You can use a macro to load Allways and establish some beginning formatting features before you add detailed formatting. The macro in Figure 14.2 shows just two examples, selecting a font list from the font library and loading a layout from the layout library.

The first line of this macro invokes Allways by using the previously written macro (**Allways**) as a subroutine. After this macro plays and Allways is loaded, the **change defaults** macro switches Allways to the text mode with the F6 label

Figure 14.2
Changes Allways
defaults by loading
font and layout
library files

```
                        ┌─────────────────────────┐
                        │    M A C R O S           │
                        └─────────────────────────┘


Change Defaults (\D)    {Allways}
                        {Window}            <---F6: Text Display
                        /fflrInvoice~       <---Font Library: Invoice
                        /llrInvoice~Q       <---Layout Lib.:Invoice
                        {Window}            <---F6: Graphics Display
```

{**Window**}. Remember, Allways does not have names for its function keys but it recognizes function key names from 1-2-3. In 1-2-3 F6 switches spreadsheet windows, but in Allways it switches the display between text and graphics mode. This switch is used with Allways macros to speed up command execution by eliminating the repainting of the graphics screen.

The third line calls the Allways /**Format Font Library Retrieve** sequence and specifies a font set called **Invoice**.

Line four enters the /**Layout Library Restore** menu and specifies the **Invoice** layout library. The **Q** at the end of this macro line returns the program to the Allways mode.

The final macro line uses the F6 ({**Window**}) toggle to restore the graphics display before halting, leaving you in the Allways mode to finish the spreadsheet formatting.

Import Formats from Other Worksheets

The concept of importing formats from existing spreadsheets for use in new spreadsheets was discussed in Chapter 5. This section shows you how to set up a macro to handle the IMPORT AND PRINT function automatically.

Spreadsheet formats are imported with the /**Special Import** function. This is a useful feature if you use a number of spreadsheets with the same format. As an example, suppose you maintain a master spreadsheet for invoice entry and add data to the master as necessary.

You could store the empty master with Allways formatting, load the file when you want to add data, then store the filled-out version to a separate file. In this case, the companion Allways file will be stored with the new file.

Another approach is to store two master files, one for data entry and one for the associated formatting. With this technique you enter data into an unformatted 1-2-3 master spreadsheet, save the modified file with a new file name, enter Allways, and import the format from the master format spreadsheet. After you print the spreadsheet, you exit Allways and call up the master data spreadsheet for more data entry *without saving the formatted version of the spreadsheet you just printed.*

A macro can automate as much of that process as you like. The suggested macro in Figure 14.3 picks up after you have loaded the master data spreadsheet and added the information you want to format and print.

NOTE: This macro uses the previous **Allways** macro that saves the current 1-2-3 file before switching to Allways. After the data is entered, you should save this file manually before you use this macro, or the edited spreadsheet will be saved to the master file. As an alternative, rewrite the macro to bypass the save operation, to hard code the file name you wish, or to have 1-2-3 ask for the file name before saving.

This macro is self-documented and uses the previously created modules. You won't be able to reuse every macro you design, but a little planning ahead will help you get the most out of your programming efforts.

The steps involved in switching to Allways, setting a range and printing the file are

≡ Save the current file and enter Allways.
≡ Use **/Special Import** to overlay the data master with the format from the format master spreadsheet.
≡ Load a font library file.
≡ Load a layout library file.
≡ Print the result.
≡ Exit Allways.

When the macro has finished its run, you can discard the current worksheet, unless you want to save it as a formatted file. Remember, using the overlay technique in this macro obviates the need to store the *.ALL format file with every spreadsheet you design.

Other Macros

By now you should have a good idea of how to use macros compatible with 1-2-3 to conduct business inside Allways. With perhaps a few exceptions,

Figure 14.3
Loads Allways, imports a format, prints the formatted spreadsheet, and returns to 1-2-3

MACROS

Format and Print	{Allways}	
	{Defaults}	<---Change Defaults (\D)
	/prs	<---Set Print Range
	{?}	<---User Sets Range
	g	<---Start Print
	{Esc}	<---Exit Allways

such as the Allways SHIFT-F4 function key and the Allways Quick Keys (ALT-key combinations), you should be able to do about anything in Allways with 1-2-3 macros that you can do manually. You should have little difficulty designing your own macros for Allways operations, especially if you are familiar with macro programming in 1-2-3.

To get you started, we have suggested some additional utilities and procedures in the form of Allways-compatible 1-2-3 macros that you may want to incorporate in your own macro master spreadsheet or use as a starting point to help you design custom macros for your applications.

Set Allways Headers and Footers

Suppose you have a series of reports that you print regularly with the 1-2-3/Allways combination. You have a prescribed format for these reports, including what information will be in the headers and footers.

The macro in Figure 14.4 can be used alone or in combination with other macros to set up the spreadsheet for printing. This **hdr_ftr** macro calls Allways, then establishes the desired header and footer. When this macro ends, you are left in the Allways program with the assumption that you may want to do additional formatting. It would be an easy matter, however, to link this macro to one or more of the previous examples to add additional formatting and print the spreadsheet before exiting to 1-2-3.

Reset Macro

You may want to start certain spreadsheet designs from a default mode. Suppose you have a formatted spreadsheet that includes the data you want but requires reformatting. Allways has several commands to return changed settings to a default. The macro in Figure 14.5 enters Allways and resets all of the attributes to the preset or default condition.

You can use this macro when you first load the spreadsheet to be reformatted, and it will call up Allways for you, set the defaults, and leave you in Allways to continue your work. Even if you are already inside Allways, it may

Figure 14.4
Sets Allways
headers and
footers

MACROS

Set Headers/Footers	{Allways}	
	/lth	<---Layout Titles Header
	Monthly Financial Report||Page: #~	
	f	<---Footer
	Report Prepared: @~	

Figure 14.5
Resets Allways to
default mode

```
                    ┌─────────────────────────┐
                    │       M A C R O S        │
                    └─────────────────────────┘
```

Reset All Defaults(\R)	{Allways}	
	{Window}	<---Set text mode
	/wcr	<---Worksheet Column Reset
	/wra	<---Worksheet Row Auto
	/wpd	<---Worksheet Page Delete
	A1..IV8192~q	<---Delete all Page Breaks
	/ffdrq	<---Format Font Default Restore Quit
	/fbc	<---Format Bold Clear
	A1..IV8192~	
	/fr	<---Format Reset
	A1..IV8192~	
	ldrq	<---Layout Default Restore Quit
	/prcq	<---Print Range Clear Quit
	/psrq	<---Print Settings Reset Quit
	/dznq	<---Display Zoom Normal Quit
	{Window}	<---Set Graphics Mode

Figure 14.6
Turns on Allways
grid lines

```
                    ┌─────────────────────────┐
                    │       M A C R O S        │
                    └─────────────────────────┘
```

Turn on Grid	{Allways}	
	/log	<---Layout Options Grid
	y	<---Yes (Use Grids)

be simpler to exit Allways to the 1-2-3 mode and run this macro if you have a complicated spreadsheet.

NOTE: As designed, this macro resets every cell in the spreadsheet to default mode. If you only want to reset a portion of the worksheet you should conduct the operation by hand or modify the macro accordingly.

Turn on Grid Lines

A simple macro, such as the one in Figure 14.6, can be used as part of a longer "setup" macro that conducts certain operations to get the spreadsheet ready for your application.

You probably would not want to use this macro in a standalone mode because you would have to invoke it through 1-2-3, and it performs only a single function. However, it is provided as a sample of the kind of functionality you can add to your macro library so you can call on the modules as you need them to perform different kinds of setup operations.

Set Outline and Shade for User-Specified Range

This macro shows how you can use 1-2-3's {?} macro command to accept input from the keyboard before continuing with more macro commands. Macros such as the one in Figure 14.7 show how you can include a setup sequence in a macro that will call Allways but permit the user to specify the exact range.

Use this user-input technique anywhere that you need the flexibility to decide what actual settings will be but want to automate as much of a given process as possible.

You're on Your Own

Okay—that's how it's done. Now think about the tasks you are repeating by hand that could be done just as well by a macro. Think about how you can save time during spreadsheet formatting and printing by letting the power of 1-2-3 macros do some of the work for you.

You could format a spreadsheet for a 1-inch page length, for example, and print mailing labels from a database. (This is necessary because Allways, unlike 1-2-3, sends a form feed command at the end of each printing operation.)

You could set bold for a range, underline a range, shade a title, set the display color for your own preference, add a graph, select another printer and printer port, set a print range, and more. Macros are time-saving tools that can help you do repetitive tasks that you might not try without them.

Figure 14.7
Outlines and
shades a user-
specified range

```
                          M A C R O S

Outline & Shade       {Allways}
                      /flo               <---Font Lines Outline
                      {?}                <---User Input
                      /fsl               <---Font Shade Light
                      {?}                <---User Input
```

Summary

This chapter was designed to get you started, to show some practical examples of how you can use 1-2-3 macros to conduct Allways operations.

Use the general techniques we have outlined here and study appropriate texts on 1-2-3 macro programming. Then start designing the program tools you need to make your Allways life easier.

Index